Faith Schools and Society

Also available from Continuum

Education and Community, Dianne Gereluk
Is Religious Education Possible?, Michael Hand
Schools and Communities, John West-Burnham, Maggie Farrar and
    George Otero
Schools and Religions, Julian Stern
The Spirit of the School, Julian Stern
Education for Citizenship, Denis Lawton, Jo Cairns and Roy Gardner
Quality in Education, Denis Lawton, Jo Cairns and Roy Gardner

Faith Schools and Society

Civilizing the Debate

Jo Cairns

Foreword by
Denis Lawton

continuum

Continuum International Publishing Group

The Tower Building   80 Maiden Lane
11 York Road   Suite 704
London SE1 7NX   New York NY 10038

www.continuumbooks.com

© Jo Cairns 2009

British Library Cataloguing-in-Publication Data
A catalogue record for this book is available from the British Library.

ISBN: 9781847062291 (hardcover)

Library of Congress Cataloging-in-Publication Data
Cairns, Jo.
    Faith schools, and society : civilizing the debate / Jo Cairns ; foreword by Denis Lawton.
      p. cm.
    Includes bibliographical references and index.
    ISBN 978-1-8470-6229-1 (hardback)
    1. Church and education. 2. Church schools. I. Title.

LC107.C35 2009
371.07 – dc22   2008045461

Typeset by Newgen Imaging Systems Pvt Ltd, Chennai, India
Printed and bound in Great Britain by MPG Books Ltd.

Dedication

This book has been many years in the making and as such it has been shaped by the wisdom, practice, and good sense of academic and professional colleagues, students and faith communities and their leaders here in the UK and overseas. My debt to so many is immense and I can only hope that they each recognize something of their particular contribution in the pages that follow.

Unquestionably, I owe the four schools at the heart of this study immeasurable gratitude. Their senior managers and teachers gave unstintingly of their time and their students engaged with the research process with a thoroughness and energy which I could not have expected. Equally Lesley and Craig Whitehead proved invaluable colleagues throughout as they helped probe the ever-growing data about faith schools which was collected over a number of years. So too the careful and continuing support and guidance from Alison, Alex, Kirsty, Ania and Janice at Continuum helped overcome much diffidence on my part throughout the editing process.

Such a lengthy process has, however, had its costs most particularly for my family. For this reason I simply wish to dedicate this book to Roy Gardner. It has been his insistence that we share our work and conversations in faith schools during the last fifteen years or more as widely as possible which has led to the writing of *Faith Schools and Society*. Moreover, his many requests that I 'describe the view' on our journeys through London, Oxfordshire and the Caribbean, southern Africa and south east Asia became the foundation for our joint development of the research design and data base which form the core of this book. Roy characteristically, however, now generously insists that his own considerable, expert and original contribution to the process should be susbsumed under the specific heading of 'the Cairns approach' to the evaluation of the place or otherwise of faith schools in contemporary plural societies. For this and so much more I shall always be very grateful indeed.

Contents

List of Tables

Foreword

One of the current educational issues in the UK and other secular or plural societies is the stance that should officially be taken towards Faith Schools. Some have argued a case in favour of all Faith Schools; others have advocated abolishing them all; a minority have seen the complexity of both arguments, justifying some kinds of Faith Schools whilst expressing doubts about others.

Dr. Cairns, whilst wanting to support some kinds of Faith Schools, has seen the need to express doubts and conditions. In the UK, for example, the position of Church of England schools has a long history, and it would be difficult to recommend a policy of complete closure. But if, in principle, Church of England schools are allowed, how can other Christian denominations be denied – and what about Jewish or Islamic schools? Can all Faith Schools be accommodated in a democratic society even if they might threaten the continued existence of that society?

Dr. Cairns examines these general arguments carefully. Her more specific task is, however, more difficult and more interesting: given that there might be a case in favour of some Roman Catholic schools, how can such schools be evaluated? Having rejected the tempting proposition that if some Faith Schools offer something different and worthwhile, then all Faith-based schools should be encouraged, Dr. Cairns embarked upon the task of establishing a set of principles and procedures by which Roman Catholic schools can be evaluated. She describes a rigorous procedure, partly based on some interesting work by Bryk and others in the USA. The result is a research Profile of each school that is quite different from the one-dimensional approach of most of the effective school researchers. The Cairns approach is based upon a view of the purpose of education which is much richer than the economic and materialist values of most earlier school evaluation research.

One outcome of her research is summarised by means of four detailed case studies of schools, all of which are Roman Catholic, but differ considerably in their organisational structure and cultural context. The study illustrates the fact that this kind of ambitious evaluation requires considerable sensitivity, as well as time, and the permission of those being evaluated. The results described in the four case studies can be used to throw light upon the Faith Schools debate in the UK and elsewhere, provided that the temptation to over-generalise can be avoided. While Dr. Cairns is very careful to point out the limitations of her research, the benefits are very clear.

This book will benefit policy-makers and others concerned with the establishment and regulation of Faith-based schools within national, plural systems. It will also enhance the debate for educationalists who wish to get beyond simple yes/no opinions on the complex question of Faith Schools.

Denis Lawton
Emeritus Professor of Education and formerly
Director of the Institute of Education,
University of London

Preface

The study of faith schools and society with which this book is concerned arose from professional development work I undertook with African Caribbean, Anglican, Catholic, Jewish and Muslim schools both in the UK and overseas between 1982 and 2002 and the insights this afforded concerning the relation of faith and education.

Among the communities with whom I had the great privilege to work during that period, reflection on the nature of the relationship between specific faiths and education was extremely intense. In retrospect this was not coincidental. On the one hand, the dominance of sociological and philosophical perspectives within educational understanding was being overtaken by an overriding concern with teacher competence and student performance. On the other hand, the engagement of religion with modernity within an increasingly globalized world gave rise to two major responses within faith communities. There was a desire among articulate believers to clarify and express the nature of their belief. There was also a desire to ensure that the new-found confidence in their beliefs and values was secured in the identities of their young people through particular kinds of education.

The professional development framework with which those communities engaged grew out of the concern which had been fostered in the PGCE programme on which I studied by the teaching and writing of Richard Peters (1966) who argued that education is:

> First, the experience and nurture of personal and social development towards worthwhile living;
>
> Secondly, the acquisition, development, transmission, conservation, discovery and renewal of worthwhile culture.

An overview of the professional development undertakings by each faith community during this period suggests the following growth points:

1. Reassessment of the nature of each faith both in the life of its community and in the individual adherent, historically, socially and as a contribution to identity.
2. Rigorous questioning about the purpose and practice of education in state schools, as well as in the part-time schools belonging to the communities.
3. Evident concern with the kinds of young people which education, both compulsory and voluntary, should seek to develop.

In addition, the extensive concerns about the existence and expansion of faith schools in England which followed the publication of the White Paper *Schools Achieving Success* (DfES 2001) coincided with the debate engendered about the place of faith communities and faith schools in the civic societies of countries caught up in the 'war on terror'. These concerns prompted me to revisit and unravel in this new context the professional development work across faith schools and the research in Catholic and Jewish school cultures I had undertaken. It seemed that the debate about faith schools never touched on the aspect of them with which my studies were concerned, namely the real educational cultures to which particular beliefs and values give rise in a variety of plural societies, and, in particular, the student voice which gives shape and direction to those cultures. In writing this study I have attempted to put individual school cultures and their student voices at the heart of the debate about faith schools.

Introduction

The purpose of this book is to develop and test the means to support a balanced and civilized civic conversation around the question, 'Should plural societies operate common schools which will ensure the full educational entitlement of all students, from whatever social, cultural, ethnic or religious background; or should there be a plurality of schools, in which religious groups are accorded the right to their own schools?' The study will involve an examination of schooling in complex plural societies through the micro-cultures of four individual faith-based schools. The examination will be situated within the overarching argument that plurality itself is central to the common good because individuals and their communities centre on the pursuit of different components of the complex human good. Case studies of the schools have been undertaken in an attempt to develop a new form of school profile which both makes clear the attitudes and values of the senior students in the schools and the differing ideologies through which the schools set about educating those students. The variety, differences and similarities within and across faith schools evidenced by the school profiles will be offered as a contribution to the wider debate about the nature and ethical purposes of public education in and for pluralism and the role of faith schools, if any, in state supported education.

The key to promoting such a civilized conversation lies in a structured examination of the nature and variety of school cultures and their influences on the lives and development of those involved in them. Readers are invited therefore to put aside for a time the current educational fashion to focus exclusively on school outcomes and results and to consider instead the nature, purpose and values of individual schools as they are experienced by their students, teachers, parents and wider communities. In order to justify such an approach to the study of schools in our present plural complex societies, this book examines the problems which arise for effective policy development concerning faith schools in the absence of appropriate evidence to illuminate Ofsted findings and league table results, following the publication of the White Paper *Schools Achieving Success* (DfES 2001). It provides summative statements arising from the empirical studies of four Catholic schools and suggests that the methodology used has three important outcomes for a civilized conversation about this matter: a basis for data modelling; a means of deciding indicators of successful school cultures; and a need to examine the culture fit between macro-education policies and micro-school cultures. It calls for a civic conversation about faith schools within a wider debate about the purpose and practice of education in plural late modern times. The concluding part signals to government and policy makers the benefits of developing educational policies whose origins lie in school practice. Most particularly it is argued that in the matter of faith schools, if comprehensive evidence is weighed before policy is made, education itself might become the catalyst for a newly emerging democratic, inclusive and normative culture of pluralism.

A glance at the Letters columns of *The Times* of 4 July 2008 crystallizes the need for a civilized public conversation about the role of faith schools in increasingly secular, global and multicultural societies. Three letters can be found there in response to the report 'In Bad Faith' by the journalist Christine Odone.

The first letter sees the Secretary of State for Children, Schools and Families, Ed Balls, responding to Odone's accusation of his instigating a 'witch hunt against faith schools' and of his alleging that they are 'selective, divisive and a law unto themselves'. The Secretary of State retaliates that 'this is absolute nonsense . . . Faith schools are popular, successful, thriving and the oldest established part of the schools system – I am 100 per cent committed to that continuing'.

In the second letter, Keith Porteous Wood, Executive Director of the National Secular Society, makes two points. The first that 'every time an Education Secretary tries to have faith schools follow the public interest, he or she gets bullied into retraction . . . Similarly, Alan Johnson was forced into the quickest U-turn in political history for the temerity to suggest quotas (in admissions to faith schools) to improve cohesion'. Pursuing further the contentious issue of social cohesion in relation to faith schools, Porteous Wood next argues 'Odone seems intent on bringing up Muslims apart from the rest of the community even though as study after study shows the best way to integrate people is by educating them together from an early age.'

The third letter from Mary Bousted notes the 'accusatory language' of Odone's report leading, Bousted believes, to the 'risk of polarising the debate, suffusing her report with a them-and-us mentality, which will do nothing to achieve what we all want'. Bousted, General Secretary of the Association of Teachers and Lecturers, concludes that 'In Bad Faith' is 'an unhelpful addition to the debate about faith schools'.

This present study sets out to be a helpful addition to the debate about faith schools as it explores how best to achieve a public conversation about 'what we all want' in the crucial matter of those schools. In order to do this, the study develops first, theoretical models by which to argue the case both for and against the continuance of faith schools; second, it includes empirical studies of a number of faith schools in different parts of the world; and third, it proposes an evaluative framework in which to judge the merits of faith schools in complex plural multicultural societies. At its heart is a concern to lend structure, evidence-based argument and civility to a frequently ill-judged, misinformed yet passionate debate about public policy and the continuing existence of faith schools in plural secular societies.

The study combines an intellectual exploration of issues raised by the existence of faith schools with empirical studies of Catholic schools in different kinds of plural societies. In particular, the study takes into account a recurring question in the current debate about the nature and purpose of faith schools; namely, the need or otherwise to ensure that the student population of each faith school represents fairly the wider make-up of the national population in terms of religious, non-religious, secular and agnostic persuasion. In three out of the four schools, students are admitted to the schools on the basis of national examination results, rather than on religious identification. Questions are therefore raised throughout the study about what makes a faith school different from other schools, when the majority of the pupils are not even nominally adherents of that faith, or the majority of the staff.

The shape of this study is in fact central to the process of answering the question as to whether or not faith schools have a distinctive and valuable role in plural societies. This is because it sets out the theoretical dimensions of the matter and employs empirical studies to illuminate both the nature of the questions which faith schools pose and the possible solutions. Theory and practice together provide a framework for discussion and evaluation of this important social and educational matter.

As Ed Balls, the Secretary of State, concedes in his letter to *The Times* (4 July 2008), faith schools have long been an established part of the education system in England. Similarly, in each of the countries included in this study, their education systems, which are currently characterized by complex cultural situations, have been at work for a long time. As a result different needs, tensions and global concerns have been incorporated into some rather elderly and fragile systems whose foundations lay in very different times from the present. The kernel of the educational and cultural problem with which such societies struggle today has the potential to be both constructive and destructive. It can be summarized in the question: 'To what extent can plural societies which comprise a spectrum of world views and cultural perspectives sustain a satisfactory common schooling for all?'

An important task of the study is to incorporate into a conversation about what we all want with regard to faith schools the possibility of 'seeing anew' the evidence, argument and policies surrounding the existence of faith schools. As Simons (1996: 237–8) argued, 'To live with ambiguity, to challenge uncertainty, to creatively encounter, is to arrive, eventually, at "seeing" anew.'

The emergence of a new incipient culture from within pluralism marks out a key role for education policy making to 'see anew' within its particular social, intellectual, cultural and educational contexts. Up to now it has been assumed that the cultures of schools were susceptible to receiving new directions in policy. The central assumption of a 'culture-fit' between individual school cultures and new central policy initiatives can no longer be taken for granted. Examination of the 'culture-fit' between macro-education policies and micro-school cultures in the four school studies described later in the study suggests the need for an intense reappraisal of the purpose of education if individual schools are to reach their potential to educate in these complex global times both for human and for economic flourishing within an overarching education system.

The study suggests that a reappraisal of the nature and purpose of education would involve a considerable amount of learning by both government and citizens at such times of cultural instability and fragility. To know what we all want in connection with faith schools presumably is begun by a conversation defining what we all want from formal education. For the conversation to flourish, would require learning from the specifics of education as they already exist; namely, those arising from the development and formation of particular kinds of human beings both at school and as they enter adulthood and in the particular achievements and characteristics of individual school cultures. Learning from such practice would stretch from and back to government, between citizens and their children and across constitutive communities which form the backbone of an evolving plural culture.

For the present author it has been striking to learn, for example, that the school profiles which have resulted from this study appear to indicate, inter alia, that:

- the interplay of beliefs, values, knowledge and behaviours found in some faith schools suggest that these school cultures can be porous, flexible and responsive;
- the added value which some faith schools seek to achieve appears to result from a carefully crafted relationship between knowledge, attitudes and values required to achieve national education standards with the knowledge, attitudes and values necessary to become a particular kind of deliberative, reflective human being.

In other words, it appears that it is the schools themselves which are finding ways of accommodating pluralism within the educational cultures which they both inherit, as a result of national education policies, and create, as a result of their particular beliefs and values. Examining schools in this way also gave rise to data which supported some comparative perspectives on the kinds of distinct school cultures which are currently sustained by a faith group, in this case, the Catholic Church and the response of the students to those cultures, whether they were Catholic, non-Catholic Christian, from other faiths or from none. Perhaps the most important comparison that the data facilitates is that between the attitudes and values of the students within each school and between different schools and across the schools. From these particular data derived from four schools, a strikingly similar profile of the school leavers from all four emerged. Most notably the students shared, or thought they shared, the following values, attitudes and beliefs:

- belonging to their school as a community;
- being happy at school;

- purpose in their learning and a desire to do well in their school work;
- acceptance of themselves as they are;
- respect for other people, whatever their race, nationality or religion;
- respect for the environment;
- recognition of the influence of their parents in their religious development and attitude formation;
- honesty in their dealings with other people;
- commitment to the disadvantaged in society;
- believing based on their own convictions and not the beliefs of others.

If illuminating evidence about faith schools was able to enter into a wider educational debate about what kinds of school cultures were best capable of meeting the needs of education in plural societies, then a sustainable point might be reached in which a plural society would be able to answer the question:

> Should plural societies operate common schools which will ensure the full educational entitlement of all students, from whatever social, cultural, ethnic or religious background or a plurality of schools, in which religious groups are accorded the right to own their own schools?

A reassessment of the purpose of education within such a framework would have as its main task the engineering of a primary focus for educational endeavour within a society deeply conscious of plurality in its ethnic, religious, social and intellectual life. Part of its task would be to encourage ways of thinking about achievement in schools through an examination of their cultures rather than an examination of their outcomes. That discussion would also provide an opportunity to assess the viability of responding to citizens' faith or attitudes to the world within distinct contexts rather than within a one-size-fits-all model of schooling.

A civic conversation about the purpose and practice of education is long overdue in societies which are more usually now expected to grapple with a top–down proliferation of policy initiatives in matters of education and social cohesion. As the Letters page in *The Times* of 4 July 2008 indicates, reports and issues concerning faith schools provoke political, ideological and professional challenge, approbation and dismay. Each of these would prove a key ingredient in any worthwhile discussion of faith schools and their place in a plural society's education system. What they lack are three rather more significant ingredients: the first, evidence of what really constitutes the educational cultures of individual faith schools and non-faith schools; second, the voice of students who have attended faith schools; and third, an engagement between the protagonists and antagonists of faith schools across society and education leaders and policy makers. If such an on-going conversation were to get underway, then at least in the matter of faith schools' practice might inform policy, and policy in turn might reflect good practice.

The Socio-Intellectual Landscape in Which the Study Is Set

The present discussion seeks to explore how judgements are made about which educational cultures and practices are best suited to the task of education in plural societies. Given that religion, faith and education are all contested concepts, there is reason to undertake an analysis of the intellectual, social and political landscape against which we make decisions about purpose and practice in education in a plural society. That landscape currently provides four different modes of thinking about how best to proceed with this decision making.

The first arises from reflection on the relationship between the individual and their community. In *Habits of the Heart*, Bellah et al. (1996) argued that many Americans now recognize that they cannot sustain themselves by themselves when facing the complexities of contemporary life. They need some degree of connection in their lives if they are to find meaning and purpose. There can thus be identified an intellectual, social, communal and personal awareness of the need for both involvement in the marking-out of the values which affect our public and social relationships, and a public acknowledgement of such values.

A second mode of thinking can be found in the approach most widely championed by Rawls (1987: 12–13), in which he advocates 'the method of avoidance' in the face of pluralism in political life. In promoting political liberalism within plural societies, Rawls argued that a just society should establish the rules by which political decisions are taken in isolation from the world views of its citizens. From such a position the view can be taken that politics is the dominant and, potentially, the only recognized discourse of a just society.

A third mode of thinking is to be found in 'Third Way' politics, a movement which was perhaps born of reflection on the impact of globalization. It is a concept, according to Giddens (1998), which proposes a rejection of both top–down socialism and traditional neo-liberalism. In response to the vacuum in guidance which has been created by a liberal concern about how best judiciously to fill the 'public spaces' of a plural society, politics, as with Rawls, becomes the dominant voice in directing what is best for given social and personal situations.

A fourth mode of thinking is now emerging which is arguing for an ethical and religious vision of the importance of community in contemporary society (see for example, Sacks 1995, 2000, 2002; Berger and Neuhaus 1996; Annette 2005: chapter 18).

The plotting of schools' individual cultures onto the intellectual and cultural landscape will not be a simple task. Schools themselves are complex institutions that serve varied and competing aims. For example, Bartelt (1995: 7) argues that it is best to see schools as 'structures that are intimately and irrevocably woven into others, all of which serve political, economic, cultural, religious and social aims'. Others such as Comer (1987) have argued that it is unwise to separate academic from social and emotional development in children and that there is a need to incorporate all the resources of the school into a common blend of care and education.

In seeking to make judgements, albeit provisional ones, about the ability of school cultures to meet the task of educating students for and in pluralism, I shall discuss the usefulness of positing postmodernism as a complex map of late twentieth- and early twenty-first century directions. In doing this, I shall follow King (2002: 6) who urged that postmodernism should not be understood as a clear-cut aesthetic and philosophical ideology that is 'taken to nihilistic extremes', or, 'a fixed extreme that denies all others'. This device permits a perspective on postmodern and late modern times which can support a looking-backwards to the influences of modernity on education and a looking-forward to the possibilities for education which global late modern times afford. From there I shall attempt to construct a map of cultural directions onto which individual school cultures can be plotted. This exercise will be carried out because I wish to argue that education for and in pluralism is as yet embryonic, resulting from the current lack of clear direction on many social, educational and political matters from within plural societies themselves.

Why This Particular Study?

The initial impetus for this work was the dilemma, whether we as a diverse, plural and multi-faith society can, or indeed should, agree that our plural societies should support faith-based schools within a state education system. This dilemma has dominated my professional life since I began teaching in a Catholic comprehensive school in 1975. There was at that time, and for many years afterwards, an almost unchallenged liberal educational orthodoxy that faith (church) schools had no particular educational place in the schooling of the young. Consequently, little attention was paid to the specific kinds of education on offer in such schools, except by the faith communities which sponsored them. Their role in wider debates about the nature and purpose of education was limited to often acrimonious discussion, supported by little empirical research, about the ability of students from those schools to take a positive role as citizens in their plural and multi-faith societies. In particular, however, the present study was generated by two related incidents: the first, concerning comments made by a senior Ofsted officer; and the second, a discussion about research into Catholic schools in the United States.

An HMI at the Office for Standards in Education (Ofsted) raised with me informally in 1997 the apparently higher examination results and better Ofsted ratings in social, moral, spiritual and cultural education to be found in a substantial number of church schools in England. Very quickly, this first finding became a dominant concern among politicians, educators, parents and students. Was there some specific formula at work in faith schools, for which parents, politicians and some educators had been searching, which might now be bottled? Might that formula not also guarantee successful examination results in all schools? For me, however, the finding about the quality of social, moral, spiritual and cultural education (SMSC) was equally impressive.

To me the nature of education rested on the particular understanding of being human which each school and, indeed each teacher, adopted. Were there therefore some weaknesses of a significant nature emerging in a large number of primary and secondary schools? What indeed was the foundation for the educational endeavour if that element of curriculum thinking which we chose to call 'SMSC' was 'badly done' or, far worse, not even discussed, let alone understood. Further, the information which Ofsted had unearthed led to another question: that of the role of the spiritual in state education. How well did the spiritual contribute to the overall concept of education in a state school? Indeed, does 'the spiritual' work if it is not 'tethered' to a specific religious tradition in a faith-based school? Related to these questions are the methods which can appropriately be employed in schools to examine how those aspects of being human, which the English system calls SMSC, are included in the life of each school. A most enlightening discussion about national methods used in England can be found in Erricker and Erricker (2000: 38–44) in which the 'political territory' for spiritual education is mapped out.

The *Handbook for the Inspection of Schools* (Ofsted, 1994) sets out evaluation criteria and evidence by which inspectors observed and evaluated SMSC at the time when the above Ofsted findings were reported. A school was said to be meeting high standards in personal development if 'its work is based on clear principles and values expressed through its aims and evident in its practice' (Part 4: 15). The final report on a school must include an 'evaluation of how the school promotes pupils' spiritual, moral, social and cultural development and how the pupils respond to that provision' (Part 2: 22). The template provided by Ofsted relied heavily both on the school's ability to articulate its values and mission within an inspection framework and on the inspectors' capacity to know what to look for. Nonetheless, the findings which provoked my own concerns about the state of SMSC provision in many non-faith schools were derived from school inspections following a common template in faith and non-faith schools and in such numbers as to suggest a certain credibility.

The other incident which stimulated this study was a seminar led by O'Keefe at the Institute of Education, University of London, where he discussed the research he had recently published. He proposed 'a renewed purpose for Catholic schools' in the United States; namely, 'the preferential option for the poor', which he described in the following way:

> In keeping alive a legacy of educating those outside the ethnic and socioeconomic mainstream, context and identity meet; the needs of the world coincide with the strengths of the organisation. . . . The future may be

uncertain, but one truth remains: the strength of Catholic schools is in mission not margin. (1996: 193)

In elaborating the 'preferential option for the poor', O'Keefe compared his thinking with the ideas of Preston Williams, an African–American Protestant theologian. Williams speaks of the Catholic Church's opportunity in the United States to demonstrate its global and not simply its Western character. He argued that if Catholic schools were prepared to change their curricula and their extra-curricular activities to reflect their global character, then 'they would become vehicles for multicultural and multiracial learning'. He concluded:

A school with such a redefined curriculum and ethos would enable the Church to become a great embodier of the Christian gospel. It would also serve as the beacon light for demonstrating how African–Americans and white Americans might come together to form a more perfect union. (1990: 315–8)

O'Keefe and Williams had thus raised the possibility of re-visiting the educational philosophies of different faith communities as they individually sought to meet the challenges and opportunities of formal school education in an increasingly fragmented yet globalized universe. In particular, their rooting of school mission in global concerns about the conditions in which many young people were growing up gave rise to important questions about the kinds of educational values at the heart of some faith schools. For example, education in such schools might offer different perspectives on economic competence and attitudes in human beings from that on offer in schools dominated by market-driven educational values.

The Nature of School Cultures

My aim in examining individual school cultures within plural societies is to discover whether those cultures can offer guidance to their wider societies about how to proceed in making decisions about the nature and purpose of living and educating in a plural situation. The study will look at each school culture in relation to the purpose, identity and practices in which it engages students and teachers in the development of their values, beliefs and behaviour. One major researcher on Catholic education, Bryk (1996), has argued powerfully that we live through our institutions. This study will attempt to track, therefore, the nature of the experience which is on offer of belonging to, and learning in, a particular school.

The study, therefore, attempts to discuss how we might examine faith schools in such a way as to guide our present thinking about the place of faith-based education in plural societies. The mapping of school cultures onto a wider map of cultural landscapes is offered as an example of how in the current educational research climate we might adopt some new and, perhaps, more subtle understandings of educational purpose and quality in education. For when Lawton pointed us to a more precise understanding of school culture through a hierarchical plotting of 'beliefs, attitudes and values and behaviours' on the cultural map of a school, he spoke of the value of such a model thus:

> Clearly this view of school culture will tend to emphasise many aspects of life, in addition to goals. Success or failure will not only be seen in terms of league table results. There is evidence that parents look for much more than academic results when judging a school. It is very important that parents are encouraged to contribute to school life in a variety of ways. (1996: 116)

Indeed, Parker-Jenkins et al. (2005: 6) found in their research into new faith-based schools that 'the role of parents was central in securing what they see as an appropriate up-bringing for their children'. The model for the thinking which supports the present study is thus derived in good part from the ideas, writings and concerns of Lawton. As such this study is particularly concerned to break away from the research methodologies employed by the school effectiveness movement when looking at school cultures. Although that movement was developed from principles of social justice and equity, it came to be characterized by many, such as MacIntyre, as making effectiveness a core virtue:

> The whole concept of effectiveness is . . . inseparable from a mode of human existence in which the contrivance of means is in part the manipulation of human beings into compliant patterns of behaviour. (1984: 71)

This study seeks to find a means of profiling particular schools through an intense examination of the internal relationships between the members of the school and the beliefs and values at work in its culture within the intellectual, social, cultural and educational landscape in which the school is situated. It suggests that greater attention needs to be paid in research in schools both to the content and to the pedagogy of religious and spiritual education, for as Hobson and Edwards argue:

> Principles and values from an ethics of belief complement democratic values to provide ethical and epistemological norms which should inform the teaching of religion and act as a guide to how religious differences should be handled in the curriculum. (1999: 85)

The Significance of School Cultures

The White Paper *Schools Achieving Success* (DfES 2001), which paved the way for the expansion of faith-based schools in England, pays little if any attention to the many differences and distinguishing features of the faith schools currently in existence. Calling for accountability from each school in a system increasingly characterized by centralized resourcing, curriculum reform, league tables and external reporting, demands attention to the individual school and its particular characteristics and culture. As Grace (2003a) has reminded us:

> Thoughtful debate about faith schooling must recognize that faith schools constitute a great variety of educational cultures, principles and practices.

Busher (2001: 76) notes that the nature of each school's culture or ethos is 'dynamic and created through the interactions of people'. He continues saying they are a nexus of shared norms and values that express 'how people make sense of the organisation in which they work and the other people with whom they work'. A warning also follows that 'organisational culture is often taken for granted by current participants who may be unaware of how a particular culture has been constructed, how it might or can be changed or how it is sustained by those in positions of power and authority'. Morrison (2002: 19) would agree for he writes that schools are 'storehouses of distributed knowledge' which frequently governs the micropolitics of the organization. Wrigley provides a useful summary, though, to such current thinking on school cultures emanating from the school effectiveness movement and turns instead to the fundamental question with which, I think, a study of school cultures should be concerned:

> We have devoted such energy to developing a sophisticated knowledge of change management, planning, assessment, school cultures, leadership. Now, in this new century, the question is unavoidably – to what end is all this? Where is the vision? (2003: 7)

Wrigley's views are supported by a growing number of school researchers, including Morley and Rassool (1999) and MacBeath (1999) who would all concur with the argument expressed by Slee and Weiner that:

> Effective schooling and the school improvement movement is blind to a searching interrogation of outcome. Test scores become ends. . . . Explicit discussions of values and the types of society to which schools articulate/ adhere are ignored. (1998: 111)

This study, therefore, within its limited scope and nature, will attempt to put the question, 'To what end is all this?' back at the centre of the debate about the purpose and practice of education specifically through the study of individual school cultures within a framework of beliefs, values and behaviours. It will explore the means by which sufficient information about a particular faith-based school culture might be collected in order to determine the influence of its specific beliefs and values on its educational purposes and practices. The information thus collected would contribute to a profile of the school. The profile would, in turn, provide a lens through which those concerned with the generation of macro-educational policies linked to pluralism and globalization might reflect on the micro-management and implementation of those policies within particular cultures and their success, failure or innovation.

Developing a process for the study of faith-based schools and their cultures

Part of the problem associated with making a study of faith-based schools is that there is an assumption that they inhabit some unknowable realm beyond the experience of most educators. That is, since these schools are seen as being concerned with religion, there is an assumption that those whose business or belief system is not religious are unable to penetrate the *genus loci* of the place. Although it is commonplace now to highlight the rankings of faith-based schools in national league tables of examination results, little headway has been made in examining the role of religion within the educational culture of successful or, indeed, failing schools. Part of the reason, I suspect, lies in the discussion above in which it was claimed that the school effectiveness concern with school cultures was restricted to questions of how best to superimpose a model of effectiveness onto the managerial and behavioural organization of each school, despite or in the face of a school's particularities in its beliefs and values, in order to achieve specific outcomes. It will take some little while to overcome this managerial model of school organization.

A further problem might well be 'religion' itself. Faced with this same problem McCutcheon (1997: 6) called for a methodological, theoretical and political analysis applied to 'a particular way of talking about, conceptualizing and constructing religion as a discussion object'. Indeed, she speaks (1997: 5) of the need to 'dispel a long-standing assumption that matters of religiosity and spirituality inhabit a privileged, unblemished realm'. Her solution (1997: 200) is to suggest that the 'way people talk about their Gods' would be more helpful to 'the outsider' of a religion if they spoke 'not in terms of theology but in more general categories'. She proposed general categories of 'social formation' and 'authorising practices' which could prove helpful in a study of this kind.

There is also, however, the reluctance noted by Arthur (2005: 152) to examine the interplay of religion and the building of a school community. At the Institute of Education, I was privileged to be able to work with a number of representatives from the major faiths, most particularly members of the Hindu, Jewish and Muslim traditions and different Christian denominations as they sought to clarify their identities and purpose(s) as communities in education. As our work progressed it became clear that our most productive and significant ideas and practices in teacher education, curriculum development and community policy, for both formal and informal education, arose from our commitment to ask educational questions first of the major faith traditions. Those questions crossed a wide spectrum but always involved issues about how best to support the child and young person from those communities in developing their identities, values and beliefs in our complex, plural societies both here and overseas. What did the child need from education and how could formal and informal education practices contribute to meeting that need? Religion and faith in this model of educational process were servants of the immediate and long-term educational questions and aims.

When some provisional decisions had been taken about educational questions and aims, it was then the task to interrogate the histories, traditions, scriptures, ethics and teachers of those traditions to examine how best to employ education in its various political, social and cultural settings to meet the stated needs. That methodology was challenging and complex for it focused the endeavour on human growth and human concerns and not on proselytism and religious point-scoring. It was also at times frustrating, challenging and painful. Nonetheless it was a methodology which permitted and sustained a continuing conversation between religion and education and between professional educators and communities of faith.

Those extended and fruitful encounters between religion and education within faith communities give some ground for optimism in employing some similar questions during the present study when collecting data about the culture of faith schools. At its centre this study will be concerned with examining the purposes of education as they are worked out in practice through the cultures of specific schools in a number of plural societies in late modern times. Through seeking to excavate the particulars of certain educational situations against a background of pluralism on the one hand, and one specific aspect of that pluralism, Catholicism, on the other, it is hoped to engage in some coherent educational and curriculum thinking about whether it is possible to argue cogently for or against the place of faith-based schools in plural societies. The international dimension to the study will help to focus reflection and conversation about this important question on the nature of education which different plural communities consider to be important both for their own future well-being and for playing a viable role in an ever-increasing globalized world. It will also present the opportunity for examining three out of four faith schools whose student populations are selected not as a result of their, or their parents' beliefs, but on the basis of national test results.

Carr has pointed out some of the considerable difficulties associated with educational thinking in postmodern times and he (1998: 14) has asserted, 'some conception of objective knowledge or truth requires urgent defence or rehabilitation in the interests of coherent educational theorizing'. At the same time Kelly (1999: 53) argued that pupils should be given much more than a curriculum which is 'a selection of the culture of the society as it exists at the time when they happen to be in schools, even if it could be identified and defined clearly enough'. Indeed, Carr (1998: 53) asks of such a model of education, where is 'their (the pupils') right to emancipation and empowerment'? Priestley has also wisely reflected that:

> A curriculum which prepares children only for the present world is a betrayal. Change is not an option. It will happen with us or without us. It is a moral option of whether that change is for better or for worse and Education is the vehicle which will help determine that course. (1996: Part V)

Examining the practice of individual school cultures from outside of the faith tradition on which they are founded in order to inform public debate about the value or otherwise of their existence in plural societies is as yet relatively untried. It is important, therefore, in this study to test the potential helpfulness of its particular methodology in the present sometimes challenging and mostly non-directional pluralism. For these reasons, it is proposed that for this study the investigation of faith-based school cultures should involve only Catholic schools. This is because a tradition has developed among Catholic researchers to study the workings of a school through its culture. Most importantly for my study, Flynn (1993: 25) proposed that a study of school cultures should be a 'mapping as well as a mining operation' and should take place within the context of the wider culture of the 'world post 1989' and national society.

The present study will advocate the development of an appropriate methodology which could be used ultimately across all faith schools, not only Catholic ones. Its aim would be to build comprehensive profiles of the social, personal, spiritual and educational capability or non-capability of state-supported faith schools in modern plural societies. Working within Catholic schools only, Flynn built up a sophisticated frame of analysis of large databanks developed from questionnaire surveys to parents, teachers, as well as the students. In this study it is argued that the analysis of the data from the questionnaire to the students in four schools is best contextualized within a theoretical analysis of the students' social, intellectual and national contexts and a qualitative study of the school's religious and educational culture.

It also stands philosophically within the broad and authoritative research of Bryk with Lee (1989) and with Lee and Holland (1993). Working with comprehensive quantitative national databases, Bryk first sought to compare the social and academic achievement of students in the United States in Catholic schools with those in public schools. The marked difference in positive achievement between those in the Catholic schools and in the rest led Bryk to examine the organizational features of Catholic schools. As an eminent statistician he then examined the contribution of specific organizational features to the social and academic achievement of the students in those schools. His analysis pointed to a number of distinctive features which merited further investigation, including the school as a 'voluntary community'; the school as a 'bridging institution'; and the 'role of religious understanding in contemporary schooling'.

From such rich data which lead to complex multilevel modelling, Bryk came to perceive the American Catholic school as significantly distinct from the American public school. This very important work emphasized for me that the distinctiveness of faith schools in the UK and elsewhere merited an articulation which gave some explanation not only of the reasons for their apparent academic success but also their sensitivity to personal and social development in a faith-based community. In so many ways Bryk's research has proved foundational to my thinking in this study and to my hopes for a future solid research base to underpin educational policy concerned with faith schools in England. My own study must, however, be different. In the first place I am not a statistician and therefore I more naturally turn to a methodology which sustains a combined small quantitative and qualitative empirical study. Far more importantly, however, I am concerned that my experience in faith schools in England and overseas teaches that different schools, even within the same faith tradition, feel different. I wished to find a way of excavating those differences in relation to the individual school.

At the same time, I wished to have a framework for reporting differences and similarities in separate school cultures which borrowed from Bryk's concept of reporting differences in levels of achievement across a wide range of schools through the instrument of using common educational indicators. For him, the research landscape was dominated by equity and access for students of all races and world views. For me the landscape in this study is dominated also by pluralism and inclusion and the role of the spiritual in personal and civic education. It was also important that this study should find a means of reporting the essential nature of each school culture which went beyond the scope of the Ofsted template of report writing found in the *Handbook for the Inspection of Schools* (Ofsted 1994). There inspectors were enjoined to report their examination of the 'pupils' personal development and behaviour' by recording how the school promotes their spiritual, moral, social and cultural development in just two paragraphs. Thus in the exemplar inspectors are encouraged to write:

> The school is a community in which the spiritual and the moral dimensions of life are taken seriously. . . . The school helps pupils to understand what is right and wrong and to appreciate the needs of others. (1993: 14)

Inspection reports must necessarily be brief but the philosophical, cultural and ethical dimensions underlying a school's approach to SMSC and therefore human formation require a more extensive and discursive template, if not rationale. The intention of this study is the development of a school profile whose template can assist government, educators and communities to test the value of individual school cultures' ability to a) offer a vision of a viable, fair, inclusive and just complex plurality to their students and local communities and b) encourage human flourishing in each of its students so they are able to take their place in democratic societies.

It is hoped that this study of individual Catholic schools, as exemplars of specifics within the general concept of Catholic education, will yield data which may point to commonalities and universals, as well as dissonances and dissimilarities in the cultures and outcomes of particular Catholic schools. If this is shown to be the case, the study will suggest that policy makers cannot afford to make generalized decisions about the value or otherwise of faith-based education. It will seek to recommend areas in which all schools, and the philosophies and cultures within which they operate, should be investigated before decisions can be taken about their worth within state supported education systems. Such an approach would have the advantage of treating all faith schools in the same manner, as well as, perhaps, secular schools. This is necessary since the spectrum of faith-based education includes schools from religious traditions which have a long history of involvement in state education and others from traditions which are new in their involvement with formal state-supported education.

By its nature this has been a small study and resources have been extremely limited. Nonetheless, the undertaking was considered imperative, first because such a study has not been attempted before and, more importantly, because globalization has seemingly forced a world-embracing, economics-driven view of education onto both the global North and the global South. It is important, therefore to consider how matters of human development are tackled within individual countries, and in particular schools within them, and to learn from the result. In this way, the study will seek to respond to the concerns of Bruner, who reflected:

> What we resolve to do in school only makes sense when considered in the broader context of what society intends to accomplish through its educational investment in the young. How one conceives of education is a function of how one conceives of culture and its aims, professed and otherwise. (1996: ix–x)

This book articulates some of the consequences for a state education system of permitting particular faith communities, or indeed any other major life-stances or philosophical traditions, to organize and sustain distinct schools for students of all faiths and none, at times of intense pluralism and a critical lack of direction in social, cultural and intellectual values. In brief it is seeking to identify and verify a process whose purpose is to facilitate a genuine conversation between faith-based education and the state, mediated through political philosophy and regulatory protocols. To this end, the profiles of each school will be used to contribute to the discussion about the appropriateness of faith schools in plural societies.

At present, however, it is sufficient to comment that the attempt to profile each school as a particular social reality in late modern times might be judged to have worked, insofar as:

1. Each complex culture seems to have proved susceptible to exposure in the matters of beliefs, attitudes and values and behaviours through an externally moderated process.
2. The continuous inter-play between the three constituents of a school culture have been demonstrated to inform both school policy and behaviours, including that of the senior managers and teachers, the students and the culture as a whole.
3. Distinctive values and beliefs of school managers were evaluated against the students' own satisfaction and happiness with belonging to a particular school culture.
4. A distinctive perspective on each culture has been gained through eliciting a separate self-review from among the student body.
5. A database has been developed of cohorts of school leavers who were about to enter their own societies as full citizens from Catholic senior secondary schools in three countries. Interrogation of the database proved worthwhile in terms of establishing a profile of the students' developing attitudes, values and beliefs.
6. Each school culture has been profiled within a historical, educational, sociological, and religion-state perspective.

In writing this book, I have attempted to remain alert to the tentative nature of any discussion about school cultures in which the developing identities of students in relation to pluralism and individual beliefs, values and attitudes are being examined. A most valuable cue to remaining alert has been taken from Jackson (2004: 17), who has argued that culture should be seen not so much as an 'entity' but 'an active process through which humans produce change'. Thus our concern with the development of the students in the schools of this study is to gauge their capacity to engage with cultures, some secular, some religious, and their ability, as Meijer (1995) would say, 'to continuously interpret and reinterpret their own views in the light of their studies'. Equally the fluidity of a school culture necessitates that at any time in a school's history an investigation could be made which achieved a fair and evaluative profile of the capability of the school within a plural society.

At a personal level, the research ethic guiding this study of the place of school culture in human flourishing is, perhaps, best summarized in the words of Pope John Paul II, in his address to the United Nations General Assembly, in October 1995:

> To cut oneself off from the reality of difference – or worse, to attempt to stamp out that difference – is to cut oneself off from the possibility of sounding the depths of the mystery of human life.

In studying differences in school cultures against the background of difference in contemporary plural societies I have attempted to develop an enquiry based on reason, sensitivity and validity, thereby hoping to avoid the stricture of Thomas Aquinas to Dante:

> He ranks very low among fools who says 'yes' or 'no' without first making distinctions . . . since often opinion, rushing ahead, inclines to the wrong side and then passion blinds the intellect. Far worse than useless . . . is the quest of a person who casts off from the shore and fishes for the truth without the art. (Dante: 115–23)

I hope that the present study will encourage many others who engage with the ambiguities and uncertainties of educational thought and policy-making to cast off and descibe the view of the varied plural landscapes along the way the better to see anew the purpose and practice of education in and for pluralism through the lens of individual faith schools and their cultures.

Part I

An Intellectual Framework to Support a Civic Conversation about Faith Schools in Plural Societies

The Purpose of Part I

First an intellectual framework in which to tackle the perplexing problem of privileging religion within education is established. Next the study raises the need for discussion about the continuance or otherwise of faith schools to have access to evidence about the nature of all school cultures and, in particular, those of faith schools. It asks what kinds of evidence would be necessary for a more satisfactory discussion than that which has taken place since 2001 and reflects on the kinds of authorities which would be trusted in the discussion to provide both raw data and interpretation of various kinds of evidence. It calls for a common audit procedure across all faith schools with an emphasis given to the student voice.

Chapter 1

The Urgent Need for a Civilized Conversation about Faith Schools and Society

Purpose of the Chapter

At present it is politicians who steer the conversation about faith schools and ultimately develop the policies by which those schools either flourish or fail. Reaction to the present British government's support for such schools suggests a profound split between those who intellectually and educationally favour a continued dual education system and those who perceive the existence of faith schools as socially and educationally divisive. The chapter argues that the matter is potentially so intricately woven into the fabric of British and other countries' pluralism that the many constituents of pluralism, including political voices, should be offered a framework in which to conduct a conversation about the benefits or otherwise of a dual system. A putative procedure for supporting such a conversation is set out which includes the establishment of particular values such as respect and real engagement with all sides of the conversation and the collection of data about individual school cultures. This latter evidence base would ensure that the profiling of faith and non-faith schools beyond the confines of examination league tables can begin to have a significant voice in the conversation.

The debate about the furtherance or abolition of faith-based schooling has the potential to cause a severe crisis for plural living for as Ranson (1994) pointed out in periods of social transition, education becomes central to our future well-being; institutions should be enabled to respond openly to periods of change and the different communities should become a source of reflective understanding.

Sutherland (1996: 47) has also argued that very close to questions about human flourishing in plural societies is the relationship between particular forms of economic strength in a society and the prospects for the acceptance of tolerance and therefore pluralism. We need to find ways of knowing as a result of evidence which types of schools best contribute to the healthy social and economic functioning of complex plural societies.

Debate surrounding the value of faith schools requires the framework of a procedural common good if it is to contribute positively to the social transition which pluralism creates. Even more, educational ideology in plural societies must find a way of recognizing and responding to the present 'predicament' of pluralism and incorporate consideration of the religious or 'spiritual' into its nature and practice. Have we perhaps in the last twenty years or so, sought to impose a way of working with pluralism, as, for example, with 'multiculturalism' without first fairly describing the norms which pluralism will entail? The question is important because it recognizes that pluralism is the perspective which all citizens of complex plural societies share. 'Muticulturalism' as a principle in present education thinking has arguably sought the integration of minorities into a culture which is as yet unconceived. This has been favoured over the development of an organic pluralism, which fully takes account of the individual citizen's perspective on pluralism, while living in a presently undefined or a-culture. Thus education for and in pluralism is as yet embryonic, resulting from the current lack of clear direction on many social, educational and political matters from within plural societies themselves.

The purpose of a civic conversation about the place or otherwise of faith schools would be to enquire whether they are or could be sources of shared meaning about living well communally in plural democratic societies. In a state education system which provides for the existence of faith-based schools alongside community schools, can we find a common learning culture which fosters inclusivity, equality and social justice? With such values could not each school, faith based or common, explore the meanings of religion, secularization, pluralism and citizenship in an epistemologically open way? For Jackson (1997: 126), if schools could achieve this, they would be developing the capability in young people to move 'between the different arenas and perspectives of religious and modern plurality'. Skeie (1995: 27–9) has powerfully proposed that that this would mean that young people become 'subjects in their own culture', representing traditions and working with pluralism rather than against it.

The Cultural Landscape in Which the Conversation Could Take Place

Parker-Jenkins et al. (2005: 6) have commented that the new faith-based schools that have been established 'reflect greater diversity in terms of race and ethnicity than previously experienced in England and Wales'. The extent of religious identification in today's plural society of England and Wales is highlighted by the Census figures of 2001: 76.8 per cent of the population identified themselves as religious, with only 15.5 per cent saying they had no religion and 7.5 per cent not answering the question. Furthermore, more than 70 per cent counted themselves as Christian. In terms of the diversity of religious belief, it is particularly instructive to examine the profile of religious belief offered by the Census in London: 58 per cent gave their religion as Christian, with the highest proportion in the borough of Havering (76 per cent); 36 per cent of the population of Tower Hamlets and 24 per cent in Newham is Muslim; over 1 per cent of the people in Westminster are Buddhist, while Harrow has the

highest proportion of Hindus, with 19.6 per cent and Barnet the highest proportion of Jews (14.8 per cent); over 8 per cent of the populations of Hounslow
and Ealing are Sikh; 16 per cent of the population of London say they have
no religion at all. The evidence from the Census is indeed of huge diversification and, particularly striking, is the extent of difference in beliefs within the
capital. At the same time, Dorling and Thomas (2007) having conducted a
comprehensive survey of the UK's population trends, predicted that London's
population, though significantly diverse, is not likely to become plural in the
near future but that at least a dozen British towns and cities will have no single
ethnic group in a majority within the next thirty years. Leicester will become
the first 'super diverse' city in 2020, then Birmingham in 2024, followed by
Slough and Luton.

The nature and practice of religious identification is, however, fluid and
yields different data according to the questions used to collect the information about people's religious identities. According to the *Third Wave of
the European Values Study* by Tilburg University (2003), Britain has become
one of the least religious countries in Europe. Nearly one-third of those
polled in Britain said that religion was not at all important to them and
70 per cent said that they never went to a mosque, church or synagogue.
Figures published by the Church of England in August 2003 also dis-
closed that the weekly adult attendance in the Church of England, which
has 13,000 parishes, has dropped below one million. Other mainstream
churches are showing a similar decline, except for pockets which are in
areas favoured by immigrant communities. For example, in an article for
Inside Out, the journal of the Council for World Mission, David Cornick
(2003), General Secretary of the United Reform Church, explained how
churches in Europe, which are haemorrhaging members, could be in the
process of receiving a life-saving transfusion from the developing world.

Large parts of London, for example, illustrate this point where religion
has become a defining characteristic. For example, there are vibrant church
groups in the capital within such informal Afro-Caribbean congregations
as Victory Church or House of Praise that pack local halls each Sunday,
even though local Anglican churches might stand almost empty. Other ethnic minorities have also established architectural, as well as communal,
landmarks in the capital. There is the Sikh temple in Southall, the Shree
Swaminarayan Mandir built by Hindus in Neasden, the mosque in Regent's
Park and the Ahmadi Muslims' Baitul Futuh mosque in Morden, which is
said to be the largest mosque in western Europe.

Thus personal and social understandings of what is meant by nominating
oneself as religious or otherwise show little consensus. Hence how great is
the capacity in such a situation to argue that religion is in decline or on the
increase or just about stable, depending on whether the criteria set for such
statements emanate from 'hard' or 'soft' understandings of religious belief
and commitment? From where does the politician or policy maker take guidance on this matter?

The Census demonstrated that the black and minority ethnic communities rose from 6 per cent of the population in 1991 to 9 per cent in 2001. This increase, coupled with the situation outlined above of a related increase in evangelical churches and Muslim-faith communities in the inner cities of England, has led government ministers to revitalize the Inner Cities Religious Council of the Office of the Deputy Prime Minister to facilitate an increased recognition of the importance of faith communities within civil society. That Office is charged with social regeneration of deprived areas, inclusion and equality of access to services. As such it has provided the outcome of the the then prime minister, Tony Blair's speech to the Christian Socialist Movement, which had announced in 2001 a year-long review that would examine how 'the government interfaces with faith communities across the range of our shared interests'.

It is important to consider against this complex cultural and religious landscape whether a diversity of educational offer is important to ensuring a worthwhile education for all students in our society. At present, *Faith in the System* (DCSF, 2007) the joint accord between the DCSF and faith communities, records that about one-third of the total number of maintained schools in England are schools with a religious character, that is, 6,850 out of a total of around 21,000. Of forty-seven academies opened, sixteen had a faith designation. Nearly two out of every five independent schools, that is, around 900 out of a total of just over 2,300, are of a religious character. Out of these, 700 are Christian, 115 Muslim and thirty-eight Jewish schools.

The numbers of faith schools might be taken to support the significance of religion in terms of personal identity in postmodern/late modern times. For example, Parker-Jenkins et al. (2005: 6) comment that 'what is particularly striking today is the importance of religion in terms of personal identity'. They note that faith-based schools are 'being chosen by parents who see them as places providing compatibility between the religious values promoted in the home and those practised in schools'. Ultimately the question raised by the presence of faith schools concerns the ability of state education in plural societies to encompass all that is worthwhile across all those schools into a common framework supported by equity, justice and respect.

Is Government Steering the Debate?

Since the nineteenth century the English education system has included schools supported by faith communities. The 1902 Education Act introduced free compulsory Christian education for all and the 1944 Education Act formalized this government/faith community partnership for school provision alongside state secular provision. The consensus that this dual system of education should remain is, however, now under challenge by many in society but not by government. Since 2001 the Labour government has championed the expansion of faith-based schools. First the White Paper *Schools Achieving Success* (DfES 2001) called on faith communities and groups to partner the

DfES in developing new faith-based schools. Second, in *Faith in the System* (DCSF 2007: 4) the government 'welcomed the contribution that schools with a religious character make to the school system both as a result of their historical role and now as key players in contributing to the more diverse school system that we seek'. Moreover, the government has committed itself to 'this greater diversity' of school providers because 'it will help to raise standards'. The document, *Faith in the System* significantly spells out that

> the Government and faith school providers believe that: all schools – whether they have a religious character or not play a key role in providing a safe and harmonious environment for all in society, thereby fostering understanding, integration and cohesion. (2007: 1)

Within *Faith in the System*, the government states that, 'our unequivocal purpose in agreeing this document is for other parties to appreciate the contribution of faith schools' (2007: 1). The question of faith-based schools' fitness for purpose in relation to the needs of the plural and diverse society of today does not appear to be so firmly settled outside of government and the authors of *Faith in the System*, according to the comments which followed its publication. The National Secular Society, teachers' unions, leading articles in *The Independent*, *The Times*, and most newspaper letters' pages provided evidence of opposition to this renewed support for faith schools. For example, Mary Bousted, General Secretary of the Association of Teachers and Lecturers, argued that 'We need schools which embrace the diversity within our community, not a diversity of schooling dividing pupils and staff on religious grounds' (BBC News 10 September 2007). Allen and West in a paper presented to the British Educational Research Association (2007) make the case that religious secondary schools in London educate a much smaller proportion of pupils eligible for free school meals and their intakes are significantly more affluent than the neighbourhood they are located in. Particular concerns about faith schools have therefore been related to their perceived divisiveness and apparent inherent inability to take full account of the cultural context and student identities in which they provide education. Such dilemmas are pressing within an unsettled, increasingly fluid multi-faith, secular and plural society and the problem they specifically pose for schools and the national education system has been helpfully summarized by Gallagher, an educator from Northern Ireland, in the following way:

> Plural societies are faced with a dilemma whether they should operate plural schools, within which all or most identities are acknowledged and recognised, or a plurality of schools, in which minorities are accorded the right to their own schools. (2005: 163)

The statement expresses the tension which is often said to exist between the rights of faith groups and religious parents to own and manage their own schools and the values of inclusion, equity and tolerance, which are currently championed as the basis of a viable, modern, plural society. It also highlights a very particular dilemma for current educational thinking. Focusing on pluralism and fractures in social composition, though central to the nature of any debate about how to work towards a healthy and just society can, however, distract educators from a more comprehensive understanding of the overall purpose and practice of educational activity. As Peters argued:

> A connection between 'education' and what is valuable does not imply any particular commitment to content. It is a further question what the particular standards are in virtue of which activities are thought to be of value and what grounds there might be for claiming that these are the correct ones. (1966: 25)

Faith in the System chooses to sidestep the fundamental issue at stake in addressing the place of faith schools in state-supported education; namely, the ability or otherwise of a common education to introduce all pupils to the values which a just society champions and facilitate such values as major aspects of students' developing identities. Instead, it describes its purpose as 'to highlight the very positive contribution which schools with a religious character make as valuable and engaged partners in the school system and beyond' (DCSF 2007: 1). There follows a short series of anecdotal examples which neither address the role of religion in all schools' curriculum nor establish evidence of on-going or strategic modes of building social cohesion through formal compulsory education. All that is offered are examples of a small number of faith schools explaining how they are attempting to meet the new injunction on schools to contribute to community cohesion in particular classroom activities.

Faith in the System records a new interpretation of the rights of faith communities and religious parents to provide state supported schools. The act of ownership of any one school demands that the faith group or religious parent ensures the civic integration of their students into the wider society through an as un-yet spelled out vision of social cohesion. At the same time, *Faith in the System* states that, 'the government and the faith school providers should teach "identity and diversity: living together in the UK" as part of the secondary curriculum'. It goes on to say, 'this is a vital agenda for all schools, whether they have a religious character or not'. No advice is offered as to whether it is known if all schools teach this agenda in the same way and if not, is one method more appropriate than another for students from some or all faith communities. The document is endorsed by fifteen religious organizations, several of which represent a particular faith tradition two and three times over, together with the Department for Children, Schools and Families. Some of the faith traditions listed do not so far own a state-supported school. Others have a long tradition of ownership of a substantial number of schools. Little wonder that there is therefore a need for a much closer engagement with core questions about the nature of education, civic society and civic values and the way in which these relate separately and together with social cohesion, integration and understanding.

What Questions Does the Establishment of Faith Schools Pose?

The dilemma outlined above can usefully be framed into a question using the words of Gallagher:

> Should plural societies operate common schools which will ensure the full educational entitlement of all students, from whatever social, cultural, ethnic or religious background or a plurality of schools, in which religious groups are accorded the right to their own schools? (2005: 163)

The question is a challenging one for plural societies. On the one hand it underlines the rights which have previously been given to faith groups in some countries, including Britain, to establish their own schools within an education system which at the same time offers 'common schools'. The role of those schools is to provide an education for all, based substantially on the principles of equity, justice and inclusion. To what extent does the existence of faith schools negate the social, civic and educational principles on which the common school is founded? On the other hand, are there some forms of pluralism which militate against the very existence of the common school? In the main, the discussion surrounding this question will focus on two interconnected questions:

1. Are there educational purposes which morally, socially, religiously and culturally support the existence of faith schools in a plural society?
2. What kinds of individual school cultures foster the types of human development which are needed, and will flourish, in a plural environment?

Responses to these two questions will be considered, first, in respect of the educational capability of each school within a plural situation and, second, in relation to the personal, social and cultural capability of each school's graduates in a plural situation. Finally the study will return to the question concerning the viability of the common school in certain plural situations. A response will be given in the light of reflection on the purpose of education within intensely plural and complex societies.

The Scope and Nature of the Study

The sweep of this study extends beyond Britain, however. It is concerned to examine the role of state-supported faith schools in plural societies alongside an emerging concern with the place of religion in civil society. Specifically the study will seek to describe and evaluate the place of religion in secondary schools in plural societies through a study of the cultures of four Catholic secondary schools. The study will be conducted against the background of the prevailing cultural perspectives experienced at national and global levels by individual citizens of the countries in which the study has been conducted; namely, in Country X, in southern Africa; in Country Y in the Caribbean; and in Country Z in south-east Asia.

Central to this study will be a recording of the student experience at the schools. Students afford an excellent insider view of those aspects of the school's culture which touch on their personal beliefs and values and their future aspirations as citizens. The students are from senior schools and in their final year. Their voices capture well a lengthy period in a faith-based school, as well as being poised to take on the full rights and responsibilities of being citizens in their own plural communities. Each of the countries in which the case studies were conducted offers a different model of pluralism and the place of secular thought within it. For example, one is dominated by Christianity but includes a wealth of denominations within it. Another is dominated by Islam but also has sizeable populations of Christians and Hindus.

What kinds of experience and attitudes has faith-based education promoted in these students? To what extent has the school been an influence over and against their homes and families? What values and attitudes do the students hold in relation to their personal and social lives and their future roles in their own countries? What are their attitudes to religion and the faiths of others?

The study, then, comprises an intellectual statement of the problems and opportunities posed by the maintenance of faith schools in plural societies, with case studies based on quantitative and qualitative approaches. This approach has been recommended by Yin (1994: 13) who suggests that case study inquiry 'benefits from the prior development of theoretical propositions to guide data collection and analysis'. The concluding section of this present study will then be concerned to set out the profiles of the four Catholic schools derived from the case studies and portray them in such a way as to, in the words of Bassey (1999: 41), 'invite others to make value judgements about the worthwhileness' of the continued maintenance and support of faith schools in present complex plural societies.

Catholic Schools and Their Cultures

In the 1950s, in the decade before I became a student in a Catholic secondary school, the Catholic church seemed to many to be increasingly out of date and out of touch. Then came Pope John XXIII and the Second Vatican Council and the Church seemingly began to re-engage with the world. Part of this process was a renewed vision of how the Church might work to change its relationships with other faiths and cultures. Bryk et al. (1993: 334–5) when discussing their own empirical study of Catholic schools in the United States have drawn attention to tensions inherent in faith schools, precisely as a result of the new approaches and workings of the Catholic Church after the Second Vatican Council, particularly in its relationship with the larger secular culture. This study will seek to make connections between general school mission and policy statements and individual school's understanding of their culture and function.

Recent research into Catholic schools and their practices, some of it relating to schools more generally, has highlighted five key areas which it will be important to examine in this present study of school cultures:

1. The school as a community: it was the research of Bryk et al. (1993) which highlighted the importance of the school as a communal organization. In a later work Bryk distinguishes three core features of the 'community structure' of the Catholic school as:
   (a) shared activities which provide shared experiences among adults and students;
   (b) a set of formal organizational features which support the community;
   (c) a set of shared beliefs
       As a result, Bryk argued that 'the basic social organization of the high-school as a community has substantial social and personal consequences for both teachers and students' (1996: 29).

2. The concept of social capital alongside human and economic capital: Coleman (2001: 90–2) argues that all social relations and social structures facilitate some forms of social capital but schools are important in facilitating specific forms of social capital.

3. The question: 'How does the Catholic philosophical world and life view influence educational practices in Catholic schools?' a key question raised by Arthur, who (2005: 152) also asks, 'Are Catholic schools theological communities of believers or are they more sociological communities of care?'

4. The impact of national educational policy on individual Catholic schools and their managers: for example, when Grace (2002: 125ff) conducted his study among Catholic headteachers in England he suggested that Catholic schools' mission incorporates chiefly an emphasis on the promotion of faith, alongside the social and communal aspects of learning. He reported at the same time that Catholic schools' prospectuses emphasized academic performance. This arose mainly as a result of government legislation. The headteachers in Grace's (2002: 142) sample, however, were not drawn to 'the domination of technical performativity' in their schools.

5. The significance of religion in terms of personal identity in postmodern/ late modern times: Parker-Jenkins et al. (2005: 6) comment that 'what is particularly striking today is the importance of religion in terms of personal identity'. They note that such schools are 'being chosen by parents

who see them as places providing compatibility between the religious values promoted in the home and those practised in schools'.

   In this study, I have been greatly humbled by the most generous support provided by distinguished and professional colleagues in the South, by the willingness of three governments and the Catholic educational authorities within three countries to permit me to conduct case studies of Catholic school cultures. The schools have been chosen because together they provided a diverse cohort in terms of religious adherence and gender. Nor do three of them represent a traditional view of a faith school, which is one in which children of a particular faith community are educated by that community separately. One is private but state supported and the other three are fully integral to their national systems of education. Two are in the same country thus offering an opportunity to compare the method and the data collected within one country.
   Admission to three schools is based strictly on examination results gained at junior secondary level. Three of them are mixed and one single sex. The single-sex school is for girls. In one school, the overwhelming majority of the students are Catholic. In each of the others, Catholics comprise less than half of the whole student cohort. Data from these studies will therefore contain information about both male and female students' attitudes to their faith schooling; students from a single-sex school's attitudes to their schooling; and a mixed 'student voice', both male and female telling of their school experience through discursive responses to open questions in questionnaires and in discussion. At the same time, the study will provide a means of articulating some of the consequences for a state education system of permitting particular faith communities to organize and sustain distinct schools for students of all faiths and none, at times of intense pluralism together with a critical lack of direction in social, cultural and intellectual values.

Developing a Procedure for a Civic Conversation about the Place of Faith Schools

Debate surrounding the value of faith schools requires the framework of a procedural common good if it is to contribute positively to the social transition which pluralism creates. The postmodern map offers guidance on developing the procedural common good. There remains the modern liberal view of the good society: a society founded on the principles of democracy, reason and justice. These principles would seem to offer a firm foundation for the procedural common good. In particular, the foundations are laid for the key principle at work within social capital, that of trust, to form the leitmotif of such a civic conversation. Equally the liberal values encapsulate the place of respect at the heart of the procedural common good. Sennett (2003) has usefully, however, pointed to three forces which challenge mutual respect in society: unequal ability; adult dependency; and degrading forms of compassion. He explores how self-worth can be nurtured in an unequal world; how self-esteem must be balanced with feeling for others; and how mutual respect can forge bonds across the divide of inequality. His conclusion is that individuals cannot sustain a sense of their own self-worth if institutions neglect them.

For the procedural common good to do justice to the schools of all faith communities, there is also the matter of how difference should be considered within the concept of religion and across religions. Sociologists and philosophers, such as Woodhead and Heelas (2000: 2–3) have identified, for example, the following typologies of religion which can each be found in our plural culture today: religions of difference; religions of humanity; and spiritualities of life. At this stage, it is only possible to speculate about how each of those types of religion would engage with education for and in pluralism. Nonetheless, the nature of variety possible in different religious responses to establishing their own schools makes the need for a common form of audit procedure of all faith-based schools an important matter for consideration if the civic conversation is to be based in sound understanding from evidence across all such types of school.

Examining the Role of Faith Schools in Bringing about Inclusion, Equality and Justice in Democratic Pluralities

The tentative nature of any answers to the main questions set out in this study is determined by the cultural times in which it is undertaken. At present there is no longer room to define knowledge as 'objective' and therefore morally neutral. For this reason a public space exists in any discussion of the purposes of education at the beginning of the twenty-first century. There is a need therefore to examine the purposes and outcomes of different types of schooling and its impact on the lives of students in two areas:

1. Their capacity to recognize and discern differences in cultural traditions and the place of difference in their own and their society's human development, including its positive or negative contribution to a sense of cultural at-one-ment with others from their own communities and the wider community in which they live.
2. Their ability to exercise their rights as citizens of a democratic society to change and contest the cultural trends at work in that society.

To some extent the answers will rely on the past experience of policy makers and the predictions to which this leads them. For example, Niblett recently predicted:

The schools . . . to which the young go, while still efficient at training the mind to reason and be critical, will need to recognise again, far more than now, the power of a loved community both to educate and discipline its members. The young need help and human examples if they are to absorb the heritage freely offered by literature, music and the arts. Schools themselves need to see that insights of great importance are given by failure as well as success and that hope which has many dimensions – matters enormously. (2001: 27)

The results from this study about how each school develops its own curricular approach to religious and plural studies must ultimately inform the relationship between the general purposes of education at the beginning of the twenty-first century and the individual cultures of the schools providing that education. To what extent do faith schools consciously relate their particular faith values to their pedagogical and curricular practices? It is also anticipated that the data drawn from the case studies will provide guidelines about how to respond to the question whether plural societies can sustain viable forms of common schooling at a time of cultural disjuncture, multiculture and cultural fragmentation. The study will, of course, also consider whether plural societies can afford not to include faith-based schools in their state provision. Longley's (1995) assertion that faith communities might never know the influence they have had in shaping their wider communities should not deter such a study. A-cultures need examples of strong understandings of community, inclusivity and personal capability. Perhaps studies of particular school cultures might provide for general educational theory what Gilbert (1980: 65) called a 'prophetic relationship with the dominant culture'.

This study is based on the belief that the existence of large numbers of faith-based schools throughout the compulsory education systems of plural societies provides an important opportunity to study varieties of distinct cultures and their ways of 'experimenting' with the interface between education, human development, religion and pluralism. Any conclusions drawn from it will, however, remain tentative and no doubt, will give rise to further uncertainties about how best to proceed with education in and for pluralism. The context for this study is not only the postmodern trend within the educational research culture but more importantly as Pring reminds us:

Living with uncertainty is not the offshoot of postmodernism. It is the essence of the perennial philosophical tradition. (2000a: 114)

We may, however, take additional confidence in this enterprise in the work of Stiltner, specifically when he argues:

Since religion involves both belief and practice, as well as both cultural and institutional expressions, a focus on religion helps us to investigate the variety of pluralism – cultural, institutional, religious, and ideological – in modern society. (1999: 9)

Thus researchers can usefully investigate whether such schools are in fact contributing to the human capital of living in a plural democratic society.

Such investigations might then form the backdrop to the question which would result from any major reassessment of faith schools in plural societies: 'What should be the balance between all schools contributing to a politically driven understanding of the "common good" and each school's particular understanding of what constitutes the most effective culture for the development of "flourishing' individuals"?' The following chapters are an attempt to make these matters the subject of a civic conversation whose ultimate purpose is to steer the policy debate about the continuing existence of faith schools in plural societies.

Chapter 2

A Reassessment of the Place of Faith Schools in State-Supported Education in Plural Democratic Societies

Purpose of the Chapter

The present complex plurality found in many societies has given rise to an a-cultural situation, that is, one in which many cultures live together without a common conscience by which judgements can be made and to which appeals can be directed. In this situation it is argued that education policy has become cut off from the beliefs and values of individuals and the communities which the schools serve: education must therefore re-establish its moral purpose.

The development of that moral purpose might begin by schools being defined as micro-cultures whose main purpose is to sustain themselves as intelligent learning communities for personal and social formation within the macro-culture of educational policy driven by economic imperatives and standards-based evaluation. Judgements about the quality or 'intelligence' of school micro-cultures would be related to their ability to yield sources of shared meanings in life, while acting as mediating institutions within the moral matrix of society.

Religion, Culture and Education: The Crucial Predicament for Schools

The Rawlsian 'method of avoidance' of personal religious and ideological stances can lead to an over-zealous attempt by government to bifurcate issues of national and human well-being, so that the public arena devalues the essential character of the private lives, attitudes and beliefs of its citizens. Carter (1993: 8) has highlighted the impact of this modern liberal approach on America, arguing that there is in American political ideology 'a magnificent respect for freedom of conscience' but at the same time a huge fear of religious domination of politics and a wariness of 'those who take religion seriously'. In addition, the Catholic philosopher Maritain (1951: 13), argued that the separation of individual and community initiatives from the political will of a society endangers both the existence and the prosperity of the political community or culture.

Traditionally education has been chiefly concerned with beliefs and values and it has been the political and philosophical values of modernity which have formed the core of educational endeavour. In particular, philosophical and political liberalism, with its location of the common good in a common morality founded on respect for universal human rights, has contributed to the view that conceptions of justice take priority over individual person's or community's understandings of the good life. Education working within this view of the just society can take two directions. Either it can foster schools which seek to inculcate the values of the common good through holding to a common morality or it can seek ways of encouraging communities of like-minded people, such as religious adherents or secular humanists, to found schools based on their principles and values. The first approach requires schools to involve teachers and students in learning about principles and values which are only evidently of use when the individual student or teacher participates in civic or social communities or in the workplace. The second requires all schools to recognize universal human rights and civic responsibilities but presumes that the schools will be more fully engaged with the development of the student as a whole person, with personal values derived from their homes, friends and social communities.

For philosophers such as MacIntyre, a person cannot be adequately educated in morality unless the school and the community it serves profess a coherent set of moral and religious values. Thus Carr has commented that:

> it has long been common on something like MacIntyre's grounds for religious constituencies and denominations in developed democracies to make their own provision for the education of their members. (1998: 248)

Herein lies a particular reason for taking seriously the historical situation of the existence of faith schools both in the UK and in many former colonial territories. In what ways do they educate the moral, religious and civic aspects of individual students and to what extent could they yield good practice in the matter of educating the whole person as opposed to each aspect? On this basis, too, it is possible to sympathize with Sidney Webb, who is quoted by Judge (2002: 43), as insisting in 1901 in a Fabian Society pamphlet that:

> It is politically impossible to abolish these voluntary schools; and whatever we may think of the theological reasons for their establishment, their separate and practically individual management does incidentally offer what ought to be, in any public system of education, most jealously guarded, namely, variety, and the opportunity of experiment.

This study is concerned to examine, in these problematic plural times, the varieties of ways in which different faith school cultures set about the task of human and social formation and the outcomes of their approaches.

In 2001 in northern towns in the UK such as Blackburn, Bradford and Huddersfield a series of extensive disturbances took place. Such towns put flesh on descriptions of British society by sociologists such as Flanagan (1999: 7) as being 'fragmented and containing a range of beliefs and values'. The Cantle Report (2001), resulting from the northern inner-city disturbances, described faith-based schools as undermining community cohesion. Such schools were seen as both exclusive and divisive.

Fifteen years earlier the Swann Report made several recommendations concerning common and faith or separate schools, which included:

1. Far more can and should be done by schools to respond to the 'pastoral' needs of Muslim pupils, to ensure that there is a real respect and understanding by both teachers and parents of each other's concerns and that the demands of the school place no child in fundamental conflict with the requirements of his faith.
2. As we have observed earlier, the right of communities to seek to establish their own voluntary aided schools is firmly enshrined in the law. At the same time, we do not believe that such separate schools would be in the long term interest of the ethnic minority communities. (1985: 496–8)

Assumptions are made in both reports that attention should be paid to the pastoral care of religious or ethnic minority students in all schools and that separate schools are inherently exclusive and divisive. Each report finds cause to criticize both state community schools and state-supported faith-based schools. Neither is thought to be equipped to meet the educational needs of students growing up in an intensely plural society. The obverse of such assumptions is that a common form of education for all could be found in a 'common school'. Unwisely the reports do not consider the steps which a plural society would need to take away from the historical position of the existence of state-maintained faith schools to their abolition in order to build a new form of common school. Nor do they consider the difficulties facing formal education as it seeks to accommodate state-supported education to the differing patterns of living and working in the new millennium. Instead education is seen as a positive concept which merely requires harnessing to the particular problems with which the reports are concerned in order to bring about a change for the better in plural communities. What is seen here is an accumulated package of goods with which education is to be concerned, without a matching commitment to a reassessment of the overall purpose of education.

Within a landscape of pluralism and diversity, Hargreaves has been prompted to judge that:

The decline of the Judaeo-Christian tradition as the prime purpose underpinning schooling and teaching in a context of greater religious, cultural and ethnic diversity raises penetrating questions about the moral purposes of education. One of the greatest educational crises of the postmodern age is the collapse of the common school: a school tied to the community and having a clear sense of the social and moral values it should instill. (1994: 58)

Hargreaves makes a critical connection here between the definition and purpose of education for the common school in former times and a religious base. At present he argues that the common school has no clear sense of the social and moral values it should instill. If that is the case, then the common school without a common moral purpose is in grave danger of operating amorally. Yet education has traditionally been defined as a moral activity. The agenda, therefore, which Hargreaves proposes for the education community is pressing. What attempts do we make to examine whether the whole state-maintained system of schools for pupils of compulsory school age is supported or not by an adequate moral underpinning, with which it might sustain its purpose? Second, are schools given clear authority by the many and diverse communities which now constitute society to teach about and instil specific social and moral values? Implicit in Hargreaves' words is a warning that without an adequate and appropriate consideration of the essential nature and purpose of education, the professional community may find itself cut off both from the beliefs and values which traditionally secured its authority to educate and from the beliefs and values of those it seeks to educate.

In this way, Hargreaves pointed to the need for the debate with which this study is concerned. He points to the requirement of a 'prime moral purpose' to undergird schooling. He reflects the view that in a postmodern society, no one tradition or world view can hold dominance in a situation of ethnic, religious and cultural diversity. In consequence, education itself is stripped of former prime sources for its moral purpose and authority. Hargreaves' lament for the collapse of the common school is indeed no less than for education itself, which traditionally since the nineteenth century has defined its nature as moral and its outcomes as the ethical inculcation of habits and virtues consistent with modernity. Second, Hargreaves highlights the traditional British indifference to religion, which was thought by Gilbert (1980: 65) to be influenced by a 'subtle assumption of rationality'. Thus a modern rational education has tackled social and intellectual problems without too much concern with religion.

He suggests that a common cultural heritage by which certain moral assumptions could be clothed in a common narrative tradition was the basis for education in the modern age. This view would reflect Gordon and Lawton's (2003: 60) definition of culture, as referring to 'knowledge, beliefs and attitudes, passed on from one generation to the next, and by definition any society possesses a culture or way of life that members of that society share'. In the postmodern age, Hargreaves, however, describes a situation in which no one set of moral assumptions holds and no one dominant narrative conveys cultural understandings of human purpose. This postmodern perspective, which holds no common assumptions about values, beliefs and human narratives can arguably be described as lacking a culture, although it houses many cultures. Wright, for example, in his discussion of religion, education and postmodernity concludes:

> Given the plurality of choices and opinions before us, it is increasingly difficult to make sense of a diverse and complex world. This has led perhaps inevitably to the collapse of a single shared high culture and its fragmentation into a diverse range of popular cultures. (2004: 3)

It is surely a matter for speculation whether a plural society which holds to the inherited conception that it has a duty to educate its children, though with no consensus with which beliefs and values, might better be described as a-cultural. Its description is adapted from the word 'anomie'; a condition defined by the Oxford English Dictionary as a 'lack of the usual social or ethical standards in an individual or group'. In an a-cultural situation, individuals have both social and ethical standards and so too do individual communities or groups, whether large or small, ancient or new. What is lacking is a set of standards in common or across the individuals or the groups. Thus the many cultures live together without a common conscience by which judgements can be made and to which appeals can be directed. Within this a-cultural society there is little, or no, opportunity to express values and beliefs in common about the nature and purpose of schooling. Any commonalities or standards can only be imposed from outside the individual's or individual community's realm of meaning.

The Impact of Centrally Driven Meta-Policy on Micro-School Cultures

The a-cultural situation, in which the political liberalism described above mixes with other cultures, seriously challenges education's interface with the variety and complexity of citizens' beliefs and values. For example, it is of little surprise that a standards-led understanding of education was imposed through the establishment of the Office for Standards in Education on the education community in Britain at the very time when this a-cultural situation was being most graphically depicted in Lyotard's theories, succinctly summarized by Wright as:

> The modernist search for universal truth, for the ultimate meta-narrative capable of explaining the totality of the order-of-things, must give way to an acceptance of a diversity of local micro-narratives whose horizons are necessarily limited by the contingencies of culture and the accidents of space and time. (2004: 24)

Standards as the defining culture of national education were centrally imposed at the expense of a coherent set of aims for schooling in general. Little room was left for each school to respond to individual pupil and local needs. Significantly, the new edition of MacGilchrist et al.'s *The Intelligent*

School (2004) begins with a critical overview of the government's standards-driven school agenda: a one-size-fits all model. The authors point out that the government's policy is derived from a particular reading of 'school effectiveness' research. This reading enables politicians to locate all responsibility for students' learning within the schools themselves, with no reference to the social contexts in which they have to function. Thus schools become mechanistic implementers of a national system of skills development and curriculum assessment. Intelligent schools, on the other hand, are characterized by certain values which the authors root in the concept of 'multiple intelligences'. These are ethical, spiritual, contextual, emotional, collegial, reflective, as well as operational, pedagogical, corporate and, at their heart, systemic.

The case made by MacGilchrist et al. makes clear that, in postmodern times, formal educational policy, which is centrally driven, seeks to engage schools in a meta-narrative, with no reference to their micro-cultures, namely, the school cultures themselves. This study proposes that in an a-cultural situation, where no one view holds sway, leeway should be given to the kind of education which individual school cultures engage in, for it is they, and not central government, which are primarily responsible for the education of the young. It is critical in reassessing the purpose of education to examine how individual cultures meet the beliefs and attitudes of their students at present. It was McLaughlin (1994: 459) who pointed out that the statements of value which emerge from Ofsted inspection visits may be ambiguous, provisional and less than totally clear. Taylor goes further:

> Unless schools make the effort to articulate their values and develop some clarity of vision, they will not be in a strong position to pursue their task of developing pupils' understanding of values . . . and their own commitments. (1996: 8)

In examining school cultures a further distinction can be made between 'culture' and 'ideology'. Geertz, for example, set out the relationship between culture and ideology by arguing that the role of culture is to provide 'extensive sources of information, templates for the organization of social and psychological processes'. Ideologies, however,

> come most crucially into play in situations where the particular kind of information they contain is lacking, where institutional guides for behaviour, thought or feeling are weak or absent. It is in country unfamiliar emotionally and typographically that one needs poems and road maps. So too with ideology. (1985: 81)

From this argument, it is possible to assert that it is the schools as micro-cultures, with mainly a standards-driven understanding of education to guide their outputs, which bring their individual ideologies to bear on the task of educating the young. A characteristic, therefore, of an intelligent, complex, plural society would surely be to take heed of the ideologies of education which are developing within the micro-cultures of schools and reflect upon them. For schools which operate in an a-cultural situation could prove to be a valuable source of information and understanding about how to involve adults and the young in education in values. That reflection would in turn examine whether each school is ethical, contextual, collegial and reflective and under-pinned by a dominant set of assumptions or values which are both inherent in the culture of the school and found throughout its mission and practice.

How this might be done is central to the present work for it is concerned to question how best education at present can proceed from its historical situation of supporting state-maintained faith schools among the variety of schools open to its young people. It is thus concerned to look at the prospects of education as a whole offering a good education to all at this time of cultural and intellec-tual uncertainty. It assumes that judgements about which school offers a good education can best be arrived at by first examining a variety of school micro-cultures within plural societies. For this present exercise, it is considered appro-priate to study faith-based micro-cultures; in time, however, such a study would be important in the micro-cultures of common and community schools.

The intention is first to test methods by which school cultures and their nested ecologies may be usefully explored in relation to the beliefs and values they espouse and to which their students adhere. Second, the study will explore to what extent those micro-studies can engage with established or developing concepts of education in plural contexts. In this way, the present study will first examine single-school cultures and their understanding of the educational enterprise. Then from an overview of how particular school cul-tures contribute, or not, to personal, social and cultural development, a case will be made that authority for each school to educate at the present time should result chiefly from their capability to educate in and for pluralism.

Any examination of a school as a micro-culture within a plural society will, therefore, necessitate judgements being made about the quality of the micro-culture as a school capable of developing students for plural situations. This study proposes that such judgements can be made validly in a plural a-cul-tural situation within two matrices. The first will be the school's position on the mediating-institution matrix; the second, will place the school within a moral matrix.

Schools as 'mediating institutions' in A-Cultural Contexts

To date, the need for a more reasoned and organic analysis of what might con-stitute an educational ideology sufficient for the challenging task of engaging with pluralism has been sidestepped as a result of the dominance of the eco-nomic imperative in current education as opposed to the moral. This trend has been helpfully summarized by Lawton and Cowen:

> Overall much of the thinking that has guided definitions of a good educa-tion in many cultures has been about the relationship of education to the

acquisition of virtue. Discussion of education has been a discussion of the nature of virtue . . . now we are increasingly used to a discourse in education that uses economic terms as the vocabulary of valuation: it is in economic terms that education is itself to be understood. That which is economic has become that which is virtuous. (2001: 18)

The arguments in this book will therefore not be primarily concerned with the ability of schools to meet the economic imperatives of globalization, presuming that national ministries of education have already devised means of inspecting schools to judge their competence in academic and vocational education and their ability to offer value for money in the process. Instead, it will seek to uncover the ability of particular school cultures to focus their efforts equally on the acquisition of virtue as well as economic competence in plural times. It will move directly to examine the relationship between the virtues which each school espouses and the values and identities with which senior students emerge from their schooling. The exact definition of a value differs among social scientists and educators but it might be summarized as a preference that is felt or considered to be justified in choosing between available ways of acting, thinking or being. Cultures, ideologies and world views help organize and direct values and identities. As such in a complex world of plurality, the individual student must select a view that best does justice to her or his experience and, ultimately, identity. Otherwise, as Nelson (1967: 48) warns, if a person does not make such choices, 'he will forever be the battlefield on which the various views struggle for hearing'. At a time of wide freedom of choice in values and lifestyles, and possible conflicts within an individual's experience of deciding values and acting upon them, education needs to find a mode by which it can assist the individual's understanding and decision making.

If schools and their particular cultures are to be examined in relation to their effectiveness as 'mediating institutions', there is a need to ask on what basis judgements might be made. An answer to this question is suggested in the writing of Pendlebury. She asserts that 'education is centrally – although not solely – concerned with opening ways for people to become members of one or more epistemic communities' and 'it helps to constitute selves'. Pendlebury's (1998: 185) definition of an epistemic community suggests judging a school in three key areas: the role of the school in articulating the kinds of knowledge and virtues with which its teaching and learning is concerned; the procedures it uses for qualifying and disqualifying evidence; and its ability to sustain a critical mass of practitioners with the appropriate virtues necessary to sustain that community.

It is a promising notion within the search for reinstating the worth of the virtuous in education to find a means of placing a school on a matrix concerned with its ability to mediate. There is the ability to mediate, for example, government concerns for students' civic, social and vocational development through a school's inherent commitment both to the value of students as individual human beings and to knowledge as a means to learning how best to be human in plural and globalized times. There is also the ability to mediate local community concerns and values with individual student's life-stances and commitments. Testing a school's mediating quotient would permit a perspective on the intelligence or otherwise of a school as a learning community capable of focusing on the knowledge and virtues necessary for assisting students to live well in a-cultural, plural societies.

Schools as Part of the 'moral matrix' of a Plural Society

Hargreaves (1994: 58) raises important questions about which compass bearings might be of use when considering whether the 'common school' can be resuscitated, as well as whether there are other alternative types of schools, which might 'instil social and moral values' appropriate to the times. Some of the broad questions which stem from the main question would look something like the following: Should schools avoid religion altogether both in their foundations/vision and curricula? Or should the diversity of religious belief in society be mirrored by faith communities having the right to own their own schools? Or should schools be places in which the fragmented nature of present society is healed and diversity integrated into a communal endeavour to find common values for living together, underpinned by shared beliefs in the nature of humanity? Or is it possible to blend some overarching moral purposes for education throughout society with the beliefs and values of particular communities, so that the students emerging from such schools may have hyphenated identities, such as British–Muslims, British–Catholics or British–Humanists? If the education community were to take on the exercise of gathering data and evidence related to the above questions, on what grounds might it, with the wider society, recognize which evidence to keep and which to discard? It is here that the concept of a 'moral matrix' in society can prove most helpful.

The former Archbishop of Canterbury, Dr George Carey, takes the view that there exists within British society ample evidence of moral commitment in all walks of life through the participation of many in public life, in the support of dependent relatives, in the increasing focus on environmental and animal rights issues, and in the continuing interest in forms of spiritual exploration. This suggests there is a substantial bedrock of commitment on which society can build in a wide range of areas, including education, although this does not depend exclusively on one ideal of the good. Each institution and each person has a role to play in developing the moral society and without that personal identification with a set of values Dr Carey argues that society could descend into disunity and anarchy.

Yet the moral purposeful commitments of many citizens described by George Carey, have brought individuals and communities within a moral matrix:

(in) the moral vision of a mature and civilised society, where do schools, churches, home life and the wider community fit in? We all fit in as part of the moral matrix through which individuals are formed or, conversely, deformed as civilised and caring people. (2000: 20)

To be placed on the 'moral matrix', therefore, a school will be required to show how it acts as a 'moral companion' to the young and to their society. Further the Commission for Social Justice (1994: 10) defined the good society as depending, 'not just on the economic success of the individual', but on the 'social capital of the community'. For Gamarnikow and Green (2000: 96–7) the concept of social capital 'represents the rediscovery of community and of the idea that social relations are an essential resource for people', with 'trust' as a constitutive element of the 'social capital' framework. In other words, the concept of 'social capital' has been built from the idea that people are moral because they live together socially. A school must give account of how it has contributed to students' attitudes and values as they engage with their own school community and with the wider community.

There is then the potential for a positive framework to support the many pluralities of people, communities, values and beliefs in appropriating for themselves a public moral culture. The question, however, arises: Will the pressures of so many communities living together obscure the opportunities for new ways of engagement in a public moral culture?

Faith Communities and the Common Good in Education

The Church Schools Review Group (2001: 3) argues that in a state which provides education for all, the purpose of the Church in education is 'not simply to provide the basic education needed for human dignity'. The Archbishop of Canterbury (2003) has also spoken of 'a real tension in educational thinking between those whose concern is primarily, almost exclusively, with imparting skills to individuals and those who understand education as something that forms the habits of living in a group'. In this way the Anglican tradition puts its weight behind defining the ultimate purpose of education as social and personal formation leading to the ability to live well in a group or community. Individuals are defined as being educated when they perceive themselves as developing humanly in community.

The Anglican Church presents a stance against the economic imperative in education. It also, however, represents a growing movement within faith communities to align themselves with the philosophical challenge to the individual excesses of liberalism set out by the communitarians. Stiltner has astutely analysed the communitarian position into three strands:

1. Narrative communitarianism highlights the pervasive role a community and its stories play in the formation of its members' characters, values and beliefs. . . . Therefore the common good in its fullness is found only within a fairly homogenous community.
2. Discourse communitarianism locates the common good in a form of society that allows all members to discuss and articulate their conceptions of the good. The strand sees community held together by

conversation . . . [it has] a preference for a procedural common good focused more on the form of the civic conversation than its content.
3. Egalitarian communitarianism focuses less on communal narratives and more on communal relationships. . . . this strand is similar to the prior one, though it identifies equality as the primary social good. (1999: 6–7)

In the United States, Miller exemplifies egalitarian communitarianism in his thinking about the role of the Catholic community. In his review of the role of religion in American public life (1986: 288–9), he has speculated whether the Catholic tradition's commitment to the idea of human interdependence in community might serve the American republic well as it faces a complex and uncertain future. Miller observes that Catholicism possesses resources that both Protestantism and secular liberalism lack. These he argues can help shape a response to both the challenges and the opportunities of a society that needs a stronger sense of life being bound up with life, if it is to flourish in a way that befits the dignity of human beings.

On the other hand, Longley, who is himself a Roman Catholic, projects a discourse-based communitarianism as having purpose in these present plural times. Writing in the Chief Rabbi's book, *Faith in the Future*, Longley argued:

[It] requires an institutional habit of tolerance that goes beyond peace between factions, and deepens into an ability to listen and to learn. Faith communities will have their own clear principles, but may find that uncompromising insistence upon those principles is possible only within their own ranks. They should not for that reason reject efforts to influence the community at large, nor should they give up if they are not totally successful. Faith communities serve the wider needs of society every time they offer moral principles that are out of step with the fashionable morality of the age, even when that offer seems not to have had any affect. In any event, how can they know? (1995: xiii–xiv)

Both authors seek to make use of faith communities' claims to absolute truths in different ways. For Longley, absolute truths can be shared in community but they may give way to cooperative affirmations of common values if the practice being pursued; namely, an interest in the survival of humanity within plurality, seems worthwhile. Miller describes the need for a more pervasive evangelization of a Catholic narrative in order to bring about fundamental changes in the social and personal attitudes of a large democratic people.

The above examples both illustrate the significance of personal and communal beliefs within the common good and point to ways in which the various strands of communitarianism might be employed to focus examinations of the role of personal belief and values in the development of a common morality in a-cultural pluralities. Gutmann (1993: 3), on the other hand, warns of the necessity for an ethics of belief when dealing with religion at present. She warns of the dangers of an over-zealous promotion of one communitarian stance over another, which required that children be educated 'to accept the singularly correct and comprehensive conception of the good life'. Further Wright, in arguing about the possible limits of common schooling in a post-modern age, concludes:

An education rooted in the philosophy of difference will strive to take alternative viewpoints with the utmost seriousness, and commit itself to the struggle to avoid any imperialist imposition of one view or another. An honest recognition of difference and disagreement is infinitely preferable to a paternalistic and authoritarian regime of cultural oppression. (2004: 218)

Education for and in pluralism therefore should not be a matter of indoctrination even in the form of a beneficent communitarianism. Wittgenstein (1953: 143) serves the argument well here for he contested that the presentation and exposition of the religious world view must come across to the student as a moral challenge. Values are not free-standing and the public arena of education cannot operate in a moral void. That is to say, education, if it is agreed to be an initiation into epistemic or learning communities, is not about an entirely neutral communication of information. As Kerr (1998: 78), reflecting on the principles which would underpin religious education within Witttgenstein's thinking, would argue, 'on the contrary, learning about it (religion) comes as a challenge to the values and practices that the learner already has, whatever they may be'.

In this regard education in postmodern times should not disregard the contribution of modern liberalism to its nature and practice. Halstead (1996: 18) has succinctly described the three fundamental liberal democratic values as:

1. Individual liberty.
2. Equality of respect for all individuals within the structures and practices of society.
3. Consistent rationality.

This particular principled view of education for liberal democracy has underpinned modernity's project of enlightenment through education. In these perplexed times enlightenment must surely be the goal of educational endeavour in the matter of living well in plural societies. Modernity itself through its concern with the development of a reasoned understanding of the world and relationships in it led to an emphasis on education fostering the growth of individuals who increasingly were able to act autonomously. For Pring the development of autonomous individuals in postmodern demands the eradication of indoctrination:

Indoctrination lies in closing the mind, to blocking out, often through strong sentiments or feeling, the possibility of contemplating the alternative view. It lies in the removal of the system of belief from the critical tradition through which those very beliefs have evolved . . . It arises as much from the secular assumptions of the media and the cold indifference to religion of the humanist as it does from the closed institutions of religion. (2005: 59)

Pring (2005: 59) recognizes the diversity of values with which education will be involved and therefore advocates reasoning as the means of working with diversity because for him 'the aim of education is not to instil particular beliefs but to enable individuals to acquire beliefs on the basis of evidence, reason and criticism'. Similarly Bryk (1996) in writing about Catholic schools argues that schooling is to nurture in students the feelings, expressions and reflections that can help them approach their relations to all the world.

In examining the mode of autonomy and notions of rationality permitted to the students within their faith-school cultures, it is helpful to couple Pring's analysis with the advice of Hirst and Peters (1970: 31–2), when they argued that ideals such as autonomy are 'vacuous unless people are provided with forms of knowledge and experience to be critical, creative and autonomous with'. In other words, this study of ways in which faith interacts with the social and cultural formation of the young, particularly in faith schools, acknowledges the importance of Carr's argument that, although initiation into a rival conception of belief or practice cannot be other than indoctrination, initiation into a given spiritual perspective may offer a valuable basis for the appreciation of its rivals.

A reassessment of the place of faith schools in late modern times is urgently required, not least when empirical studies, such as the present one, uncover radical approaches to the building of school communities and the use of curriculum in personal, social and cultural education by faith communities. Some traditional images of faith schools as inward-looking powerhouses of indoctrination and exclusivity have certainly been shattered. Catholic schools featured in the study provide evidence of integrating their approaches to teaching and learning nationally agreed curricula with concern and understanding of their young people's very real personal and social predicaments. So too Catholic schools are described whose student and teacher populations are predominantly non-Catholic, yet whose students insist that the schools are meeting their needs both as human beings and as future workers who are economically competent. In addition, the great majority of students at the four schools confirmed their pride at attending those schools. In England, for example, pride in a school has become a pressing concern in re-vitalizing schools, which have been perceived as failing by students, parents, teachers and local communities. Any reassessment of faith schools would therefore encourage a variety of ways to discover: Just how does this or that particular faith school encourage and sustain such distinct models of good practice in personal, civic, academic and vocational education?

Chapter 3

To What Extent Can Plural Societies Which Encompass a Spectrum of World Views and Cultural Perspectives Sustain a Common Schooling for All?

Purpose of the Chapter

A deeper analysis of pluralism is presented as central to understanding, and inherently constitutive of, the common good. Such analysis highlights the fracturing of national education policies, in which some aims are grounded in the economic imperatives of global late modern trends, others in modern liberal humanistic considerations. A conclusion is reached that pluralism itself is central to the common good and that a normative pluralism could itself become the source of agreement about what is important in human and civic life. Critical to this success is the fostering of Sandel's (1994: 1794) deliberative engagement across civic society with key cultural and faith constituents. In these bewildering times, all types of schools, whether common 'community', faith based or specialist, have the capacity to contribute through a deliberative engagement with civic society to a wider and more satisfying understanding of an ethical education for plural societies. Their method of contribution to this debate would be through a new particular of educational thinking, a meta-narrative of educational school cultures.

The Problem Faced by the Common School in Late Modern Times

A society in which many cultures jostle for attention and dominance can find itself without any one influential culture, which as Heelas (1999: 64) argues would 'differentiate values, to distinguish between what is important and what is not, and to facilitate coherent, purposeful identities, life-plans or habits of the heart'. At such a time, within an a-cultural situation, there is the possibility of three alternatives developing: wholesale alienation among the general populace; cultural stagnation within the many existing cultures; or thoughtless cultural blending. Some plural societies, embraced in a series of cultural trends or philosophical modes, remain curiously a-cultural in terms of social perspective, world views, and, generally, ways of being human. Sutherland offers a powerful analysis of the problem which this descriptive rather than normative form of pluralism presents for education:

> The problem facing teachers is a very serious one. Unless the society in which they live and work gives some coherent account of what it considers important in human life then teachers have no real framework in which to operate. (1996: 48–49)

This chapter's concern is to respond to Sutherland's critical analysis of the teachers' and their society's predicament, and to propose a framework for education which might facilitate a more purposeful environment for their efforts in the face of a continuing absence of a coherent account. To what extent is the common school offering a satisfactory social, moral and spiritual education at present to each of its students? Moreover, if a coherent account could be given of what is important in human life, would the distinctive faith school be redundant? Both questions are vital at this time of cultural fracture and fragility.

Answers cannot be provided in haste. Some, such as in the Cantle Report (2001) will attempt to offer solutions from above, that is, without due regard to the complex nature of a plural democratic society. Others will insist that all sections within society must have their voice heard from below. Those who urge a Third Way will seek only political solutions. As Sacks, the Chief Rabbi, (1991: 11–12) has wisely commented, there exists at present 'a tenacious modern fallacy' that politics is the only form of activity capable of bringing about change in modern society. This chapter will argue that a central government community cohesion imposed from above cannot do justice to the plural culture experienced from below. Instead, this chapter will attempt to search out the beginnings of a solution by first addressing the nature of the pluralism and second setting out means by which some form of agreement might be reached across the breadth and depth of a plural society.

The individuals and the communities who face and tackle the challenges of distinctiveness, alienation and frustration in plural societies represent a wide spectrum of values and life-stances. Equally there are many different roots from which their values and moralities rise. This is the difficulty about which Taylor (1989: 495–8) wrote so convincingly; namely, that the moral roots or 'sources' of common human values are at least threefold, and each source is 'continually borrowing from and influenced by each other'. He offers excellent advice to those who might seek moral justifications in common in diverse, plural societies:

> My point here . . . is only to show how understanding our society requires that we take a cut through time – as one takes a cut through rock to find some strata are older than others. Views co-exist with those which have arisen later in reaction to them. (1989: 498)

Taylor's analysis of moral authorities within present society underlines the need for this study's concern with an analysis of the strata of world views which together constitute present-day complex societies. For any worthwhile debate about common values within pluralism there will need to be a recognition by all those in the debate of each of those sources, or authoritative traditions. Without that there seems little chance of moving such a debate from some generalizations about the quality of life in a plural society to its real substance. That substance has been examined so thoughtfully yet provocatively by Taylor. For him the search for moral sources in which to root many of the values at work in present society is imperative. He also argues significantly for this study that aspects of a potential common humanity are denied by current tendencies to ignore or deny spiritual aspirations. As he says (1989: 520) 'we tend in our culture to stifle the spirit'. He questions whether moral sources today can be sustained without a vision of hope or a religious dimension. For him the search for moral sources in both modern and postmodern times can lead ultimately to an emphasis on the 'disengaged individual self' as the source of morality:

Because of the plurality of social worlds in modern society the structures of each particular world are experienced as relatively unstable and unreliable. The . . . modern individual's experience of a plurality of social worlds relativises every one of them. . . . Therefore, the individual seeks to find his foothold in reality in himself rather than outside himself. (1989: 499)

Taylor leaves open the role of communities and faith in that search for the sources of morality. He does warn, however, as does Gutmann (1993: 3) when discussing the communitarians' position, of the dangers of an imposed view of the personal and social order as found in policies such as that derived from the Cantle Report. For him there is much to fear from a consensus imposed through persuasion or even force.

Taylor's seminal work suggested that the human search for an ethical identity in modern times is complex and often dispiriting. It is possible to hear echoes of Taylor's concerns while analysing a plural society's attempts to reach agreement on what it considers important in human living, both personal and social, civic and global. Those attempts are concerned with placing values on aspects of living and behaving. Valuing is an ethical activity but without an agreed ethical base how might a society composed of many cultures, religions and life-stances put discussion of the virtuous onto its agenda? The traditional view has looked to education but without a coherent understanding of education which includes the fostering of a virtuous life. How might education meet the moral and social expectations which society still holds? It is necessary first to contextualize the reasons why these questions have arisen. This will be done as a means of setting out the socio-intellectual cultural pluralism which at present runs alongside and, frequently, cuts through the religious, philosophical and ethnic pluralism with which most commentators are concerned. These secular aspects of pluralism which are called modern, postmodern and global late modern in this study will therefore be described more fully below.

The Three Cultural Modes and Their Particular Influence on Educational Thought

The modern cultural mode

The modern cultural mode has been described by Pring as having the following characteristics:

1. There is the ideal of a complete and scientific explanation of physical and social reality.
2. In pursuit of this ideal the progressive development of knowledge can be divided into intellectual disciplines, based on their distinctive concepts, verification procedures and modes of enquiry.
3. These bodies of knowledge provide the secure knowledge base for social action and improvement.
4. The educational system is crucial to the initiation of the young into these different bodies of knowledge and forms of rationality. This is achieved by teachers who have become 'authorities' within these different forms of knowledge. (2000a: 110)

The modern secular mode impinges on students in a further significant way in relation to their attitudes to religious education. Such attitudes are described by Hammond et al. as 'minds . . . tightly closed against the possibility that reality might plausibly be seen in any other way than that transmitted via the dominant culture' (1990: 108). Moral education in modern times also persistently championed the separation of religion from morality, thus ensuring the continuation of the modernist tradition of privatizing religion and zealously secularizing the moral.

In general, liberal political philosophies accompany this traditional modernity. That political liberalism can perhaps best be illustrated by the thinking of Rawls. In his *Political Liberalism*, Rawls (1993) distinguishes civic or political virtues, which are necessary for the functioning of a liberal plural society and other virtues which human beings may possess, rooted in religious and philosophical stances. Although he acknowledges that the more personal virtues may be necessary for religious and cultural formation, only those of tolerance, fairness, respect, reasonableness and civility are required for a good civic life. Young (1990: 116) reflects that the thinking of Rawls necessitates within the 'politics of difference' the creation of what she calls a 'heterogeneous' public.

On the other hand, Callan (1998: 14) advises that 'liberal politics must include a project of cultural assimilation'. For this a common education for all is required which teaches knowledge and habits of thought and feeling 'that participating competently in the government of a free people requires'. Gaining this 'civic perspective', however, does not proscribe 'many kinds of separate education' and he astutely advises that 'liberal theorists and ordinary citizens may disagree about what measures a state can justly pursue in support of the assimilative process of education'.

The postmodern cultural mode

Postmodernity is defined by Lyotard (1984: xxiv) as 'incredulity towards narratives'. Gellner (1992: 24) speaks of it as seemingly 'in favour of relativism . . . and hostile to the idea of unique, exclusive, objective or transcendent truth'. Pring examines 'what typifies the postmodern world' and asserts that:

> We live in a culturally diverse society which makes us question the dominance of any one view . . . Therefore, we need to come to terms with pluralism, not simply in recognizing that there is a diversity of culture, but also in recognizing the diverse modes of rationality and perspective. (2000a: 110)

For Young a fine example of the postmodern cultural trend is her 'ideal of city life':

> City life signifies the bringing together of strangers. Citizens learn to find the free play of difference both within and without, as their kaleidoscopic social world arouses a restless longing for the strange and the exotic. (1990: 236–41)

According to Wright (2004: 146), at the centre of postmodern educational thought is 'the desire to resist, subvert and deconstruct modern approaches to the theory and practice of education'. To what extent are young people conscious of the choices which postmodernity presents to them? For Alexander the challenge facing contemporary education in 'an emancipated, postmodern age' is:

> To promote only those putative ethical visions that embrace the conditions of moral agency and that are, therefore, at home in open societies. (2000: 308)

Global late modernity

Giddens has defined the 'global' cultural mode as:

> not only, or even primarily, about economic interdependence, but about the transformation of time and space in our lives. Distant events, whether economic or not, affect us more directly and immediately than ever before. Conversely, decisions we take as individuals are often global in their implications. (1998: 30–1)

Cowen spells out what he believes to be the consequences for education of the 'globalization' cultural mode:

> The contemporary crisis – globalisation and the relative increase in the powerlessness of the 'nation-State' – is not merely an economic crisis. It is a cultural one, which requires historical, sociological, anthropological, cultural and philosophical analysis. If the social and human sciences are impoverished by technisisation – by performativity, by pragmatism, by an excessive concern for the immediate and the useful – then one of the defences of the nations to understand what is happening to them will be dramatically weakened. (2000: 101)

Cowen astutely provides the context of global late modernity for one of the most serious consequences for education; namely, the stripping bare of the traditional humanistic concept of education itself, grounded in historical, philosophical and cultural analysis. That concept can be summarized and exemplified by the writings of many key philosophers and educators; for example, Peters and the London school of post-war philosophers of education in their setting of aims for a liberal humanistic education and their criteria for education for autonomy. Within this same humanistic tradition, Pring (1984: 30) and Maritain elaborated the centrality of recognizing that students are persons. For example, Maritain with Gallagher and Gallagher described the purpose of education as:

> Education directed towards wisdom, centred on the humanities, aiming to develop in people a capacity to think correctly and to enjoy truth and beauty, is education for freedom or liberal education. (1976: 69)

Global trends in culture and education have been seen to challenge this liberal understanding of education. Neave (1988: 274) for, example, has argued that education is 'increasingly viewed as a sub-sector of economic policy' and less as 'part of social policy'. Lawton and Cowen characterized a late-modern educational system in the following way as it:

> locates (a) the moral as the concern of the family, (b) the national principle as the concern of a homogenizing regional agency (NAFTA, MERCOSUR, the EU) and (c) defines the 'values' of the education system as those of effectiveness and efficiency. (2001: 25)

They continue (2001: 25) by offering a haunting commentary on the late-modern mode, arguing that performance and surveillance have then 'become the main values that educational processes signify and institutionalize'.

These dominant motifs of global late modernity can be seen in the educational planning and policies of a number of countries in recent years. For example, in Country X, the National Development Plan 8, 1997/8–2002/3

(Government of Country X, 1997: 337) states that, 'a productive and highly motivated workforce is fundamental to achieving sustainable economic diversification' and spells out the strategy to achieve this, partially (1997: 339) through an 'effective preparation of students for life, citizenship and the world of work'. This example well illustrates the description of education as a sub-sector of economic policy and dominated by 'technisisation' and 'performativity'.

The test for any school in global late modernity must be to establish by what means it responds to the challenge of preparing students for global economic reality and their own economic concerns, while taking account of their other values, such as altruism and the importance of belonging to a cooperative community. This is why it becomes imperative to enquire of individual schools whether they have theorized the character of knowing how to be human as well as that related to how to be economically successful. Perhaps it is within each school's epistemology of social and personal formation that centrally driven curriculum policies take flesh and can be evaluated for their role in developing certain kinds of human beings and citizens of plural societies. Investigating how a school tackles the education of an individual human being in late modern times would seem to be a fruitful means of beginning to resolve the cultural problem with which this chapter is concerned.

Before examining the individual school, however, it is worth spending a brief time examining some of the tensions which an interplay of the three cultural modes can create within the education systems of plural societies at present. In the 'Foreword' to its Education Act, Country Z's government sets out the following purposes for education:

> To inculcate in young minds the respect for human rights, for cultural pluralism and learning to live together, promote morals and character building as well as unity in diversity in the spirit of brotherhood and solidarity . . . The government recognizes the importance of education as an investment in human capital formation that lays the foundation for future economic growth and development in Country Z. (Government of Country Z, 2003)

This statement encapsulates the diverse nature of the tasks demanded of educational systems in the global, late-modern cultural mode. Education is to work with key values foremost in all its activities and concerns. It is also to ensure that certain personal, social and spiritual values are acquired by young people and put into practice. Above all it is to ensure that young people become well informed and productive workers, contributing at all times to the economic development (and growth) of their national economies. The UK government in *Teachers Meeting the Challenge of Change* sets out no less a diverse task for its teachers who are to ensure that their pupils receive:

> education for a world of rapid change in which both flexible attitudes and enduring values have a part to play. (Great Britain 1998)

Education in the UK as elsewhere in the world is set a problematic task without being given the solution. It seems that education is being asked to reconcile through its curricula and pedagogy opposites such as inculcating both 'flexible attitudes' and 'enduring values' into the personal and social development of their students. The statements are positive and expect certain outcomes but none in themselves speaks of any innate worth within education or examines its nature. Both statements presuppose that 'education' will 'deliver' the stated aims, with the first seeing education as 'an investment in human capital formation'. None begins, however, with a statement about the nature of education; rather, they choose either to set out the nature of the culture in which they perceive the educational system working or the culture to which they would wish education to propel the young.

The question posed by the discussion above is the extent to which educational activity is able to recover as its central purpose the development of human beings within plural societies in which the modern liberal vision of education apparently packs no greater punch than global technological trends. The problem is whether education systems within present plural societies, which are simultaneously pushed and cajoled in modern, postmodern and late modern directions, can achieve and sustain a common moral purpose; indeed, from which directions in society might these systems take their purpose for their common schooling?

Towards a Resolution of the Problem (1): Satisfactorily Defining the Common Good in and through Pluralism

The question of how to arrive at a satisfactory definition that constitutes the common good in a plural late modern society is central to the outcomes of this present study. Stiltner (1999: 6) presents one method which is firmly located in the modern cultural mode. He has argued that 'the liberal tradition generally locates the common good in citizens' agreement to live in a society structured by respect for rights and by common pursuit of liberty and individual opportunity'. He goes on to examine the role particular communities should play in a society that favours individual rights and protection. In a particularly stark manner, Stiltner poses the question thus:

> Should the state accommodate, protect, or remain neutral towards the interests, practices and mores of various religious and ethnic sub-communities? Some have framed this debate as a stark choice: modern societies can strive to protect primarily either rights and freedom or values and mores. It is often assumed that this is a zero-sum game. (1999: 7–8)

Others, along with Stiltner and the present researcher, believe that it should be possible to achieve a consensus. The two main proponents of how to achieve consensus are Rawls and Sandel but they, too, disagree about how this might be achieved. According to Rawls, citizens must achieve agreement on the political ordering of society, and they must agree to disagree about their beliefs and the different values by which they live. For Rawls (1993: 226), public reason refers to the way citizens in a democratic society should explain, defend and promote their political views, by employing reasons which are accessible to all reasonable citizens. Rawls places reason at the heart of a process he calls 'political construction'. In the ensuing structure, according to Stiltner (1999: 59), public reason is used in such a way that 'its judgement accords with the fundamental ideas of the political culture'. This establishment of the 'method of avoidance' by Rawls for the modern state sets up a political liberalism, which Stiltner (1999: 75) rightly concludes is 'counterproductive to the kinds of public discussion and political deliberation that promote a society in which citizens are truly tolerant and mutually respectful'. In particular, 'it removes from our political deliberations those moral and religious views citizens find most germane to the debates'.

Sandel understood Rawls to be the successor of Kant in his particular liberalism:

> Its core thesis can be stated as follows: society being composed of a plurality of persons, each with his own aims, interests and conceptions of the good, is best arranged when it is governed by principles that do not themselves presuppose any particular conception of the good: what justifies these regulative principles above all is not that they maximize the social welfare or otherwise promote the good, but rather that they conform to the concept of right, a moral category given prior to the good and independent of it. (1982: 1)

For Sandel, then, the individual possesses basic human rights which are not dependent on society's view of what it means to be good or of how to belong to a society. His arguments here also highlight a problem often encountered in the debate about the existence of faith-based schooling in contemporary plural societies; namely, that the concept of a political right when directed to forms of schooling appropriate for plural societies will frequently dismiss the rights of faith schools to exist, despite the good which such schools might promote. Sandel (1994: 1794) later concludes that political liberalism is unable to contain 'the moral energies of a vital democratic life'. He, therefore, sets out to develop a 'more spacious public reason' which is connected by 'a deliberative conception of respect'. That respect, he defined thus:

> We respect our fellow citizens' moral and religious convictions by engaging, or attending to them- sometimes by challenging and contesting them, sometimes by listening and learning from them- especially if those convictions bear on important political questions. (1994: 1794)

In *Man and the State*, Maritain prefigures both of Rawls and Sandel's arguments, when he comments in the following way on the possibilities of pluralism within the state:

> The national community, as well as all communities of the nation . . . [are] comprised in the superior unity of the body politic. But the body politic also contains in its superior unity the family units, whose essential rights and freedoms are anterior to itself, and a multiplicity of other particular societies which proceed from the free initiative of citizens and should be as autonomous as possible. Such is the element of pluralism inherent in every truly political society. Family, economic, cultural, educational, religious life matter as much as does political life to the very existence and prosperity of the body politic. (1951: 11)

With this argument, too, Maritain foreshadows Carey's concept of the 'moral matrix', through which pluralism can be seen to be central to the common good because different communities, as well as individuals, pursue different aspects of the sum total of the common good. For the concept of the common good to be of practical and ethical value in post and late modern societies there must be serious attempts made to furnish it with both political and social/community meaning.

Perhaps the most appealing definition of the common good for help in resolving the present concern is that resulting from Sandel. For Sandel political questions can best be treated by listening to citizens' moral and religious convictions. Faith-based schooling is a social reality at present in many plural societies, generally as a result of historical circumstances. The fact that so many religious adherents and non-religious believers argue that the education of children is best handled in schools in which faith is taken seriously suggests that the common good in post and late modern times is best served by 'engaging, or attending to them – sometimes by challenging and contesting them, sometimes by listening and learning from them'. Equally there is a need to engage with those students who have attended a faith school for there is much to be learnt about the role of an established community working as an epistemic community in offering the individual student a base from which to perceive different understandings of personhood from her/his own.

Towards a Resolution of the Problem (2): Establishing an Ethics of Personal, Social and Civic Education

Personhood implies a conscious development of an individual towards that which is considered good or bad both for the individual and for society. Individuals source their identities and values from different traditions and cultures – society also. For convenience the distinction is often drawn between a private person with differing attendant interests, beliefs, attitudes and values and a citizen whose behaviour, values and attitudes are shaped by the civic society.

Pring's (1984: 21–4) thinking about what constitutes a person and the kinds of values and knowledge which are relevant to this or that sort of person represents an essential principle in resolving the present problem. In the plurality of socio-intellectual cultural modes, Taylor points out that it is the individual who will ultimately make decisions about the source of moral authority. It is therefore the duty of education to seek purposeful ways of helping the individual student become the person s/he is most capable of becoming. Pring sifts the attributes of a person to be educated into intellectual and moral virtues, character traits, social competencies, practical and theoretical knowledge, and personal values.

Pring here makes a clearing in the ground which has been tested and examined by Rawls, Sandel, Young and Maritain but he does not as such posit a definitive answer to the core question of the present study. Instead he provides a framework by which it might be possible to analyse data about the education which young people receive concerning their values, identities and characteristics in particular schools of a plural society.

A common schooling cannot afford to ignore the choices which living in plurality offers for the individual and society. It follows, therefore, that education must concern itself both with an education which promotes intellectual and moral virtues as well as particular character traits. For Aristotle the moral person is unable to practise the virtues, unless s/he is cognizent with the situation in which they are to be practised. He argues:

> An agent has a moral obligation to know the facts of the case. This does not preclude the use of general rules, but they are at best, only rough guides, summaries of past actions, a part of a web of background knowledge useful in understanding a case. (NE 1106b36–1107a3)

Taking Aristotle as a guide to what might indicate that a school had taken seriously its duty to promote personal, social, moral and civic virtues in its students, it is clear that a good school in a plural society will need to create the circumstances in which students would exercise intellectually and emotionally their understanding of a situation which demands an ethical response. At the same time, it would promote circumstances in which the students might exercise their responses in practical ways.

If schools are genuine epistemic communities in which learning about the human condition and living well in plurality is a priority, then they must also consciously provide situations in which individuals, or moral agents, might as Sherman (1999: 38) says, 'know the facts of the case'.

The distinction between a private person and their citizenship has served modernity's project, as exemplified in the writings of Rawls and moral educators such as Wilson (1990). Education in late modern times, however, cannot presume that it can successfully engage all students in only one form of enlightenment. As Taylor has argued it is the individual who will decide which sources of authority to accept. How then might schools best support their students in studying virtuous lives within the Aristotelian tradition? In the confused and perplexing times so eloquently described by Sutherland above, educators have sought means of re-establishing their concern with values education. One major direction for a return to an ethics of education has recently emerged among a number of educators; namely, the pivotal role of hope as foundational to the education enterprise. Wrigley, for example, proposes the following model of hope in education:

> To examine school improvement using the touchstone of hope is not a vaguely utopian moralism but an attempt to reconnect to core issues. Hope is a principle which unites the actions and aspirations of teachers, parents, children and headteachers. . . . It articulates connections between the five key areas of school development, curriculum, pedagogy, ethos and the wider community which school leaders need to align in order to bring about significant change. (2003: 8)

For Freire (1998: 47) hope 'is not just a question of grit or courage. It is an ontological dimension of our human condition'. Roberts writes of Freire that he:

> Theorized an intimate connection between education and the process of becoming more fully human. (2000: 1)

Freire's theories opposed a 'banking' model of education and called for a problem-posing approach, with students engaged in an interested, questioning stance to education.

In respect of their duty to plurality and pluralism, the schools might turn to Freire's concept of conscientization for a guide for how to make plurality and pluralism a key focus of their epistemic communities. In his essay, 'The process of political literacy', for example, Freire (1985: 107) suggests that 'conscientization' involves 'a constant clarification of what remains hidden within us whilst we move about the world'. It cannot ignore the transforming action that produces this unveiling and 'occurs at any given moment'. Conscientization remains in Freire's (1998: 55) words 'a requirement of our human condition'. For Freire, (1998: 55) humanization occurs through praxis and that process is 'inevitably incomplete'. Freire (1972: 28) saw praxis, that is, reflection and action on the world in order to transform it, as the synthesis of reflection and action. Thus, from this critical definition of praxis, Freire explains that conscientization occurs at the transforming moment when critical reflection is synthesized with action:

> All social institutions have a meaning, a purpose . . . to set free and to develop the capacities of human individuals without respect to race, sex,

class or economic status . . . the test of their value is the extent to which they educate every individual into the full stature of his possibility. (1972: 28)

Heightening awareness of the human condition has been presented here as an indispensable component of an ethical education in plural societies. Indeed, it is suggested that a sensitive awareness of pluralism in education might itself lead to a normative pluralism in the wider society. Such a step would place the defining of the common good firmly within the moral matrix of a plural society.

Towards a Resolution of the Problem (3): A New Perspective from Educating Humanity in Community

In continental Europe, a shift of emphasis among philosophers can be discerned as they seek to include 'Bildung' once again in educational discourse. The word 'Bildung' has been used to bring together those complex aspects of education which constitute its humanistic character. For example, Gadamer commented:

> But if in our language we say Bildung, we mean something both higher and more inward, namely the attitude of mind which, from the knowledge and the feeling of the total intellectual and moral endeavour, flows harmoniously into sensibility and character. (1989: 11)

Here the resonance with Alexander's position (2000: 308) and Pring's (1984) is clear. With 'Bildung', education is integral to the development of the 'whole person'. Standish in the 'Preface' to *Educating Humanity: Bildung in Postmodernity* also clearly addresses the question of the cogency of the idea of *Bildung* in contemporary conditions of postmodernity and late modern globalization:

> It is not cultural initiation alone that is important but something like the education of character and the kind of personal growth that this implies. And if this is a growth towards self-possession, self-mastery, autonomy of a kind, it can be achieved only through an alienation that unsettles that same quality. (Lovlie and Standish 2003: vii)

The authors have very clearly here re-focused the liberal modern concept of education so that it proposes a specific purpose for learning and teaching in plural times, that is, the education of character and the promotion of personal growth. Learning about others and difference demands a personal response from the student and an informed pedagogy from a school so that the student is intentionally transformed into a particular kind of person through engagement with the vast array of information and values which a plural society affords.

Biesta (2003: 62) explores the 'double face' of *Bildung*: one face is educational, the other is political. He argues that *Bildung* as an educational ideal emerged in Greek society. Then through its adoption in Roman culture, humanism, neo-humanism and the Enlightenment, *Bildung* became one of the central notions of the modern Western educational tradition. He underlines the centrality in this tradition of the question of what constitutes an educated or cultivated human being. His answer to this question is not given in terms of discipline, socialization or moral training, that is, as 'an adaptation to an existing external order'. Instead, he concludes that *Bildung* refers to 'the cultivation of the inner life, that is, of the human soul, the human mind and the human person; or to be more precise, the person's humanity'.

Biesta adds that 'the Enlightenment brought a further development'. Kant (1992: 90) developed the classical definition of Enlightenment as 'man's release from his self-incurred tutelage through the exercise of his own understanding'. Kant argued that in order to reach the state of rational autonomy education was a necessity. Any attempt to block this ideal would be for Kant a crime against human nature. Biesta (2003: 62) has pointed out that for Kant *Bildung* was more than an educational ideal: it was also, and primarily, an answer to the question about the role of the person in the emerging civil society, that is, a subject who can think for himself and who is capable of making his own judgements.

The importance of autonomy as an aim of education is frequently held to be a self-evident truth of a modern education. Pring sets out, however, the following persuasive analysis of the concept, as it is understood in modernity:

> Autonomy is not a straightforward concept. In what way can one be said to be thinking for oneself or thinking independently? The defenders of autonomy are themselves both empowered and constrained by the philosophical traditions they belong to. (2005: 59)

Pring's argument that the concept of autonomy relies on philosophical or cultural modes or traditions suggests that its place in different school cultures will vary according to how each school understands the role of the individual student in acquiring and making knowledge their own.

Autonomy underpins aims in education which seek self-determination and self-direction for students. As Pring (2005: 59) indicates above, there is room for discussion about the way individuals can be said to be thinking for themselves, or thinking independently, particularly in post or late modern times. Gill (2005: 500) reflects on this problem in the context of late modernity. She argues that secular post-Enlightenment ethics 'underestimated the power of religious belonging/believing to motivate individual moral agents and overestimated its own power to resolve public moral disagreements'.

There is little doubt that in England the present tensions experienced among and across different ethnic and faith groups have propelled the need for education to take action in the matter of personal, social and civic education. At stake is the ability of a plural community to act for the common good as well as on behalf of the rights of the individual. Unfortunately, there is as yet no major study of the effect of different forms of education on the values and beliefs of young people. In particular, in plural societies in which faith-based schooling co-exists with common schools there has been no coherent attempt at mapping the kinds of individuals who emerge from each sector, either in their values and identities or in their civic propensities and involvement.

The closest research to the brief outlined here can be found in the recent important work of Francis (2001). He has profiled the values of nearly 34,000 students between the ages of 13 and 15, partly against the backcloth of the key stages 3 and 4 learning outcomes for personal and social education and those for citizenship education. His instrument covers fifteen areas related to the students, which include personal well-being, worries, counselling and school.

Francis points to the need for mechanisms to know and understand the identities and values of students and how they perceive themselves at particular times. The need to understand the students' voice is important as well if the basic purpose of education outlined thus far, that of human formation and economic capability, is to be examined formally. Significantly for this concern, Francis (2001: 15) has also set out afresh the concept of school as a 'community of persons'.

The concept of developing identities and forming humanity within community has become integral to the current preoccupation with hope in education. It stands in stark contrast to the educational purpose of modernity in which the development of the person as an autonomous individual was seen as critical. Education for personal and social formation is now understood to be largely dependent on the quality of the educational community to which the student belongs. Such an approach to the worth of educating students as individual human beings, whatever their ethnicity or belief system, responds positively to Pring's concern that:

> To teach without coming to grips with how the learner understands things, would be to impose a system of ideas or a set of values that disrespect the learner as a person . . . as someone with a conscious view of things and of what is of value. (1984: 30)

The abhorrence of hatred and violence in towns and cities in England rightly leads to pressure on schools to participate in programmes of civic education. The argument presented throughout this chapter leads to a conclusion that a successful civic education cannot afford to fracture the identities of the students involved. If lack of clarity in educational direction has led to fractured education systems, there is a need to protect each student from becoming disengaged from the civic process. An important basis of successful civic education would seem therefore to lie in examining the role and practice of individual schools in negotiating a community of learning for living well in plural societies. Francis' work provides a sensitive backcloth to a further important task. That task is the evaluation of the purposes and practices of individual schools in contributing to the common good through personal and social formation in distinctive educational communities. Such analysis would most fittingly concentrate on the nature and practices of the whole-school community, or as, in this study, the whole-school culture. Through a review or evaluation of each culture there might be established those aspects of it which best support personal and social formation in plural societies.

At a time when the certainties of modernity in education are less sure and the rigidity of the economic imperative of late modernity dominates most educational values, the opportunities provided by postmodernity for education become clearer. With no grand narrative dominating educational thinking, it becomes ever more important to ensure that the micro-narratives of each school are told. In that way the particularities of individual school cultures might be better understood. In that way the excellence found in some cultures, whether in common schools or faith-based schools, might be more generally disseminated within a new particular, a meta-narrative of educational school cultures.

School cultures which derived their purpose from the need to educate the individual person in community, their ethical base from the virtue ethics of Aristotle and their ways of knowing about, and acting in pluralism, within the general concept of 'conscientization', or heightening awareness and understanding, surely have much to contribute to the discussion about the nature and practice of 'common schooling' in plural societies. Without such a discussion, it is difficult to see a way out of the cultural problem for education set by pluralism in complex modern societies. Without a review of individual school cultures' capacity to alert students to the consequences of difference and pluralism in an a-cultural society, together with an ability to prepare them for an active role in their own and others' understanding of being human at such times, no such discussion can validly take place.

The next chapter will consider the importance of a sensitive analysis of the role of faith in civic societies and their schools. Such an analysis might contribute to some level of agreement about the ability of faith schools to contribute to a democratic development of a normative pluralism.

Chapter 4

The Role of Faith in the Schools
of Civic Societies

The Purpose of the Chapter

Faith and schools are both contested notions. This chapter will consider the role of faith in schools and its ability to work with civic society to contribute to the common human and social good. The differences which faith and belief can or do make to the schools of contemporary pluralities will be discussed against the background of the cultural trends which predominate in them. This discussion is developed as a means of coming to terms with the question whether faith-based schools contribute or not to the social capital of living in complex pluralities. The chapter sets out the premise that religious and secular plurality, with its characteristic motifs of difference and indifference, must be confronted by education systems directly, if the central question about the right to existence of faith schools in this study is to be met with ethically.

A decision has also been taken to limit the illustrative materials in this chapter to the Roman Catholic tradition. Catholicism is presented extensively because it is the faith tradition found in the schools in the case studies. Equally importantly, however, it contains a common core of beliefs and principles about education, from which individual Catholic schools derive their particular cultures. As such it is a suitable denomination through which to examine the profiles and cultures of specific faith-based schools.

The Impact of Modern and Postmodern Cultural
Modes on the Place of Religion in Civic Society and
Education in Global Late Modernity

The present discussion about the place or otherwise of faith-based schools is set within global late modern times. It is sensible therefore to look back at how the interplay of modern and postmodern modes has impinged directly on the field of religion in late modernity. In modern times, Nietzsche (1969: 41) declared the death of God:

Could it be possible! This old saint has not yet heard . . . that God is dead!

Later, Kung (1980: 372) in commenting on Nietzsche, argued that he pro-claimed the death of God in order 'not simply to describe the spiritual situ-ation of man and world but . . . to make people aware of the vast consequences of the murder of God'. Theology was no longer able to argue that it provided the roots of truth and meaning.

Then came postmodernity and Wright (2004: 69) succinctly draws atten-tion to two very different consequences for religion. He refers to Berry (1992: 4) who argues that 'the contributions currently being made by many theolo-gians to the changing orientation of postmodern thought appear to herald the end of theology's long intellectual marginalization'. On the other hand, Ingraffia (1995: 1) warns that 'modernism tried to elevate man into God's place, (while) postmodern theory seeks to destroy or deconstruct the very place and attributes of God'. Intellectual uncertainty and ambivalence can therefore be argued to be the attributes of the postmodern in religion.

In her 'history of God', that is, the way men and women have perceived God from Abraham to the present, Armstrong argues that:

> The human idea of God has a history, since it has always meant something slightly different to each group of people who have used it at various points of time . . . The statement: 'I believe in God' has no objective meaning, as such, but like any other statement it only means something when pro-claimed by a particular community. (1993: 4)

Armstrong's warning that belief and faith should be situated in their indi-vidual social, intellectual and communal contexts relates directly to the pre-sent study. The significance of beliefs and faiths as drivers of individual and social values, as well as their place in the overall cultural composition of plur-alities, must not be ignored in this discussion of the role of faith in the schools of civic societies.

Defining Faith as a Means of Understanding Its Role in Education in Civic Societies

Armstrong, Hare and Rodger have each pointed out that faith is to do with an overall attitude to reality, that is, whether life here on earth is good or benefi-cent. In Hare's (1992: 3–4, 37–39) language, it is a person's 'blik'. He argued that religious language is different from ordinary language and that religious language speaks of human beings' attitude to their life, their evaluation of it and their opinion about how they should react to it. Through Rodger's writ-ing (1982: 15) there is a further strengthening of the notion that 'faith is less a possession than an orientation of life'.

The differences which emerge in the living out of religious beliefs and values between, for example, one Catholic and another and one Muslim and another point to the need for careful scrutiny of the way in which human beings are educated to live out their faiths and values. If one person professing the same belief is able to act so differently from a fellow co-religionist in a whole spectrum of political, social and global affairs, then it follows that their attitude to life, or faith, should be a primary educational concern of any society which is seeking to ensure human flourishing. O'Keeffe (1992: 45) makes a very similar point when she argues that faith, rather than denomination, should 'seek to achieve the integration of differences into a collaborative and fruitful whole'.

For educational stakeholders to decide what might constitute the difference which an education in faith might make to an educated person, they might usefully turn to the work of McKenzie (1991: 31), in discussing the construction of world views in adult education. He makes a sharp distinction between different types of world view, including those which are provisional or fixed, active and passive, and critical and uncritical. School communities built on different types of world view will look very different and respond differently to the civic society in which they work. In this matter also McKenzie (1982: 65–6) proves a wise guide for he draws on the differences between formative education and critical education. McKenzie understands formative education as stressing the learner's acceptance of society's ways. Critical education, however, permits the learner's 'cultural furniture' to be taken apart and 're-assembled in new ways'. Additionally, he argues (1982: 66) that 'formative education that excludes critical education is little more than indoctrination'.

Perhaps ultimately, it is a lack of congruence between a person's faith or attitude to the world and their cultural belief system which leads in these a-cultural times to an unarticulated recognition by many of the phenomena described by anthropologists and sociologists as lives lived in 'cultural contradictions' or as 'patterned desperation'. If this is indeed the case then this in turn may be one of the major reasons why there has been a re-surgence of interest in the matter of religion in a-cultural late modern times. It is the presence of such conditions that must surely underlie the poet Seamus Heaney's (quoted in Pine 1990: 13) drawing attention to the need for 'a search for images and symbols adequate to our predicament' and Kolakowski's (1982: 194) argument that the idea of religious belief is 'born not out of a collection of statements about God, Providence, heaven and hell', but rather that 'religion is indeed the awareness of human insufficiency, lived in the admission of weakness'.

Religion, Difference and Indifference in Civic Pluralities

Young's (1990) vision of the ideal city involved people with different stories living well together in postmodern times. Their stories would be complex ones, some involving participation in religious traditions, others involving strong consciousness of and attachment to ethnic differences; some would combine both, others would not. The city itself would be host to people living together without a common story. In imagining such a city, it is useful to refer back to the picture of religious and secular diversity painted by the 2001

Census of London mentioned earlier. Although Young does not claim that the ideal city exists, her vision is dependent on the value of difference as a contributory factor in the making of the city. For Young, individuals feed and flourish on difference and choice. All cultures and values, all world views and beliefs are on display.

In such circumstances, however, the individual is faced with difficult choices by living with a set of paradoxes or in Bell's (1996: 2) phrase 'cultural contradictions'. According to the prism or world view through which individuals make sense of the world in which they find themselves, they may choose to turn to nihilism and aculturalism or to select an eclectic mix to taste, sample, accept or reject. The postmodern city sets its own standards, irrespective of individual choice or commitment. It can be argued, however, that complex pluralities ignore at their peril those strong reactions or challenges which some people may experience when in contact with different forms of faith and belief, including the postmodern trend to compartmentalize faith as an exotic, to be enjoyed through such philosophies as Kaballah or meditation. Callan captures the significance of a particular form of reaction to such abundance of difference in present pluralities:

> A world in which we unambivalently celebrate difference could not be a world where those differences are invested with ethical meaning. But because many of the differences we find in our world both within and across cultures are ethically significant for us, enmeshed with rival understandings of right and wrong, good and evil, we cannot without bad faith respond to them with the welcoming embrace that connoisseurs of difference would evince. (1998: 15)

Thus for Callan differences in belief and faith are invested with ethical meaning.

So too the Archbishop of Canterbury (2003) who in the passage below challenges the response to difference he perceives in many young people:

> I don't think I'm the only person to have struggled with groups of teenagers, trying to get them to articulate values that really matter to them, to discover that practically the only thing they will agree in voicing is the importance of tolerance – usually seen as an incurious co-existence, even a bland acceptance of mutual ignorance and non-understanding, in the name of not passing judgment.

Callan argues that differences of this nature arouse a response in many which is ethically based, for such differences arise out of widely contested understandings of right and wrong, good and bad. The Archbishop of Canterbury's position relates to the difficulties which young people seem to have in articulating any specific values other than tolerance. In particular, he points to, in his view, a deficit definition which seems to underpin the value of tolerance; namely, an incurious co-existence, in the name of not passing judgement. A certain sympathy with the Archbishop's position poses a significant question for education in a-cultural times: how might education effectively engage with the religious differences of pluralism, while fostering the value of tolerance?

Educating for and in Difference in Civic Societies: The Role of 'deliberative respect'

The American Jesuit Hollenbach (1996: 97) proposes that differences in civic society should be confronted, not avoided or tolerated. He contends that education 'shapes the values that become operative in the public affairs of a republic by helping to shape the virtues and character of its citizenry' and, therefore, education must consciously choose its principal values and purposes and prioritize them.

Cantle's Report (2001) was concerned directly with the strong reactions and violence found between members of different ethnic and faith groups. It condemned 'monocultural' schools, as well as faith-based schools whose admissions policies do not require that at least 25 per cent of the pupils should not belong to the faith. It sought instead 'community cohesion', which it defined as 'situations in which individuals are bound to one another by common social and cultural commitments' (2001: 15). The report adds that community cohesion 'is closely linked to other concepts such as inclusion and exclusion, social capital and differentiation, community and neighbourhood'. Forrest and Kearns (2000: 9), however, question whether cohesion is a virtuous and a positive attribute in ethnic or religious-based communities. They argue that such cohesion can 'create divisions between those communities and others'. Their argument would seem to be derived directly from the Rawlsian method of avoidance. Ordinary citizens' private personal identities and community commitments must not be allowed to compromise the politicians' view of social cohesion in civic society. Not only does such a stance seem unreal and unworkable, but it once again devalues the personal values and identities of citizens.

A more real and purposeful solution is provided by Modood (1997: 359), who comments that 'equality and social cohesion cannot be built upon emphasizing difference in a one-sided way. The emphasis needs to be on common rights and responsibilities . . . It has to be a form of citizenship that is sensitive to ethnic difference and incorporates a respect for persons as individuals and for the collectivities to which people have a sense of belonging'. Forest and Kearns (2000: 8) argue that social cohesion includes the domains of 'common values and a civic culture'. The question for this study is in what ways can schools, either faith or common, foster a sense of common values and civic culture in their students which are sensitive to ethnic difference and incorporate a respect for persons as individuals? Questions such as these cannot be answered by rhetoric or persuasive oratory. They require careful longitudinal studies of cohorts of students in different kinds of schools and colleges.

If the faith of citizens in plural societies can be divisive, and a negative factor in the building of social cohesion, then, according to Hollenbach's argument, the place of faith in the schools of plural societies must be the subject of direct debate, not avoided. Earlier Sandel's (1994: 1794) contention was commended that respect is shown for fellow citizens' moral and religious convictions by 'engaging, or attending to them – sometimes by challenging and contesting them, sometimes by listening and learning from them – especially if those convictions bear on important political questions'. Such a basis of engagement became Sandel's definition for 'deliberative respect' within complex pluralities. Leicester and Taylor (1992) take this concept forward when discussing moral education as teaching children to maintain the common human condition of dialogue as the foundation to dealing with value differences and giving them concepts, knowledge and skills necessary to being equal partners in the on-going debate about how the pluralist society and education should be. Leicester here sketches out a model for how deliberative respect might become both a curriculum reality and an essential practice in learning communities dedicated to human flourishing in plural civic societies.

With the ability to critique differing cultural modes, and to recognize their differing roots, from both within a tradition and outside it, there is the possibility that those engaged in this conversation about plurality might actively make and remake ways of living. That possibility may result according to Jackson (1997: 81) with a 'move from static descriptions of people's cultural characteristics to dynamic accounts of the processes in which they are involved'. As noted earlier, Jackson's account of culture has consolidated and given impetus to considerations in this study concerned with the purpose and the methods of the case studies which will follow.

In the first place, it signals that a study of individual cultures of faith-based schools is important in order to develop a dynamic account of the processes in which they are involved and the differences which separate them, since difference is itself a characteristic of world views which share the same symbols. Second, such studies might contribute to a fuller picture of the ways in which faith-based schools actively make and remake ways of life in present complex pluralities and thereby secure further evidence as to whether it is possible to create a methodology to respond to the underlying question in this study. Third, data arising from the case studies might profitably be included in a discussion about the permeability of the walls between an individual's personal private space and the civic space of the common good for it follows from the above argument that the boundaries between public and private spaces do not have to remain static. Fourth, in schools which perform the role of mediating institutions the boundaries between public and private space can be experimented with and any resulting permeability concerning common values for the common good can provide feedback into civic society.

Educating in Faith in Faith Schools: The Catholic Example

This book seeks to examine the philosophies, cultures and outcomes of different school cultures on the faith, world views, attitudes and values of their students within the map of a multicultural society drawn by Baumann:

A multicultural society is not a patchwork of five or ten fixed cultural identities, but an elastic web of crosscutting and always mutually situational identifications. (1999: 118)

Such a map provides a legitimate representation of the pluralities which form the content of this study because the often secular intellectual and social pluralities continuously interact with religious values, beliefs and cultures globally, nationally and locally. In this situation of intense plurality within a democratic society, Jackson (2004: 131) has drawn attention to the need to maintain 'mechanisms that raise awareness of the debates and maximize dialogue and communication, identifying common or overlapping ideas and values, but also identifying and addressing difference'. For Jackson the overriding aim for education in religion and *for the promotion of the cultural development of students* (my words and italics) is:

to develop critical skills in order to achieve the goal of developing a knowledge of the language and wider symbolic patterns of religions. . . . Thus the debates about the nature of religions and cultures become part of religious education: preconceived definitions are no longer taken as received wisdom. (1997: 129)

How therefore do schools in civic plural societies work with faith in compulsory education? And how might particular ways of engaging faith with education achieve the kind of worthwhile religious education discussed by Jackson? There is an urgent need for an examination of the whole spectrum of faiths involved in education in order to respond to these important questions. This book, however, chooses to explore primarily one faith and its articulation of its attitudes and values in formal educational settings. By so doing it seeks to develop a fair and just means of such an examination and goes on to propose that this method would be equitable across the spectrum of faiths represented currently in compulsory education.

Thus a general overview will be offered of how Catholic educators involve their faith and values in the nature and practice of Catholic education. This is presented both as an example of how particular faith communities might contribute to such a public conversation about the schools which they own and manage and as a precursor to the study of four specific Catholic school cultures which will be developed later. Hulmes (1979: 17) has succinctly summarized the Catholic theory that 'religion lays claim to the whole person and at the same time refuses to be classified as just one of many possible ways of apprehending reality'. He has also listed the values that characterize that Catholic perception of wholeness as:

> affirmation, authority, autonomy, beauty, belief, choice, community, con-science, detachment, discernment, discretion, enjoyment, esteem, failure, faith, freedom, integrity, justice, love, order, peace, perseverance, pluralism, quietness, reconciliation, relativism, reparation, responsibility, self-control, success, suffering, tolerance, tradition, truth, uncertainty, unity. (1994: 4)

The values listed are seemingly diverse but can each be traced either to gospel or traditional Church teaching. In education, Hulmes insists, 'coher-ence is provided only by reference to a moral centre'. If this is not the case, then 'education corrupts if that moral centre is lacking'. The research find-ings of Bryk et al. into Catholic schools in the United States appear to con-firm Hulmes' assertion. Their research data found that Catholic schools are effective with many children but particularly with the poor because of each school's commitment to children, to peace, to justice and to a living Catholic social ethic:

> Underpinning these organizational tenets is a vital social ethic. First is a belief in the capacity of human reason to arrive at ethical truth. An imme-diate implication of this belief is that education must aim to develop in each person the critical consciousness which enables and motivates this pursuit. The Catholic school's emphasis on an academic curriculum for all is one direct consequence of this stance. Moreover, such an education involves nurturing both spirit and mind, with equal concern for what students know and whether they develop the disposition to use their intellectual capacities to affect a greater measure of social justice. This is the Catholic conception of an education of value for human development and democratic citizen-ship. (1993: 23–4)

McClelland in concluding an article concerned with the 'wholeness, faith and distinctiveness' of the Catholic school argued that:

> This internal ethos of the Catholic school merges with an external pos-ition that is open, welcoming and cooperative, helping to break down what Christopher Dawson (1967) once described as 'the closed, self-centred world of secularist culture', with which it has to have a meaningful encoun-ter. (1996: 160)

These articulations of the distinctive ethos of the Catholic school culture, both within cultural modes and also within formal education, are invalu-able guides to what kind of particular features might emerge from a study of Catholic school cultures. The list of values developed by Hulmes from an analysis of Catholic teaching on education fits well into the domains of social capital. As such the Catholic school as a learning community could certainly be placed within a matrix of 'mediating institutions' in a complex plural society. On the face of it, a genuine Catholic ethos supports a pluralistic and ecumenical openness to all faiths and to secular pluralism. Deliberative respect appears to be a guiding principle. The test, however, lies in examining the ethos of individual schools within the varying contexts in which such Catholic distinctiveness might be manifest.

Grace (1998: 194) for example, has argued that 'the space, identity and voice of contemporary Catholic schooling in England is now more directly challenged by individualistic and market values than ever before in its history'. Similarly, Pring (1996: 57–69) has argued that the education reforms of the 1980s, although emphasizing the common good, would work against Catholic values in education with their emphases on the market and individual self-interest. Further, Grace (2002: 237) insists that the most significant future challenge for Catholic schools is that their leaders will not have the same amount of spiritual capital with which to respond to the social, cultural and economic challenges facing Catholic schools. Arthur (1995: 253) sees the challenge raised by the parents' values as a significant problem for Catholic education. He argues that if parents increasingly demand that a Catholic education assures good academic results and competes in the market, then Catholic schools will increasingly lose their distinctive ethos, especially at the secondary level.

The above discussion reflects the importance and the difficulty of setting out the distinctiveness of Catholic school cultures within complex pluralities. In addition, Arthur's (1995) argument in *The Ebbing Tide* relies upon a version of Catholic distinctiveness, one of whose chief characteristics is the exclusion of non-Catholic pupils. For some authors, too, there have been serious concerns about levels of racism found in Catholic schools. For example, Basil Hume (1986) alerted the Church to widespread unhappiness among black parents about the 'raw deal they get from the Church in education'. Haldane has also called for more precision in the values and direction of Catholic schools:

> Catholic education must establish a social conscience as well as one concerned with individual well being . . . the first task for a Catholic philosophy of education is to identify the good. The social good is only a part of that but it is a sufficiently large and central part to justify making it a focus of attention. (1993: 11–12)

Grace (1996: 75), however, found significant differences between headteachers in their understanding of the role of Catholic schools in developing pupils' spirituality and morality. He also questioned the impact on parental choice of schools of the kinds of spiritual and moral development they witnessed in their children. In other words, when articulating a Catholic school culture through empirical research, it will not necessarily yield data which would satisfy all Catholic philosophers, educators, parents or students that a particular school is Catholic; nor indeed might specific schools cultures adhere to such specific philosophies of Catholic cultures as described above. The nuances in foci and in practices, such as admission policies, themselves become the content of debate about the extent to which the school may be considered Catholic. For example, some such as Lacey prefer to find the Catholic focus through an emphasis on social formation. She (1996: 268–9) proposes that, as a response to the 'steep challenges in continuing to promote an empowered community of adults committed to social analysis and educational transformation for the common good', Catholic schools should be all the more intentional in:

1. Seeking out ways to develop truly collaborative communities of hope and inquiry among lay and religious teachers of varied religious, philosophical and cultural backgrounds.
2. Witnessing to authentic alternative purposes and practices of schooling.
3. Promoting a community of critique and agency among women.

Lacey, with Bryk and Haldane, delineates those aspects of the practices of Catholic schools which arguably both contribute to their distinctiveness and offer a complementary pedagogy to the work of fostering the common good and building social cohesion in all schools. That is, those three writers identify significantly the concern of the Catholic school to analyse the social structures and relationships in which they are working and seek educational transformation for the common good. The latter part of this book will therefore focus on four Catholic school cultures and 'community cohesion' and explore whether a young person in them might become 'a skilled cultural navigator' or display 'multiple cultural competence' or possess 'an integrated plural identity'.

Can All Schools Provide an Adequate Education in Faith and the Spiritual Dimension?

A serious problem arises for the students of a plural society. According to Taylor (1989: 499) they experience a disengaged instrumental mode of life because identity in modern life is 'peculiarly differentiated' for the 'plurality of social worlds relativizes every one of them'. At school the nature of most modern curricula means that they are continuously subjected to looking at the meaning of experience in a fragmented way. There is nowhere it seems where they can attempt to come to terms with, what Cox (1986: 85) called, 'the overall meaning of the different glimpses which we get of substantial reality'. This dilemma was characterized by MacIntyre thus:

Enquiry has become finally fragmented into a series of independent, specialized and professional activities whose results could, so it seemed, find no place as parts in any whole. (1990: 216)

In postmodern times there are those who would argue that there are no grounds for seeking 'any whole'. A study such as this should therefore enquire whether there are individual school cultures which do or do not reflect a more holistic approach. In complex pluralities, the purposes of education do often reflect the need for students to examine human life as a totality. For example, in England, schools are responsible for the development of the 'spiritual' in their students. For Priestley (1997: 29–30), and for this present analysis, 'to dwell on the spiritual is to emphasize the subjective, to dwell on the process of being and becoming'. For Macquarrie (1972: 40), also, it is about 'becoming a person in the fullest sense' and therefore the whole of the curriculum or, indeed, the whole of the school experience, might be expected to contribute to its achievement. How the spiritual is tackled in the schools of civic society is therefore critical to an education for human flourishing. Priestley (1996: Part IV) would wish the spiritual to be found, not only in 'notions of teaching and learning' but also in 'thinking, creating, imagining, becoming'. Later he (2005: 211) enhanced the notion of becoming by connecting it with 'utopias', with 'what we might become and not just what we are'. It is also crucial to enquire whether the distinctions laid down by McKenzie (1991: 65–6) above between formative and critical education are observed in the practice of spiritual education.

Some (such as Beck 1991: 63–4) have experimented with the development of a list of the key characteristics of the spiritual, which include: 'awareness'; 'breadth of outlook'; 'a holistic outlook'; 'integration'; 'wonder'; 'gratitude'; 'hope'; 'courage'; 'energy'; 'detachment'; 'acceptance'; 'love'; 'gentleness'. Priestley (2005: 211–2) has emphasized that the core of the spiritual is 'dynamic', and concerned with the 'communal' as well as the 'personal' and the 'holistic'. Clive and Jane Erricker (2000: xi) through listening to children's stories have found that 'young children are perfectly capable of being active participants in their own social and spiritual education'. Wright (2004: 178) has argued for a framework, which, 'starting from the given nature of our local knowledge and striving to move our understanding to that which is ultimate and universal', supports 'critical education' becoming 'a fundamentally spiritual process'.

Research in schools in south London has shown a serious confusion on the part of teachers as to their role in spiritual education and development (Schmack 2006). Further, Ofsted reporting has uncovered evidence that primary schools are more than twice as successful as secondary schools in promoting spiritual development. In addition, this particular piece of Ofsted research records that 'provision for spiritual development in primary and secondary schools is strongest in voluntary aided and voluntary controlled schools (types of faith-based schools), with county schools falling far behind in quality of provision' (Wintersgill, 2000: 74–5).

A significant number of schools are therefore failing to support their students in this aspect of their whole development. One reason given by Wintersgill (2000: 75) is that teachers are uneasy in a plural situation of assuming the supremacy of any one single spiritual tradition: others are unhappy with introducing a form of spirituality divorced from the student's own faith tradition's roots. That is why a third possible form of spirituality on offer in schools has been described by McLaughlin (2003: 192) as 'untethered'. This is because, although it deals with matters and questions pertinent to the human condition and considered traditionally by religions, it relies on no specific religious or spiritual tradition for its articulation in the curriculum. McLaughlin (2003: 195) ultimately concluded that some forms of 'education in spirituality' are defensible with teachers who 'must be certain sorts of people' in the common school. Mott-Thornton (2003: 208), however, has argued that, against the context of social and moral diversity, there is a tension between offering an adequate opportunity for the development of the spiritual and the ideal of common schooling, proposed by social democratic liberals. Carr (2003: 224) reaches the conclusion that a traditional conception of spiritual education, often rooted in religion, provides the most philosophically coherent account of the promotion of the spiritual in education.

Priestley (2002), when leading a discussion on 'the spiritual dimension of the curriculum' recalled Wittgenstein's (1921: 6. 43) comment that 'the world of the happy man is an altogether different world from the world of the unhappy man'. He argued with Wittgenstein that we perceive the world in one of three ways: materially, morally and spiritually. We need to know how a school perceives the world in each of three ways and whether it chooses to inculcate such views through its curriculum and culture in the lives of its pupils; how it chooses to employ these perceptions in developing the autonomy and critical faculties of its teachers and pupils; and how it judges it has been successful in its work. It is important that research begins to throw light on the arguments recently put forward by McLaughlin (2003) in Carr and Haldane (eds) that evidence should be collected which can contribute to settling the matter of the optimal context for dealing with the spiritual in the schools of a plural society. For Schneiders the matter is already settled. She has concluded that 'religion is the optional context for spirituality'. She continued:

> The great religious traditions of the world are much more adequate matrices for spiritual development and practice than personally constructed amalgams of belief and practices. (2000: 13)

From the Ofsted perception presented above, it is clear that a substantial proportion of those primary and secondary schools included in the sample did provide opportunities 'for pupils to gain an understanding of their own and other people's beliefs'. Wintersgill comments here that 'this was mainly provided through religious education although not exclusively'. This exposure, she added:

> Made a positive contribution to the pupils' spiritual development by exploring ultimate questions, for example about God and suffering. . . .   These

opportunities make an important contribution to pupils' spiritual development, because they enhance pupils' awareness of the spiritual dimension of
life, and encourage them to think about how people of different religions
express their spirituality. This also raises the pupils' understanding that
spirituality can affect the whole of life. (2000: 81)

Wintersgill (2000: 81) commented that 'SMSC has assumed an identity of
its own in isolation from its original context in the Act'. She thereby highlights the need for any study of how these essential aspects of a student's development are managed and contextualized and the cultures, and curriculum,
hidden and explicit, in which they arise, are to be identified. This is a very
serious problem raised by Wintersgill, in which she draws attention to the
separation of knowledge and skills in the curriculum from the developing
identities of individual students.

The discussion above indicates that the relationship between the spiritual
aspects of education and the formal curriculum area known generally as religious education, religious knowledge or religious studies is a variable one
and some of its variety will be investigated within the case studies of the four
Catholic schools.

Defining the Religious Content of the Curricula of Schools Providing an Adequate Education in Faith and the Spiritual Dimension

As the names given to religion in the curriculum differ, so too do definitions
of 'religion' used in schools. Given that the traditional formative academic
disciplines and methodologies associated with religious education are theology and religious studies, a way of approaching the definition and practice of religious education is by reference to the benchmark statement for
Theology and Religious Studies produced by the Quality Assurance Agency
for Higher Education (QAAHE). That statement (2000: 3) contains a possible guide to potential unifying principles underlying the asking of questions about, within or between religions, when it states: 'some would affirm
as a core the intention of raising questions of meaning and truth, beauty and
value'. Thus statements produced by religious groups or bodies wishing to
own or manage schools about the basis for their approach to the possibility
of meaning and truth, along with their concern with placing value on differing forms of experience, might be scrutinized in order to decide whether
such religious groups might gain public validity and authority to be formally
involved in providing schools.

The QAAHE statement (2000: 1) also argues valuably for this discussion of
the role of religion in schools' curricula that 'it is vital that any definition of
the subject does not constrain future innovation, whether in response to global trends and issues or new intellectual climates'. Very succinctly, the authors

describe the possible nature of engagement with the field of religion through religious education. Students will explore the religious thought of one or more traditions and analyse the historical, social, cultural and artistic role of religion or belief systems. The core of the subject is committed to developing knowledge and information about religion, and to learning from it. In both contexts, students explore both an 'inside' and an 'outside' perspective.

It is of further interest that the authors argue that the field of Theology and Religious Studies has developed in dialogue with modernity and note that it is also responding to postmodernity, concluding:

> Once the European Enlightenment set an agenda that profoundly shaped Biblical Studies and Modern Theology. Increasingly hermeneutics, critical theory and post-modern agendas have informed all aspects of the subject. Global perspectives, interfaith and ecumenical issues, issues of gender, race and culture, as well as fundamental debates about methods and study, figure large in discussions about the nature and parameters of Theology and Religious Studies. (2000: 4)

From the analysis of the disciplines combined in religious education, there is the possibility that religious education in a-cultural pluralities might contribute to the content and processes of a developing culture of education. This might happen, not least, through its commitment to exposing ways in which human culture has sought to identify the sources of its authority and open up knowledge of the diversity of values and beliefs. To that extent, Hull (1999: x) has rightly asserted that 'insofar as it is a legitimate heir to the Enlightenment, offering an image of a social and cultural life lived in peace and justice, religious education may be described as the Utopian Whisper in the ear of modern society'.

The above discussion of the dimensions of religion and faith in education has highlighted the need for thorough assessments of the possible contributions which faith and religion might make to the curricula of all schools in plural societies. It has been the tradition of mainstream religious education in the UK since the 1970s to respond to the plurality of the wider society by asserting that educational religious education should involve students learning about and learning from religion. This latter aspect of the curriculum subject tends to involve a personal search which begins from where the individual student is and involves a journey, with no specified destination. Some educators such as Cox (1983: 135–6) sharpened this focus by asserting that religious education should assist students 'to move towards coming to terms with their own life problems by means of a coherent and conscious set of beliefs'.

Some would argue that this approach has fostered a pedagogical agnosticism. Teachers understood their work to be that of introducing students to information about religions and other world views and then tackling the major themes within religions, such as suffering and evil, in ways that fostered

individual reflection and interest. The judgement of Carr on such a pedagogical approach is salutary and resonates with many teachers' experience:

> the complete agnosticism which is here implied about the possibility of reli-
> gious truth must call seriously into question the very possibility of genuine
> religious enquiry and hence render the idea of religious education inher-
> ently problematic, if not actually null and void. (2004: 28)

In other words, if religion and faith are matters of real difference in complex pluralities, in which educational sites might such matters and their
accompanying impact on the identities and values of their adherents be studied effectively? One indicator of such an effective site in a plural society would
surely be where the teaching of religion and discussion of faith is set within
a teachers' code of conduct or in the words of Hobson and Edwards (1999:
85), above, an ethics of belief. This would seem to be another way of defining
the moral matrix. Teachers in schools fit within this moral matrix through
which individuals are formed or conversely de-formed. Thus teachers become
'moral companions of their students'. Teachers in this model would reflect
Hare's assertion that:

> At the end of it all the educator will insensibly stop being an educator, and
> find himself talking to an equal – to an educated man like himself – a man
> who may disagree with everything he has ever said; and unlike the indoc-
> trinator, he will be pleased. (1992: 129)

This important idea about the kind of education which is crucial for an
a-cultural plurality is taken up with approval by Priestley when discussing the
ideas of Whitehead:

> There is no need for moral education as a subject when Education itself is
> properly conceived as a moral concept. . . . It was [for Whitehead] adher-
> ence to dogma which closed off enquiry and inquisitiveness, arresting
> growth and demanding dependence. (1996: Part V)

With such an alliance in place faith in education might provide one potential base from which a learning community could examine the experience
of living in plurality and learn in McKenzie's (1982: 31) words to participate
in the 're-construction' of experience 'which points to ideas of formation,
growth and the development of social capacity'.

No Imagination: No Faith in Education

This chapter has argued for the need for an education in faith through deliberative respect for all young people in the schools of plural civic societies challenged by difference and plurality in intellectual, personal, social and civic

values. It has also provided an overview of Catholic approaches to education in these complex times as a stimulus to a wider conversation about how faith communities might begin educating young people for their social, moral, spiritual and cultural development. A conversation about the purposes and practice of education concerning faith and pluralism will be limited, however, if there are few examples of real and good practice in it as part of the agenda. Similarly education itself will be limited without a common imagination about the kinds of people society wants to emerge from its schools.

It was Sutherland who warned twenty years ago that:

> Much of what goes on in theology and education involves holding at arms length what is most naturally and appropriately held in embrace . . . beliefs and values . . . [that] are . . . matters of deep-seated conviction which involve emotion as well as intellect, soul as well as mind. (1985: 140)

Of course, just how personal images, beliefs and values are handled in schools is the origin of much of the contention related to schooling and education. The rules of such educational engagement fixed by modernity have been described by Halstead (1996). In this all too brief final section of this chapter, however, the very large question is raised as to how emotion and the soul, or 'Bildung', can ethically permeate education for and in pluralism.

Faith has no role in the re-construction of experience through education, and the growth of plural communities built on cohesion cannot be achieved, unless pupils, parents, teachers and politicians have the imagination to see the possibilities for different or better ways of living together. This in turn cannot be achieved unless there is a sharing of common values and human insights. Imagination, therefore, becomes a key factor in educating for and in plurality.

For Warnock (1976) 'the cultivation of the imagination' should be the chief aim of education. Hardy (1975) cites Isocrates (436–338 BCE), the student both of Socrates and Plato, as a champion of the imaginative function. This renowned teacher of rhetoric believed that discourse is a common human possession which differentiates human beings from animals and enables humankind to 'come together and found cities and make laws and invent arts'. For him discourse is not only verbal expression but also reason, feeling and imagination. Following a discussion about the differences in understanding of the imagination by Plato and Aristotle, Price (1997: 12) concludes that they both can be seen as 'concerned with an epistemological assessment of imagination – that is, the role it plays in the promotion of truth or falsehood' and for Aristotle 'ideas are derived from the sensible world itself through the mediation of images'.

Price makes the case that imagination stands as an intermediary faculty residing, somehow, between the faculties of sensation and reason because as Kearney and Sanders (1988: 107) state, 'the image serves as a bridge between the inner and the outer . . . it is both a window on the world and a mirror in the mind'.

If schools are to serve as 'mediating structures' in complex pluralities, then they must work with and through the imagination of all who learn in valued learning communities. The experience of difference in plurality raises the consideration for education whether it should be 'held at arms length' or 'held in embrace' since it involves as Sutherland argues (1985: 140) issues of 'beliefs and values . . . that are . . . matters of deep-seated conviction which involve emotion as well as intellect, soul as well as mind'.

Engaging with difference in faith through education has been the dominant theme of this chapter. Its starting point has been the belief that religion, faith and education together form the basis of a worthwhile conversation about what human beings should best gain from formal schooling. Perhaps a stimulus to a preliminary conversation might be a discussion of Hare's assertion that:

> One's attitude to religion will impinge powerfully on one's approach to education. This is because the irrational side of our nature, from which none of us can escape, needs to be educated, and religion, interpreted broadly to include humanistic beliefs, is the only way of doing this. (1992: v)

The next part of the conversation would be to enquire what value education should put on difference. This chapter has argued that the value of difference in faith, religions and life-stances provides one of the key principles for education in plural societies. Such a value could lead school communities to invite their students to participate in the reconstruction of their personal, social and cultural experience through the perspective of difference in order to stimulate formation, growth and the development of social capacity. Faith schools within this conversation, in their valuing of deliberative respect for difference in civic societies, might then be seen both as teaching others and as learning from others about education for the common good.

Faith is both a way of describing an individual's response to the world and a concept which embraces the commitment and trust shared by communities holding a world view in common. It is therefore a core element in the identity of individuals and their communities. All schools have a duty to articulate their ethics of belief so as to make clear how they educate for difference in religions and faith. The wider community would then have a basis from which to judge whether all schools, including those which are faith based, either in their practices and/or their outcomes had lessons to offer education for all students within post or late modern plural civic societies. This study has argued that such decisions cannot be made without some way of assessing the worth educationally of the means by which the faith and world views of young people, and the societies in which they live, are met and included in formal education by a) the fostering of the imagination in the provision of spiritual, moral, social and cultural education and b) the study of provisional and fixed world views and critical and uncritical world views.

Part II

Developing a Process for the Study of Faith-Based Schools and Their Cultures within Plural Societies

Purpose of Part II

The following two chapters act as a bridge between the theoretical presentation of the problems associated with the privileging of faith schools in late modern plural societies and possibilities for their potential role found in Chapters 1 to 4 and the case, which will now be made, for the value of empirical studies of faith schools in taking forward the debate concerning their abolition or continuance. Chapters 7 and 8 in Part III will then set out the information and perspectives gained from empirical studies conducted in four faith schools in three countries. As such, Part II identifies a research/audit process which can support a genuine conversation between faith-based education and the state, mediated through political philosophy and regulatory protocols. Most importantly it draws attention to the need for an audit of faith-based education which results in non-political profiles of individual schools.

Chapter 5

Towards the Establishment of an Evidence Base for Use in a Civic Conversation about Faith Schools in a Plural Society

Purpose of the Chapter

The work of developing a research/audit process is crucial if government, educators and communities are going to be able to test the value of individual school cultures' ability to a) offer a vision of a viable, fair and just pluralism to their students and local communities and b) encourage human flourishing in each of its students so they are able to take their place in a complex plural society. This chapter, therefore, proposes a process for the gathering of information about the nature and culture of faith-based schools.

The Aims of the Process

The aim of the process is to produce a profile of individual schools at particular times from an outsider's perspective. For the purposes of this book, the outsider is the author but a proposal is made which calls for school profiles to be developed ultimately by competent and impartial auditors. Their task will be to present an analysis in the words of Le Miere, editor of *Jane's Country Risk* (quoted in Evans 2008) 'with no politicisation of the intelligence'. The trialling of such a process is a necessary preliminary to forming a proposal that such a method be considered by complex pluralities as part of the evidence used in considering the question of the continuing existence of faith-based schooling, whenever it becomes a matter of contention.

Thus, the chapter sets out the methodology employed by the author in fieldwork carried out in two Catholic schools in Country X, one in Country Y and one in Country Z in which she attempted to profile the particular constitutive elements of each school's culture. The collection of data for the profiles employed both quantitative and qualitative methods. The means by which the data is presented and analysed in later chapters is also explained. The chapter thus contains a methodology within a methodology. The attempt to validate each on the basis of the purpose for which it has been constructed will be the work of the following chapters.

The content of this particular study of four faith schools contains data that have been collected over a number of years at times when it was both possible to visit the countries involved and, more importantly, to receive invitations from relevant ministries and schools which permitted the study to take place. For the purposes of the study the timing of the collection of data was not important since its chief purpose was to evaluate the particular form of data collection being used. At the same time it seems reasonable to state that the school cultures as such may not have changed significantly since the data collection was undertaken, although the school in the Caribbean suffered very severe physical damage during the hurricane of 2005.

The Problems Involved in Developing a Worthwhile Design and Process for the Study of Faith Schools

Developing a process by which policy makers and citizens of plural societies gain an adequate profile of the cultures of faith-based schools is particularly complex in societies in which politics has become the dominant discourse. Parekh (1989: 100), when discussing Gandhi, puts the problem succinctly:

> For Gandhi the modern age was the age of politics par excellence. Almost all aspects of individualism and social life were directly or indirectly organized and administered by the State . . . Since politics was so pervasive Gandhi advanced the fascinating thesis that it was the central terrain of action in the modern age . . . and no religion could be taken seriously that failed to address itself to its political challenges.

In other words, religions and the activities in which their members are involved, including education within the state sector, cannot presuppose that the mission, values and practices contained within their schools are readily understandable to those not within the faith. Equally, the modern state must declare its difficulties in understanding the relationship between religion and secular education and explain what it needs to know and understand about any such activities. The nature of this engagement between politics and the religions which organize faith-based schooling must be carefully structured. The basis of this structure is a philosophical analysis of the situation presented to societies of many cultures and beliefs by the existence of faith-based schools. Thus the first four chapters of this study have set out the educational, philosophical, cultural, religious and political landscape against which political decisions about faith-based schooling are currently made and outlined suggestions about how such decisions might be taken in the future. The argument has also been presented in this study that educational philosophy should once more establish its roots and purpose in the search for truth. The case for regaining elements of that truth via Aristotelian modes of practical wisdom has been argued. In brief, such arguments have led to the present position that pluralities, lacking a dominant cultural mode, should seek to establish the truth involved in complex political issues, such as the existence of state-supported faith-based schools, through both a general discussion about the nature of the problem and an ethical empirical examination of the 'facts' to be discovered from the particulars of individual schools.

This chapter is therefore concerned to develop for testing an ethical empirical examination of faith-based schools in complex pluralities. An ethical examination would permit and enable members of plural societies, in their role both as citizens, inhabiting the public space proscribed by the state, and as private individuals, living their religiously or secularly 'tethered' private lives, to participate in community decision making on a matter of both public and private concern. Such a process would lead to the a-cultural mode of complex pluralities becoming itself the conscious context for both public and private choice. In this sense the dominance of politics in the modern cultural mode and the strength of the 'condition of being left only with micro-narratives' (Wright 2004: 25) are met head on by the making of such a choice when living in the community of a-cultural pluralities. Would the facility to make such a choice lead a-cultural complex pluralities to meet the challenge posed by Alexander?

> To promote only those putative ethical visions that embrace the conditions of moral agency and that are, therefore, at home in open societies. (2000: 308)

Such an outcome of the development of a viable and ethical design and process for enquiry into faith-based schooling seems rather grand. Nonetheless, Finch (1986: 148) has argued that research is 'most likely to make an impact on policy in an indirect way by creating an agenda of concern'.

Some further difficulties were encountered as a result of this being a multi-country study. Care has been taken to contextualize each school in its country's social, cultural and educational ecology. The strains and stresses, however, associated with most education systems differ in each country. Thus the emphases which government policy dictates in the schools which have been studied will vary. Nevertheless, the greatly supportive ministries and schools involved provided wise guidance during this multi-site study. In Country Z, with the additional problem of my inability to speak or understand the national language, I was given invaluable guidance and support by the Ministry of Education and the country's Embassy in London and by members of the local Jesuit university in the city in which the school was situated. They and my Catholic colleague from the Curriculum section of the Ministry both helped in the translation of the questionnaire and school documentation, as well as providing a sounding board for the results of the study.

Developing an Appropriate Research Ethic: Establishing the Truth in Educational Research

Eisner reflected that objectivity has a particular role to play in educational research, when he proposed that:

> It is in the transaction between objective conditions and personal frames of reference that we make sense. The sense that we make is what constitutes experience. (1993: 53)

In order to establish 'objective conditions' for the development of the process of enquiring into the educational value or otherwise of faith-based education, it is important to undertake fieldwork within faith-based schools. An earlier chapter has described schools as epistemic communities within complex pluralities. Thus analysis of the information gathered will question whether the group of four faith-based schools exhibited sufficient characteristics of epistemic communities which can be considered ethically viable in complex pluralities.

The question also arises about how best to establish those necessary 'objective conditions' through which transactions might be made with the personal frames of reference of a researcher. As a quality assurance officer, in the latter part of my professional life, I had been much occupied by the judgements reached by inspection/audit teams in schools and higher education institutions. To what extent was data collected at different institutions the subject of forensic investigation via an externally defined template for the individual inspector/auditor, or to what extent was it, instead, the object of an individual inspector's educational connoisseur's preference or taste? Thus the question of which personnel might be deemed appropriate for developing profiles of faith-based schooling becomes a recurring theme within the development of an appropriate research process.

Taylor Fitz-Gibbon provides a staging post, in responding to this last question, in terms of thinking through the kinds of data which should be available from any field study of faith-based schools:

> much of my support for performance indicators stems from my belief that data empowers people, promotes a spirit of rational investigation, and provides an important bedrock for systems that are fair to staff, to students, subjects and society. It is my belief that education is more in danger from the arrogance of unsubstantiated opinion than from management moderated by good quality data.
>
> Of course, misinterpretation of data is always a problem, whether by researchers or by teachers, or particularly by politicians. But at least when there is data available the debate can be joined on the basis of the data, and the error in the data can be easily demonstrated. (1997: 320)

Finally Fitz-Gibbon adds a cautionary note, which is of real value when considering the nature of evidence about faith-based schooling to be consulted by policy makers for decision-making purposes:

> Dr Paterson expresses dismay at the lack of accountability of policy-makers and politicians. Actually if indicator systems were in operation policy-makers would be much more accountable than at present because they would find it more difficult to make unsubstantiated claims and the results of their latest initiatives would quickly come on stream. (1997: 319)

Fitz-Gibbon's arguments suggested that quantitative as well as qualitative data should be collected from each of the schools. The question as to how best to handle the transaction between that data and the researcher's/auditor's personal frames of reference when seeking to establish truth about how to answer the key questions about faith schools was chiefly settled by reference, and indeed commitment, to the epistemological values enunciated by Walsh:

> Sensitivity to the local and circumstantial, freedom to follow one's bent, a decent humility considering our fallibility, an acknowledgement of the tacit, intuitive and visionary, and a sense of the inevitability of value disagreement. (1993: 80)

The broad landscape against which information and data is to be collected, according to Walsh's epistemological values, was a comparative study of four Catholic schools in three countries, undertaken in the light of wisdom gained from available comparative literature.

The dilemma at the centre of this study is not easily resolved. It is a problem described by Tulasiewicz and Brock in the following way, in relation to Christian schools:

> The question of freedom of manoeuvre to produce a legitimation to the Church's continuing claims to the right to provide such education (involving more than mechanical instruction in doctrine and literacy, but affecting the whole socio-political reality of society) is a complex one. (1988: 331)

Our concern overall is with the choice facing policy makers in multicultural and multi-faith societies throughout the world at the beginning of the twenty-first century. That is, should they abolish religion from state-supported schools? Or should they create a unified system of schools which are open to all and which teach knowledge and understanding of all the major faiths and non-faith life-stances? Or should they sustain faith-based schools which concentrate through their individual cultures and their religious education curricula on the teachings and commitments of a specific faith, while developing students to contribute to the wider, globalized world in which they find themselves? In dealing with these questions, what evidence should policy makers use in making their decisions?

A Tentative Process

A starting point for any consideration of these questions should surely be a historical review of the status accorded to religion, in general, within any state and of the particular situation of religion within a state-supported education system. The work of Judge (2002) on the place of religion in the schools of England, France and the United States and that of McClelland (1988) on the developing concept of Roman Catholic voluntary effort in education in England and Wales are fine examples of the detailed and critical historical analyses of specific situations concerning faith-based schooling to which all such examples of faith-based schooling could profitably be subjected. The studies of schools presented in the next two chapters would have benefited from such detailed historical research. Instead, an attempt is made to set out the general historical context of each school and a proposal is made that the historical nature of a faith-based school's existence must be taken into account when seeking to resolve questions about the place of faith-based schooling today. For example, McClelland (1988: 61) points out that to understand 'the tortuous relationship between the Roman Catholic Church and the State in relation to the education and schooling of Catholic children . . . and the emergence of the dual system itself', it is necessary to understand the philosophy of Catholic education which was prevalent at the time. Thus McClelland (1988: 61) refers to John Hedley, the Bishop of Newport and Menevia (1881–1915), from whose speech at Ampleforth College in 1877 McClelland includes the following statement:

> To educate is to cultivate, develop and polish all the faculties – physical, intellectual, moral and religious – and to give to a boy's whole nature its completeness and perfection, so that he may be what he ought to be and do what he should do, to form him as a man, and to prepare him to do his duty in life to those about him, to his country, to himself; and so by perfecting his present life, to prepare him for the life to come.

Hedley set out a specifically Catholic philosophy of education and schooling, derived not only from the Church's teachings but also from the context of the time in England which was just fifty years on from Catholic emancipation. That teaching set the Catholic school firmly within the body of the Catholic Church itself, where there were common beliefs and interests, and where all members were expected to work for the common good. Norman (1984: 33) asserted that emancipation brought about a Catholic 'organised and articulate middle class', which sought to retain a religious, social and cultural identity in harmony with the spiritual leadership of the Vicars Apostolic. In turn, this movement forced through with increasing impetus the urgency of a specific Catholic education. That education was in part, also, according to Cardinal Manning (1888: 309–22) to help fulfil the key mission of the Catholic Church to save England from the secular liberalism that was about to engulf it. This he argued could only be achieved from a position of intellectual strength and cohesion.

McClelland (1988: 82) has concluded that the 'concepts of wholeness, unity and spiritual integrity which lay at the heart of the nineteenth century philosophy of Catholic education' were directly endorsed by the Second Vatican Council. For the Council there was a need for religious formation which 'sought to strengthen Christian attitudes to encounter threatening social manifestations of modern society – abortion, euthanasia, genetic manipulation, violence, unemployment'. During the Council, McClelland (1988: 83) writes, Magor Andrew Beck, the spokesman on education among the English and Welsh bishops, emphasized that the continuing role of Catholic schools was to take 'the full richness of faith out into the community, to shed new light on the truths in whatever discipline they belong to, and reflect the one eternal truth that is God Himself'.

Bryk et al. (1993: 276) identified three main sources of the philosophy of Catholic education in the United States. These were Neo-Scholasticism, especially the example found in the writings of Maritain (1882–1973); the Second Vatican Council; and the National Conference of Catholic Bishops. Bryk et al. (1993: 51) argue that Neo-Scholasticism made two important contributions to the thinking of the Catholic church:

A belief in the capacity of human reason to arrive at ethical truth and an affirmation of the place of moral norms and principles in public and personal life.

Maritain remains, in no small way, instrumental in the present author's search to find a process by which to respond to the dilemma posed by the state maintenance of faith schools.

Such a brief overview of the relationship of nineteenth- and twentieth-century expositions of Catholic philosophies of education points to the need to engage with the historical circumstances by which faith schools came into existence. A further helpful starting point in the consideration of the kind of evidence, and the means of acquiring it, which policy makers might use in responding to the particular dilemmas which faith-based schools present to complex pluralities is the work of Preston. She (1997: 426–7) has pointed to the growing recognition of 'the importance of process in the understanding of social realities'. Her case is based on the view that:

This practice (research) is grounded in the belief that by extending other people's understanding through the process and outcome of research, I make a contribution to our collective knowledge of reality through the repetition of long since established knowledge, however new it is to me, as much as through sharing intrinsically new information. (1997: 421)

Preston explains that the work of the researcher is therefore to contextualize the 'streams of information' produced by research, which 'relate to theory, practice and process (separately or in combination) at different historical moments'.

This present book has therefore attempted to offer a contribution to our collective knowledge of the social reality of faith-based schools in three particular contexts. As Grace (2003b) has pointed out, the Catholic schooling system is probably the largest faith-based system serving students in a wide range of socioeconomic, political and cultural settings worldwide. The four schools under study are therefore Catholic and the study itself has been informed by important studies of Catholic schools since the late 1980s (see, for example, Flynn 1993; Flynn and Mok 2002; Bryk et al. 1993; McLaughlin et al. 1996; Scholefield 1999; Grace 1996, 1998, 2000, 2002; Grace and O'Keefe 2007; Mtumbuka 2003).

Those studies have each contributed in major ways not only to a general understanding of Catholic schooling but also to the shaping, development and theory underlying the design and process presented in this section of the book. For example, Bryk et al. have recorded and analysed the value of large-scale research projects in gaining a sophisticated picture of Catholic schooling and extrapolating the key themes which lie at the heart of Catholic education. From such rich data which lead to complex multilevel modelling, Bryk came to perceive the American Catholic school as significantly distinct from the American public school. This was a very significant finding for me in relation to the Ofsted data discussed in the preamble above. The process discussed in this section, however, is distinct from that of Bryk for it proposes means to explore some possible reasons why schools, even within one-faith tradition, feel so different. What makes one school so different from another, and therefore differently successful or failing?

At the same time, McLaughlin et al. have demonstrated the value of extrapolating the major philosophical issues involved in state-funded Catholic education against a detailed landscape of the present realities of Catholic education. Grace has detailed through extensive research the realities of Catholic schooling as they meet up with, and evolve through, government-driven initiative-based policy making, such as foci on school leadership, school-mission policies and market-driven educational values.

Equally, though on a smaller scale, Scholefield's (1999) lucid story of two faith-school cultures, one Catholic and one Jewish, and Mtumbuka's (2003: 17) exploration of Catholic secondary education in Malawi whose purpose was to aspire to 'an atmosphere of information sharing and collaborative investigation' have provided fertile ground in which to grow this present process for the study of faith schools.

In choosing to study individual Catholic school cultures as 'social realities', it should also be noted that Garfunkel (1967) explained the concept of reflexivity as 'the ways in which our portrayals of social realities simultaneously describe and constitute the realities'. As Miller (1997: 25) reflects, 'our descriptions of social realities cannot be separated from the objects, persons or circumstances that they describe or the languages we use to describe them'. Miller (1997: 26) continues:

> Postmodernism . . . also treats social realities as embedded in generalized discourses into which interactants enter in conducting their everyday activities and interactions. Indeed Foucauldian discourse studies might be characterized as moving from the 'top down' (from culturally standardized discourses to the reality-constructing activities of everyday life).

The Significance of the Study of School Cultures

This study begins from the hypothesis that each school is different because of a number of factors, including the cultural traditions and sometimes cultural pluralism at work in each of the countries in which the study has taken place. It also wishes to challenge the almost universal hypothesis that has underpinned educational activity and development for more than a century; namely, that all schools within any structured and formal system of education contribute positively to the social and economic development of the individual, their community and their nation state. Such a thesis tends to favour the positive influence of education in general, as opposed to examining the interpersonal and inter-cultural nature of much micro-educational endeavour within macro-educational policies, including the significance of the cultural relationships involved between knowledge and its status and between individual students and their peers and students and their teachers.

As Le Vine and White (1986) point out, for education to have a positive effect on social and economic development, there needs to be motivation to realize potential and effect change, and this has to be culture-specific and local in scale. Culture is a construct for survival but for it to be a vehicle for change, then culture has to be mobilized which means, in part, the generation of a capacity for change within its own integrity. A study of a number of particular Catholic schools' cultures will therefore permit the question to be asked whether each of those cultures, or only some, or none at all, contains within it the capacity to bring about specific educational changes and outcomes within its own cultural integrity.

The Value of Comparative Studies

The process involves a broad comparative survey strategy. Cohen and Manion (1994: 85) explain that:

> Typically, surveys gather data at a particular point in time with the intention of describing the nature of existing conditions, or identifying standards

against which existing conditions can be compared, or determining the relationships that exist between specific events.

The understanding of comparative education adopted is based first on Thomas (1998: 1) who has argued:;

> In its most inclusive sense comparative education refers to inspecting two or more educational entities or events in order to discover how and why they are alike or different. An educational entity in this context means any person, group or organisation associated with learning and teaching. An event is an activity concerned with promoting learning.

In addition, Arnove et al. (1992) have put forward the view that comparative education's greatest strength is the belief that, by looking at developments in different societies, lessons can be learned that will lead to reform and improvements in one's own system. It is therefore to be expected that because of the common structure of each study of four schools in three different contexts this process will offer a comparative analysis of the social realities of each school and of the processes through which faith schools may usefully be judged and evaluated in the light of current social, cultural and educational contexts, particularly within present English legislation. Thus the dilemma at the heart of this book will be open to further interrogation, and this in turn will provide the basis for developing a more informed process for making relevant judgements.

Studying the Vision and Mission within Individual School Cultures

Arthur (2005) has argued that the sociological–economic perspective in school effectiveness studies has become dominant in recent years because it relies on quantifiable data that are accessible. Thus to measure the effectiveness of Catholic schools we need to evaluate the extent to which they accomplish what they set out to do. Arthur concludes that this must include questions about the integration of human learning with religious faith, but few studies have been sophisticated enough to achieve this aim, for he argues:

> There appears to me to be two main levels of explanation for the effectiveness of Catholic schools in public examinations that could be briefly raised or characterized under the more diffuse headings of the religio-philosophical and the pedagogical. (2005: 153)

Nor has there been an international study of Catholic school effectiveness in terms of academic performance and/or religious mission; rather, there have been a series of national studies. In the United States, for example,

Coleman (1981; Coleman and Hoffer 1987) reported that generally Catholic schools promote:

- more effective education than public schools;
- students from less advantaged backgrounds;
- higher levels of discipline and academic standards.

Allied to these three areas of distinctiveness, Coleman reported that Catholic schools achieved better cognitive outcomes than public schools. He linked this to more effective school discipline, fewer student absences, higher enrolments in academic course work, and the setting of roughly 50 per cent more homework.

Neal (1997a, 1997b) repeated Coleman's research. Neal reported that 97 per cent of students graduated from Catholic schools and 94 per cent of these went on to college, while African and Hispanic Americans who attended city Catholic schools had a higher graduation rate than whites in city public schools. Neal (1997 a), interestingly however, concludes 'these results do not indicate that Catholic schools are superior to public schools in general. Rather, they suggest that Catholic schools are similar in quality to suburban public schools, slightly better than the urban public schools that white students usually attend, and much better than the urban public schools that many minorities attend'.

As indicated above, however, Bryk et al. (1993) attempt to interpret the success of American Catholic schools by pointing to certain characteristics of the Catholic school itself including the school as 'a voluntary community'; 'a bridging institution', together with the 'role of religious understanding in contemporary schooling'. In Australia, Flynn (1985) studied 2,041 pupils in twenty-three schools in 1982 who sat the Higher School Certificate of that year. He discovered that Catholic school pupils were more highly represented in the top 1 per cent of overall Higher School Certificate pupils. Flynn therefore concluded that Catholic schools have unique positive effects upon the academic results of pupils and he sought to explain such academic achievement by linking it with the dominant values of each school. Flynn attempted to break down the composition of each school's culture or climate, arguing that when students are exposed to such cultures their results in their final examinations are improved. Flynn's 'map' of school cultures included the following areas:

- the pervasive values of the school;
- the morale and spirit of the pupils;
- the importance of the development of each pupil;
- the pastoral care of the school.

Flynn (Flynn and Mok 2002: 11) more recently published the results of a longtitudinal study of pupils in Catholics schools for the years 1972, 1982,

1990 and 1998. In this study Flynn, with Mok, concluded that pupils attending Catholic schools were generally happy.

Finally, Arthur (2005: 152), in reviewing research among Catholic schools in South Africa, concludes:

> Many schools in South Africa face similar problems to schools in Third World contexts where a great deal of education time is lost due to weather, large classes, crop harvesting, teenage pregnancy, hunger and disease. There is often little homework and low morale among teachers. Evidence (Christie and Potterton, 1997) indicates that Catholic schools, particularly in rural settings seem to ride these problems and spend substantial time on task. There is an ethic of care in Catholic schools where teachers know their pupils even with large classes. There is also an ideal that motivates staff and pupils that is often absent in State schools.

The information collected about faith schools in this process may yield data which point to commonalities and universals and dissonances and dissimilarities in the cultures and outcomes of particular Catholic schools. Unlike, many of the studies outlined above, the research described in this book will also present findings of detailed interviews with school managers and principals, religious education staff and final year students in each of the four schools, alongside the quantitative data gathered through a questionnaire. If the data points up commonalities and universals and dissonances and dissimilarities in each culture, a conclusion will be reached that policy makers cannot afford to make generalized decisions about the value or otherwise of faith-based education. Recommendations will also will seek to propose areas in which all schools, and the philosophies and cultures within which they operate, should be investigated before decisions can be taken about their worth within state-supported education systems.

A Viable Process?

A variety of means is used to capture the culture of each of four schools including observation, interviews with students, parents, school managers, headteachers and teachers, documentary analysis and questionnaires. The questionnaire to students forms a major part of the process. As in the work of Flynn, it is a means of collecting a large amount of information about the school-leaving cohort of senior secondary schools in the three countries in the study. Each school in the study outlined in this book was asked to identify a large group of thirty to sixty of its final year students and arrange for them to answer the questionnaire at the same time during one school day during my visit. The questionnaire's primary purpose was to find a way into the student's own understanding of the place of the school in their personal, social and educational development, as well as their particular view of their school.

At the same time, the questionnaire itself can be evaluated as a potential tool to capture the student voice in individual school cultures and thereby contribute to the policy debate through analysing students' reactions to the development of their identities in school through faith-based education. As such the analysis will be concerned with the tool's effectiveness in bringing about an understanding of the relationship between particular faith-based school cultures and the developing attitudes and values of students to their education, their future concerns and their present understanding of the place religion should, or should not, have in that education. The results from the questionnaire can therefore be used to indicate what the students value, such as their happiness in being at a school or their pride in belonging there. Its use is integral to the process of a combined quantitative and qualitative study of individual school cultures. It is not, however, a tool whose purpose is to compare, for example, which school makes a student happier or more proud. In that sense there will not be later in the book a statistical analysis of the survey of the four Catholic schools. Instead, the data from the questionnaire will be used as indicators of the student experience of each school culture.

The student questionnaire proposed for the suggested process originates from the work of Flynn in the Catholic schools of New South Wales. As yet, that survey of Catholic schools in Australia mainly through questionnaires remains the largest and most comprehensive project of its kind in the world. In this book, the findings of Flynn in Australia will provide a benchmark for the outcomes which can be achieved in Catholic schools in Anglophone countries and their attendant cultural modes.

The actual content of the questionnaire differs little from that of Flynn. Some sections have been merged and the number of questions reduced from 370 to 184. After question 184, three open questions were presented concerned with (i) what the students appreciate and value about the school; (ii) any changes which the student would like to make at the school; and (iii) the unique spirit which exists in the school. The questionnaire included an abbreviated section on 'Knowledge of Catholic Teachings and Terms' but as Flynn himself argued:

> In an effort to assess student's knowledge of Catholic faith, they were presented with 24 multiple choice questions related to various aspects of that knowledge. . . . It quickly became apparent that Year 12 students were not familiar at all with the theological concepts and language used. (One student in a large Catholic high school asked the writer: 'Who is this person Grace?' . . . Whether students really understood basic concepts of Catholic faith, therefore, we were unable to determine. (1993: 446)

Similar problems occurred in the shorter version of the questionnaire used in this study; hence, Flynn's advice was followed that any analysis 'could not be undertaken on grounds of validity'. Equally it became apparent that the proportion of Catholics in three of the schools in this study was low and there-fore extensive questions about Catholic teachings were inappropriate.

Making this discovery, led me to refer back to the advice of Sudman and Bradburn:

> Keep asking why do I want to know this? It would be interesting to know is not an acceptable answer. (1982 in Foddy 1993: 32)

The research literature, however, is alive with warnings about the problems associated with information collected from questionnaires. Belsen (1986 in Foddy 1993: 2), for example, highlights five 'likely principal causes of error' when relying on questionnaires and interviews:

a) respondents' failure to understand questions as intended;
b) a lack of effort or interest on the part of the respondents;
c) respondents' unwillingness to admit to certain attitudes or behaviours;
d) the failure of respondents' memory or comprehension processes in the stressed conditions of the interview;
e) interviewer failure of various kinds (e.g. the tendency to change word-ing, failures in presentation procedures and the adoption of faulty recording procedures.

Foddy (1993: 3) reflects in the light of c) above that 'the relationship between what respondents say they do and what they actually do is not always very strong'. He (1993: 6) also highlights a further problem, when he argues:

> Respondents commonly misinterpret questions . . . It would seem reason-able to assume that, if a question–answer sequence is to make sense, the question given by the researcher must be understood by the respondent in the way intended by the researcher and the answer given by the respond-ent must be understood by the researcher in the way intended by the respondent.

In response to the concern raised in c) above, that of the unwillingness of the respondent to admit to certain attitudes or behaviours, it is of utmost importance that all who answer questionnaires and participate in interviews, both students and staff, are certain that confidentiality will be strictly observed at all times, as well as in the recording of the interviews. Second, question-naires should not be seen by anyone in the school but should be returned directly to the researcher/auditor after the general class session in which they are completed. Only when the data had been analysed and recorded would the school have sight of the overall findings. At each of the schools, the ques-tionnaire was completed after a discussion with the group to explain the pur-pose of the questionnaire and the information-gathering process in general.

The present research involved each school using an RE lesson for the work to be done. It is unclear whether there would have been different responses recorded if the questionnaires had been completed during secular periods or during students' own time.

Francis (Francis and Robbins 2005: 3) argues that there are 'strengths and weaknesses' in both qualitative and quantitative methodologies but for his own major survey (with Robbins) opts firmly for self-completion surveys, based largely on selecting pre-coded responses or rating intensity of responses. For Francis:

> The real strength of this method is that the responses the young people give to well-honed questions can be analysed with precision and confidence levels can be established regarding the reliability and generalisability of the information generated. The weakness is that it may be difficult to penetrate behind the well framed questions to establish the deeper underlying meaning. (2005: 3)

Francis' method (2005: 9) originated in the 1970s when he undertook a research project to 'generate insights into the world views of young people living, working or studying in London's city centre. The values map was designed as the primary tool through which to gain access to those world views'. The concept of a values map is significant for this study in which it is argued that the 'faith' of an individual is their particular attitude to life or world view. The research and writing of Francis throughout the last thirty years or so has generated illuminating and often disturbing accounts of the attitudes and values of young people in urban areas, in church schools and others. His recent account has been able to supply helpful information about students in non-faith-based schools, groups of students in faith-based schools and differences in students in differing types of schools who belong to a variety of faiths and none. He has also developed a schema (2005: chapter 10) which separates Catholic students in Catholic schools into four distinct types and differentiated each type's response to their views of the school, religious education and religious goals of the school.

The quality of the data generated by Francis and Flynn through the use of self-completion surveys establishes this method as a key means of identifying the world views of young people. Moreover, it points to the value of having a databank of the values, beliefs and aspirations of students in schools. As has been argued earlier, schools are complex institutions and achieve their identity through their population, their structures and their links with parents and the wider community. Looking at the world views of the students in one school against the wider landscape of students' world views in the same geographical area, specialist group of schools or those with faith-based connections will be useful if we are to analyse patterns of schooling which seem to be constructive or destructive of students' identities and values as they mature and become full citizens in complex pluralities. To be able to do this, however, a much wider survey would be necessary across many more schools, probably on a national or regional basis. If that were to occur, then statistical analysis could be undertaken of the data, probably beginning with a standardizing statistical analysis in order to establish the comparability and generalizability of the information from across the schools.

Powerful as such a tool might be, the questionnaire can only provide a partial understanding of the role of individual schools on the developing lives and identities of their students. There can also be widely differing views of the purpose of the collection of such data and its subsequent analysis. For example, the Catholic bishops of Australia may wish to interrogate Flynn's data in order to ascertain the attitudes of students in Catholic schools to Catholicism and from such analysis they might wish to project future membership of the Catholic Church. In other words, had the Catholic Church's investment in school buildings and teachers had a direct pay off? Similarly, the Anglican Church in England may wish to investigate whether its commitment to educational mission in urban areas from Victorian times to the present had had some direct influence on the spiritual lives of the students taught there. Such concerns are wholly appropriate for the individual faith bodies. However, if the data are to be used as a tool in responding to questions about the ethics of state maintenance of faith schools in plural civic societies, they must be collected in such a way as to facilitate real comparison between schools. Similarly the self-completion surveys must be as accessible as possible to all the students required to complete them.

If there can be clarity of the aims of such data collection and equally confidentiality guaranteed to student respondents, it seems feasible to propose that such self-completion surveys could be introduced into the schools, provided their generation and collection methods were authorized by the appropriate national and local authorities.

There are, of course, also major differences in the pupil populations and the prevailing religious, economic and social contexts of the four schools in this study and those of the Catholic schools in Australia with which Flynn was concerned. First, the Australian schools' pupils numbered over 50 per cent Catholic within the overall school population. This is not always the case in the present study. Second, the schools in this study are situated in the Global South. Thus analysis of the data will refer to work in Malawian schools by Martin Mtumbuka, which again used questionnaires based on Flynn's.

In so many ways the data and analysis found in the work of Flynn and Mtumbuka provide a valuable baseline for the analysis of the data in this study. This is because:

1. Australia has been a frequent and respected partner with Country Z in developments in its education system since the1980s, thus itself providing models for educational development and modes of measurement and evaluation. The learning of English is a compulsory aspect of school leavers examinations in Country Z.

2. Country X and Malawi both experienced educational missionary activities in colonial times and took charge of their subsequent educational developments following independence.
3. Country Y is presently poised between its historical roots in Africa, its periods of colonial occupation and its present close Anglophone ties at national and family levels, particularly with the United States.

Flynn's development and use of the questionnaire was part of a longitudinal study to evaluate the effectiveness of Catholic schools for the Catholic community which supported them, although his questionnaire was also used throughout all schools of New South Wales. Mtumbuka's research sought to examine 'the character of Catholic secondary education in Malawi . . . within the wider context of Catholic education, which among others promotes a particular view of a human existence and the world centred on the teaching of Jesus Christ'. This study is concerned with a question which faces all educational policy makers who not only seek to develop strong national identities through their education systems but also foster the growth and development of their citizens as active participants and competitors in a world made more focused, and in some ways smaller, through globalization. A major focus of global awareness, other than an economic perspective, is the place of religion in personal and national identity. This study aims to produce a profile of each school's culture within its national and local context, as well as the voice of each school's students, as both global and local citizens. Part of the accompanying narrative to the profile will be deliberately 'thick' with many different voices being included.

Thus the method adopted for this study involves an extensive use of the questionnaire, adapted from Flynn's original format, and also individual interviews with headteachers, teachers, parents and individual and group interviews with students. Thus, a number of interviews were conducted at each school in order to engage with teachers, parents and students as they reflected on the culture in which they participated, worked and studied. For example, the headteachers were asked among other things:

1. How does your school differ in mission from the schools in your local community?
2. Do you interpret the 'national' curriculum which you are obliged to teach differently from other schools and in what ways?
3. What would be your description of the ideally educated school leaver at this school?

By making the decision to use interviews as a further means of distinguishing the individual school cultures, it is helpful to be aware of Reissman's (1993: 11) concern that 'the story is being told to particular people; it might have taken a different form if someone else were the listener'. Throughout the interviews teachers and students were made aware of the author's plurality of identities: first, acting as a non-participant observer in each school; and second, as a teacher who had worked in Catholic schools and who now trained teachers, some of whom worked in Catholic schools. In Country Y, in addition, questions about attitudes and values in students and teachers took place during the perplexing and often emotional times following the events of 9/11. The visits to the school were made about three months after the events.

Miller and Glassner (1997: 101–2) also point out that adult researchers should exercise caution when assuming that 'they have an understanding of adolescent cultures because they've been there'. Fine and Sandstrom (1988: 66) argue, however, that as adolescents become increasingly oriented to adult worlds 'age begins to decrease in importance as a means of differentiation, and other dimensions such as gender and class [and race] become more crucial'. Miller and Glassner (1997: 102) ultimately point out, most valuably for this particular process for the study of the nature of school cultures, that 'adolescents' discourse towards and with us (and for themselves) is much about where and who they are'. They conclude:

> Our approach is to treat the adolescents' reports as situated elements in social worlds. . . . The interviewees typically seem to enjoy the chance to 'think aloud'. . . . Ways of thinking and talking derive from their daily experiences and are also used in these. (1997: 102)

Thus for the purpose of exploring a school culture, interviewing students, in particular, provides further insight into the social realities of the modes of working of their individual school culture. As Holstein and Gubrium argue:

> The analytic objective is not merely to describe the situated production of talk but to show how what is being said relates to the experiences and lives being studied. (1997: 127)

In this way, Holstein and Gubrium alert us to setting the words recorded in the interviews within the cultures and experiences lived by the interviewees. Thus the challenge for this proposed process of studying faith schools will be to analyse the data derived both from the questionnaires and the interviews with the students against the landscapes of the micro-school cultures in which the students study and the macro-intellectual, economic and social cultures in which they live.

Chapter 6

Faith School Profiles

Purpose of the chapter

The chapter is concerned with the tools which can appropriately be used in analysing the information gathered through empirical studies of faith schools and the manner of presentation of such analysis which best leads to 'non-politicized information' being available widely. The chapter therefore sets out to meet the challenge of how to bring fresh evidence to the case for re-considering how to deal sensitively with the questions raised by a state's maintenance of faith-based schools in late modern times through the development of faith-school profiles.

What Can School Profiles Offer?

In the context of this study, a school profile has been defined so far by the author throughout this book as 'sufficient information about a particular faith-based school culture might be collected in order to determine the influence of its specific beliefs and values on its educational purposes and practices'. The profile, in turn, 'provide[s] a lens through which those concerned with the generation of macro-educational policies linked to pluralism and globalization might reflect on the micro-management and implementation of those policies within particular cultures and their success, failure or innovation'. The proposed profiles are to be used ultimately across all faith schools, not only Catholic ones. The overall aim is 'to build comprehensive profiles of the social, personal, spiritual and educational capability or non-capability of state-supported faith schools in modern plural societies'.

The question must be addressed as to how best to develop adequate profiles of a number of faith-school cultures in order to contribute to discussion of the question, 'Should plural societies operate common schools which will ensure the full educational entitlement of all students, from whatever social, cultural, ethnic or religious background or a plurality of schools, in which religious groups are accorded the right to their own schools?' To borrow Miller's (1997: 24) words, the design and process will be interrogated as to their ability to link 'two or more analytic formations, and make them mutually informative, while also respecting the distinctive contributions and integrity of each perspective'. Can the design and research process set out so far, which combines quantitative and qualitative methods, describe adequately the specific values underpinning a particular school's culture, as well as provide insights into the values and attitudes which inform students' and teachers' world views, or faith?

The research/audit methods to be used and how their findings are to be analysed and interpreted raises key questions for politicians, educational researchers and faith communities which maintain, or wish to maintain, state-supported schools if the proposals put forward in this book are taken forward. Patterns of 'social interaction' with and about the data will have to be considered, such as those discussed by Heritage (1997: 161), who gives this very succinct account of the writings of Goffman (1955, 1983):

> the institutional order of interaction has a particular social significance. . . . The political, economic, educational and legal conduct of societies is all unavoidably transacted by means of the practices which make up the institution of social interaction.

It is precisely the lack of a distinct 'social interaction' in complex pluralities, in which many cultural and a-cultural modes vie to determine the 'practices' through which political and educational institutions interact with which this book is concerned. In the matter of deliberation about whether faith schools should receive state support, what kind of social interaction might most usefully and ethically be developed and validated as appropriate for complex pluralities?

In other words, does the research or audit process described here prove adequate to provide the basis for a genuine conversation between faith-based education and the state? If a genuine civic conversation could follow from evidence collected in this way, then a set of indicators might arise which could be used by policy makers in judging the value or otherwise of faith schools. If the present process is validated, then profiles of school cultures could be used to contribute to the discussion about the appropriateness of faith schools within state education in late modern times. The work of developing such a process is crucial if government, educators and communities are going to be able to test the value of individual school cultures' ability to a) offer a vision of a viable, fair, inclusive and just complex plurality to their students and local communities and b) encourage human flourishing in each of its students so they are able to take their place in democratic societies.

Presentation of the Profiles of the Four Catholic Schools

The profiles of the four Catholic schools are developed from information presented over the next two chapters. Chapter 7 maps the main constituents of each culture from observation, interviews and documentary analysis. Chapter 8 is concerned with the data from the student questionnaire and interviews with the students. Both chapters, however, share a common map for the presentation of the information, using the headings of 'Beliefs', 'Attitudes and Values' and 'Behaviours'. As stated in Chapter 1, there is a need to have a framework for reporting differences and similarities in separate school cultures which can usefully borrow from Bryk's concept of reporting differences in levels of achievement across a wide range of schools through the instrument of using common educational indicators. For him, the research landscape was dominated by equity and access for students of all races and world views. For the present study the landscape is also dominated by pluralism and inclusion and the role of the spiritual in personal and civic education.

The profiles which emerge place heavy emphasis on the responses of the students about themselves, their identities and values, and their particular views of the schools in which they study. There still remains the matter of how to excavate the meaning attached to the students' responses and, as importantly, how to compare their picture of their school with their teachers' and headteachers' view. In this matter, qualitative methods are employed.

Methods and Processes Involved in the Study/Audit of Four Catholic Schools

First, the case studies of the four faith schools were not conducted in order to furnish an additional 'list' of the features which improving or successful schools must include; rather, they were undertaken to examine the possibility of exploring individual school cultures and reporting on them as a means of testing whether a school can be judged good or poor educationally within the social and cultural contexts in which it operates. The schools in which these particular studies took place admitted students according to their nationally tested junior-high certificate grades.

The collection of data from the schools and the framework for its presentation

Each school study involved three days' attendance on campus. Either immediately before, or during the visit, relevant school documentation, such as the school prospectus, statement of philosophy, curriculum and pastoral policies, timetable, RE programme, newsletters, etc was made available.

The study schedule took the following form:

1. Interviews, each lasting about 30 minutes, of as many as possible of the headteacher, the bursar, the curriculum coordinator, the pastoral coordinator, the head of religious education, some other heads of department, a recently arrived junior teacher, the chair of the Parents' Association, a school governor. In some cases it was not possible to meet with a parent. A list of suggested topics and questions which were to be covered during the interviews were sent to the headteacher in advance.

2. A questionnaire, to be completed by final year students – either the whole cohort or a random sample of 30–40, which took one hour to complete;
3. Observation of some timetabled classes in RE and of some communal events, for example, coffee in the staff-room and school lobbies at morning arrival.

Lawton (1996: 116) argued that his particular hierarchical plotting of the constituents of a school culture would result in emphasizing 'many aspects of life, in addition to goals . . . and success or failure will not only be seen in terms of league table results'. Thus, for the purpose of this exercise, interview data and analysis of school documentation and procedures will be recorded against the framework headings which are taken from Lawton's concept mapping. Bartelt's (1995: 161–2) concept of 'nested ecologies of education' gave rise to the possibility of superimposing the profiles gained by using Lawton's technique onto the wider landscape of the intellectual–cultural backcloth of a heavily globalized world. Thus the functioning of the micro-educational culture can be viewed against the macro-ecology which both sustains, and is affected by, that which it surrounds and nourishes.

The work of both Lauwerys and Holmes below suggests that the ecology of the schools will have been affected by the work of the Christian missionaries who were usually, in two countries in this study, the first to establish formal educational institutions. Lauwerys (1967: viii) wisely commented that 'often in education the problems of today cannot be understood without taking account of the way in which they were generated'. Since the case studies are situated in countries in which European colonial rule was dominant in the eighteenth, nineteenth and twentieth centuries, it will be important to evaluate, in the words of Lauwerys (1967: viii) 'the missionary effort, where policy decisions were taken in the early days and institutions created. The effects were permanent and still persist.' Holmes (1967: 1) noted, for example, that the mission schools were naturally modelled on those familiar to missionaries at home – the charity schools and the English public or grammar schools. Lauwerys' conclusion is set out here simply because its references to modernization, science and freedom resonate with many of the statements included in the data recorded in Chapter 7:

> Among the general results of missionary activities, shaped as they were by religious and humanitarian purposes but deeply influenced by the cultural background from which they drew nourishment and largely controlled by an administration not always sympathetic, we could stress above all the political consequences. . . . . The missionaries, so often misguided and short-sighted, were in fact pioneers of modernisation, of science and of freedom. (1967: ix–x)

At the same time, in-country documentation is used to facilitate observation and understanding of some of the many micro- and macro-ecologies which sustain, and sometimes grow from, each of the four school cultures.

Listening to 'The student voice'

Throughout the study and in the bibliography the four schools are referred to as A, B, C and D. Questionnaires were completed by a total of 186 final year students in these schools. Their distribution by gender and school is presented in Table 6.1.

Schools A, B and C were state-maintained Catholic schools, whereas school D was private but supported also by the state. Only in school D was the majority of the population Catholic. In the southern African country, other Christians made up the majority population and in the Caribbean country Catholic students were still less than half of the total.

The low count of individual students of no religion makes it difficult to make generalizations about their responses in the following chapters. This is one of the problems of looking at aggregate scores from the data. Nonetheless, when

Table 6.1 Student survey population by gender and school

	School A	School B	School C	School D	Total
Gender					
Male	15	36	–	23	74
Female	16	30	49	17	112
Total	31	66	49	40	186

Note: Schools A, B and D were co-educational and C single-sex.

Table 6.2 Schools by religious adherence and gender

	Gender	
	Male	**Female**
School A: southern Africa		
Catholic	5	3
Other Christian faith	8	11
No religion	2	2
School B: southern Africa		
Catholic	6	6
Other Christian faith	24	22
Non-Christian religion	5	1
No religion	1	1
School C: Caribbean		
Catholic		20
Other Christian faith		27
Non-Christian religion		1
No religion		1
School D: south-east Asia		
Catholic	23	14
Other Christian faith		2
Non-Christian religion		1

examining the qualitative material in Chapters 7 and 8, as well as the open-ended questions in Chapter 8, it is important to bear in mind the provision made by the individual schools for these members of the student body, as well as those same students' response to the school experience.

Analysing the questionnaire data in order to record 'The student voice'

The data arising from the questionnaire distributed in the four faith schools and its partial analysis will be included in Chapter 8 under the heading, 'The student voice'. Further analysis will be undertaken in Chapter 9 and in the concluding chapter. Questionnaire data was analysed using the Statistical Package for the Social Sciences (SPSS) and is presented in tables with a five-point scale. Three forms of cross tabulation of data were undertaken: by gender, by religious affiliation and by school. The calculation of scores and overall scores in the questionnaire data were necessary to establish any trends, patterns or indicators. A sample of approximately one-third of the responses from the three open questions placed at the end of the questionnaire were analysed. An attempt has been made to include in these samples of discursive answers from each school, a fair distribution by gender and by religion. Hence, if there are a small number of students from non-Christian religions or from no religion in the group, then a representative script from each religious/no religious group has been included.

Some of the data which emerged from the questionnaire, and some major trends within it, were compared with Flynn's and Mtumbuka's research analyses. A particular concern in the analysis was to examine data which informed an understanding of the 'cultures' of Catholic schools. In particular, these were:

1. What are the life-goals and values of school leavers in four Catholic schools (three co-educational) in three countries?
2. What are students' expectations of Catholic schools? How important are the school's religious goals to students?
3. What is the students' experience of the culture and life of Catholic schools? What are their attitudes towards their school, teachers, headteacher and the curriculum of their schools?
4. What are the attitudes of students towards religious education?
5. Are the students happy at school? Are they depressed?
6. What can we know of their beliefs, faith and values?

The analysis of the data therefore seeks indications of whether there are differences between student responses in the individual schools and across the schools. The religious affiliation or otherwise of the respondents is also presented. An opportunity is also taken to compare differences in values and attitudes between a mainly Catholic population in one and a very mixed population of Catholics, other Christians and students who have no religious adherence in another.

The data are also analysed to evaluate whether responses from students in each of the three developing countries were similar, whether they were also similar in part to the findings recorded in Malawian Catholic schools, and whether they differed in part from the students' responses in Australia. Through this approach the data informs a statement about the cultures of these Catholic schools against the background of the prevailing religious, social and economic cultural conditions found in the countries which participated in this study.

Presenting 'The student voice'

The data arising from the students' response to the questionnaire are presented in two ways: some on a school-by-school basis, others through composite tables of cross-tabulations of overall scores by school, gender and religious affiliation. The data will present the information derived from the questionnaire completed in the four schools as a means of indicating the values students placed on education in their own lives and aspirations and on some of the key behaviours presented by the school culture.

The data presented on a school-by-school basis is contained in four tables. They are headed: (i) 'School life and climate', containing responses to questions 35 to 71; (ii) 'Agents of community spirit', containing responses to questions 113, 117 and 65 spread throughout the questionnaire since the responses to these statements across the schools showed heavy emphasis placed upon them by the students as agents of community spirit; (iii) 'The curriculum', containing responses to questions 72 to 84; and (iv) 'Religious education', containing responses to questions 86 to 108. Tables present the students' response to each statement within the questionnaire, each of which elicited a five-point response. The level of response will be in percentages. At the right-hand side of the table there is a sixth column, which presents an overall mean of the percentage responses.

The overall mean is included there to act as an indicator of the trend in the responses as to whether they are moving up or down on the five-point scale. The SPSS package did not permit such estimation of an overall score within the data generated for the tables from each school. Items in the tables have been presented in descending order according to the mean. In all the tables 1=least positive and 5=most positive, except where the statements presented to the students were of a negative nature, such as 'I think that saying prayers does no good'. In those cases a low mean represents a positive response. The responses to negative statements such as this have been clustered together at the bottom of the tables.

It is hoped that the method of formatting each table permits a clear picture of the patterns emerging from the data in each school. Comment on the data found in these four tables from the four schools introduced in Chapter 7 is made within the sections on each school, and such comment will be found to be chiefly concerned with positive trends within each of the tables.

In recording the data derived from the students in Chapter 8, a problem of presentation arose. These data both complement and enrich that found in Chapter 7 in which the four school cultures are introduced under the headings of 'beliefs', 'values and attitudes' and 'behaviours'. The qualitative data discussed in Chapter 7 are to a large extent amenable to this presentational device. In Chapter 8, however, the data derived from Flynn's questionnaire tool sit more comfortably under the section headings found within the questionnaire. Nonetheless, the shape of the presentation of data continue to use Lawton's headings, even though some artificial devices for marrying the insights afforded by the different tools have become necessary.

Flynn's tool was devised wholly as a means of encouraging the students to make clear their beliefs, attitudes and values. The analysis of the tables for each school is therefore informed by data presented in four separate composite tables concerned with the students' personal beliefs and values as well as their attitudes to their schools. Thus each section under the heading of 'beliefs' contains two parts. The first presents tables of the religious adherence both of students and their parents. The second section reports students' highest expectations of their schools and a table is provided of their experience of each school's life and climate. The next section headed 'students values and attitudes towards the school' reports in a table headed 'agents of community spirit' on the students' responses in each school to three questions. The data from these are used to suggest which aspects of school life contributed most to the building of the school community.

The second part presents findings from the students' answers to the three open-ended questions in the questionnaire which asked them to identify three aspects of their experience of the school: what they most appreciate and value about the school; what changes they would like to make; and how they would describe the unique spirit which exists in the school. Not all students completed these three tasks. For each school, about one-third of the responses received have been selected. Coupled with this selection from individual student voices within the questionnaire is a selection of comments made by students in group interviews. The comments that they made are ascribed by gender and religion. The third section headed 'behaviours' will record students' highest personal goals and present two tables concerned with curricular matters: the first, headed 'the curriculum' and the second 'religious education'. By dividing the presentation of the data from each school into each of Lawton's three domains, it is possible to speculate more coherently about the overall contribution of each of these within a particular school culture to the human flourishing or otherwise of the students.

The first part of the presentation of data in Chapter 8, however, begins with an overview of the students in the four schools who took part in this study, whose careful and thoughtful response to the questionnaire has permitted a significant and constructive voice to emerge from each of the school cultures.

The overview takes the form of four composite tables relating to the students' expectations of Catholic schools; the influences which the students have felt on their religious development; their goals for their personal futures; and their values, beliefs and faith. The four tables are labelled: 8.1 'Students' expectations of Catholic schools' containing their response to questions 24 to 31; 8.2 'Influences on students' religious development', containing responses to questions 141 to 152; 8.3 'Personal goals', containing responses to questions 174 to 184; and 8.4 'Values, beliefs and faith', containing responses to questions 109 to 140.

The four composite tables show a cross-tabulation of SPSS generated overall scores, by gender, religious affiliation and school. At the right-hand side of the table there is an eleventh column, which presents an overall score of the percentage responses, presented in descending order of positive response. Similarly at the bottom of these four tables an overall score is found in each column, helping to indicate the levels of exuberance displayed by gender, religious adherence and school in the students' responses.

Those first four tables are offered as a means of establishing some general aspirations for faith schools in the minds of young students today in the three countries, alongside their beliefs about the particular influences which they see as having impacted on their religious development so far. They also offer an insight into the aspirations, together with a profile of the values and beliefs, of those young people whose comments this survey has sought to elicit about the nature and practices of the school cultures they inhabit. Sometimes their responses are examined by gender or religious adherence, sometimes by school or country. On the whole the tables are presented as evidence of what can be learnt about the developing attitudes and values of diverse groups of final year students in individual Catholic schools through the use of a self-review tool.

The Significance of Cultural Context in Presenting Information about Individual Schools

Earlier chapters attempted to discuss the educational, political, socio-intellectual and religious cultural context for the current energetic and sometimes acrimonious debate about the future of faith schools in Britain. The religious/secular landscape which had once tacitly supported a dual system of education is now seared by a global resurgence in interest, if not adherence to, religious faiths. A late modern intellectual preference for uncertainty in grand narratives at the same time as a heavy reliance on managerialism and performativity as indicators of successful performance in education, industry and political activity has provided the backdrop for discussion of the Labour government's encouragement of the maintenance and expansion of faith schools. At the forefront of that same discussion, however, were immediate concerns with inner-city tension among different racial and religious groups and the dominance of Islam in the consciousness of the post-9/11 world. Couple such intellectual and social schisms with an intense concern about the quality of education for all children and it is clear that information about faith schools will be at times both subject to rhetorical manipulation and potentially used as a means of attacking particular religions and their adherents.

Against this background it is important that information provided about faith schools is related to their immediate local, as well as national and global contexts. Current cluster groups of similar school characteristics and contexts used by Ofsted and the DfCSF for analysis of provision, attainment and value-added offer a specific example in England and Wales. Achieving such fine-tuned statistical clusters, however, does not necessarily point to a means of contextualizing faith schools and their local and national counterparts in terms of indicating how faith is employed in individual schools to direct mission, define values and dictate practice. Nor does it provide a sure means of comparing contexts characterized by urban tension and community strife. Other factors which would lead to consideration of a weighting system of contextual factors might include the length of time in which a particular faith tradition had been involved in compulsory state-maintained schooling; the involvement of that faith tradition in further and higher education; the capacity of any one faith group to support quality school leaders as well as teachers of religion, ethics and citizenship; and the currently contested matter of school admissions.

The Swann Report (1985) noted that the pastoral needs of Muslim pupils were not always met by common schools yet still advocated that religious minorities should not seek to establish their own schools. The Cantle Report (2001) resulted from a study of the inner-city areas in which religious and ethnic tension has led to serious disturbance and concluded that faith schools were not contributing to community cohesion. As a result, by September 2007 both faith schools and community schools in England and Wales were required by law to promote community cohesion. In November 2007, an initial report from the Runnymede Trust was published. Its author, Audrey Osler, examined ways in which schools, both faith and non-faith, can contribute to community cohesion. The research team met with headteachers, local authority officers, members of faith networks, humanist groups and regeneration projects, police officers and youth organizations.

The Report highlights some of the problems identified throughout this book when information about faith schools and their contribution to education in general, and community cohesion in particular becomes the subject of P/politicization. First positively, the report observes that although there are shared challenges in the overall task, a school system that includes faith schools produces diverse and particular responses to educating young people successfully for living in a multicultural society. The Report also raises two critical issues which have been highlighted here. The first is that in many communities people expressed concern about the government's community cohesion agenda, and it noted how Muslims, in particular, have come under critical media and government spotlights. Second, it focuses on concerns about marginalized young people who are unable to make their voices heard in the often heated debate about schooling. It also notes that many teachers are ill-prepared to take on their new role in promoting community cohesion.

Cultural Context and the Study of the Four Catholic Schools

The significance of cultural context as the key determinant for the success or failure of faith schools was a key focus for the study/audit of the four Catholic schools. This was of particular concern since recent comparative literature has highlighted the failure of educational transfer to developing countries and has thus become a major concern to comparative and international educators. See, for example, Leach and Little (1999) and Crossley and Watson (2003). The national context and the dominant cultural tradition are examined in order to determine what each school is contributing to the specific factors which cohere to create the 'national and cultural contexts' of senior secondary education. This examination started from the premise that there are both universal characteristics and local aspects to the broad term, 'Catholic education'. In this way this study has been in the tradition of those writers such as Horace Mann who have wrestled with the concept of 'cultural borrowing'; for Mann, according to Watson (2003: 323), studied education in Prussia, France and England 'with the express intention of borrowing those ideas which he felt would lead to the improvement of education in the United States and . . . . as a result was often referred to as the father of American education'. The following descriptions of the four Catholic schools therefore include discussion about the universal aspects of Catholic education within specific national and cultural contexts.

This study has been undertaken against the background of specific pieces of previous and on-going research into Catholic schools in the United States, Australia and Malawi. This study could not have been undertaken without the very generous collaboration offered by the relevant national ministries, Catholic authorities, governors, headteachers, teachers, parents and students. Thus it was conducted in a spirit of enquiry together with the communities which went to make up each of the schools. In that situation, the aim was that the evidence presented from the study would not be simply impressionistic but rather in the forms of school and data profiles which would inform not only the researcher but also the ministries, schools and local and national faith communities which supported the schools.

This particular study of four Catholic schools and their cultures employed a variety of perspectives as a means of providing a structured view of Catholic school cultures, including:

1. Literature on patterns of colonial education (Watson 1982); the place of missionary schooling (Holmes 1967); and the continuing educational

dependence of poorer countries on their former colonial authorities (McLean 1983).

2. Changes observed in the general educational culture of Catholic education since the reforms of the Second Vatican Council (1962–65) and the prism which that now offers for any study of Catholic schools at the present time. For example, Bryk et al. (1993: 341) have concluded from their own research that:

> Traditional arguments against public support for Catholic schools – the fear of religious establishment, social divisiveness and elitism seem ungrounded. We discern nothing fundamentally undemocratic about Catholic schools, educational philosophy of person-in-community and their ethical stance of shaping the human conscience towards personal responsibility and social engagement. To the contrary, these religious understandings order daily life and its outcomes in very appealing ways. It is not a narrow, divisive, or sectarian education but rather an education for democratic life.

The work of Grace (2002: xii) also supports a revised understanding of Catholic education following the Second Vatican Council for he argues:

> A third mis-perception is based upon outdated but still tenacious images of traditional Catholic schooling as a process of authoritarian indoctrination rather than a process of education per se. The existence of what might be called the Antonia White, James Joyce, Frank McCourt versions of Catholic schools have obscured the extent to which new forms of Catholic education have developed as one consequence of the reforms of the Second Vatican Council (1962–65).

3. Research findings about Catholic schools concerning their promotion of a democratic life and of less prejudiced attitudes in their students. This can usefully be contextualized within a further perspective which has emerged from the American study of Bryk et al. (1993: 340–1), Catholic Schools and the Common Good. He describes this specific form of contribution to the good of society as a whole, both local, national and global, in the following way:

> Although we have emphasised the education of disadvantaged students, we note that Catholic schools also advance an important agenda in the education of their more advantaged counterparts. In schools with large proportions of low income students, the social justice mission of Vatican II is tangibly manifested . . . the concern for social justice, however, is also manifest in the schooling of the advantaged. Catholic schools deliberately strive to inculcate an understanding for, and a commitment to, social

justice in all their students. Many of these students are likely to move into powerful positions in society as adults.

4. The concept of the contribution of Catholic schools to the common good of their own societies and, perhaps, to the global common good, and the contribution of the four schools in this study will be examined later against the writings of Sandel, Maritain and Stiltner who, it has been argued in Chapters 2, 3 and 4 of this study, set out the possibility for an ethically sound education for all citizens within plural communities.

5. The Aristotelian tradition of practical wisdom, whose definition this study borrows profitably from Nancy Sherman (1997: 39). The prism of Aristotelian practical wisdom will be used to filter the results of the examination of the missions and pedagogies of the four schools and the related survey's findings about the attitudes and values of the students in them. Thus the understanding learnt from the findings about one school's culture, with its distinctive setting and values' perspective on education, will be built onto the findings from the next. In turn this cumulative narrative about the nature of each school's culture will be examined within the overall context of the need for an ethical approach to political policy making.

6. The existence of particular relationships between religion and the state and the place of religion in state supported education. Haynes (1998: 10–11) sets out five models of 'Church-State' relationships from a political perspective. These are:

   - confessional states – here ecclesiastical authority takes precedence over the secular government;
   - generally religious states, which are 'guided by religious beliefs in general where the concept of civil religion is important but not tied to any specific religious tradition';
   - states with an established faith – here the established faith is recognized as the state religion even though society is largely secular;
   - liberal secular states – these 'encapsulate the notion of secular power holding sway over religion';
   - Marxist secular states.

In other words, the description and articulation of individual school cultures as nested ecologies are presented here and in the following chapters in this deliberative and extensive mode in order to underline the need for transparent reasons for undertaking research/audits of faith schools, together with specific contextualization of the individual schools involved. The presentation of the information in the format which follows permits:

- a rigorous explanation of what information it is possible to collect using the research design and process described in the previous chapter;
- a detailed account of the information which is required to develop a school profile which offers comprehensive information about the social, personal,

spiritual and educational capability or non-capability of a state supported faith school in modern plural societies;
- a reflection on what can be learnt from faith school cultures in the Global South about the continuing presence of faith schools in multicultural societies in the North;
- a questioning of the appropriateness and viability of developing profiles of faith school cultures in England in the near future.

The scale of the research described here cannot by itself generate any authoritative guidelines on the vexed issues outlined above. The research design and process do, however, through their particular means of studying the social reality of faith-based schools, offer a base from which more sophisticated models for a wider audit of faith schools might be generated.

Part III

Profiling Faith School Cultures: A Means of Practice Informing Policy

Purpose of Part III

Profiles of four faith schools are developed partly to understand the ways in which a school's faith foundation impinges on the education it offers and partly to discern the distinctive epistemological and communal bases found in faith schools for learning about the human condition in plural societies. Clear evidence emerges of distinctiveness in each of the four school cultures. Even though each school stands within the broad tradition of Catholic education, the individuality of each one points to the need for careful scrutiny of the microcultures which together sustain and are sustained by the macroculture of Catholic education. The story told by one school culture, when layered upon the story told by another, and so on, will provide a means of writing a meta-narrative of school cultures in Chapter 9. It is from that meta-narrative that some guidelines for civic engagement with faith schools will be developed in Chapter 10, together with suggested criteria for evaluating their place or otherwise in plural late modern societies.

It is expected, therefore, that the evidence from the four profiles will permit a worthwhile discussion of:

1. the extent to which the school culture sustains, and is sustained by, an effective epistemic community;
2. whether the school culture exhibits evidence of social cohesion between its members and whether such cohesion created by a faith-based school necessarily contributes to divisions between school communities and the wider community, as suggested by Forrest and Kearns (2000);
3. the overall contribution of each of Lawton's domains within a particular school culture to the human flourishing of the students as they prepare to join their societies as young adults;

4. the consequences for education in each of the three countries of the 'glo-balization' cultural mode and the consequent increasing powerlessness of the nation-state described by Cowen (2000: 101), above, as not merely an economic crisis but 'a cultural one, which requires historical, sociological, anthropological, cultural and philosophical analysis'.

Chapter 7

Four Catholic Schools and Their Cultures

Purpose of the Chapter

This chapter aims to map the cultures of four Catholic schools resulting from discussion with headteachers, senior managers, pastoral and teaching staff, parents and related documentary analysis. The data from each school is set within a statement concerned with some important socio-cultural, religious and economic features of each country in which the schools are found. The information acquired during the study will be set out within a framework built on Lawton's hierarchical plotting of school cultures into (i) beliefs, (ii) attitudes and values and (iii) behaviours. By this means it is hoped to present the findings from each school in such a way as to, first, determine the authorizing beliefs and practices which a faith group uses to define its educational purposes and, second, gain information about how such beliefs and values inform behaviours found in the school. Plotting the data in this way will give rise to substantial elements of the school profiles which the empirical studies are seeking to develop.

Country X: A Southern African Country

Richard Dowden, the Executive Director of the Royal African Society, has warned that generalizing about Africa is as hard as generalizing about Europe or Asia. Nonetheless, he has commented that 'even in the worst starvation camps . . . and homes where Aids has reduced families to small children and grandparents, there is always a vitality that seems superhuman'. There is he argues, 'an instinct for survival that grows out of faith and hope (and) this is Africa's greatest strength'. His argument continues:

> The flipside of the survival instinct is a fear of risk. Better to stick to tradition and respect the keepers of tradition, the elderly men, than risk change. Young people cannot break that tradition in Africa so they flee. One of Africa's many tragedies is the brain drain of frustrated young professionals to Europe and America. (2002)

One of Dowden's key concerns about the difficulties facing Africa is not, surprisingly, concerned with the 'debt and economic reform policies of the

World Bank and the IMF' but with the 'tough physical environment which induces deep conservatism' and the need for Africa 'to discover an identity for its nation states'.

He concludes that:

> Discovering that identity is the first step in Africa's path to development. It will take a long time, decades rather than years, and it can only be done by Africans. (2002)

The themes captured so succinctly by Dowden of inherent conservatism, leading to feelings of uselessness in the young, and the need for Africans themselves to discover their own national identities are reflected in the conversations and questionnaire data yielded by the case studies of two Catholic schools in Country X. For the purposes of this case study it is also useful to refer to Dowden's estimate of the place of Country X along the spectrum of Africa's poverty:

> Most of Africa's 800 million people are poor and the gap between them and the rest of the world is getting wider. Yet Africa's poverty is neither inevitable nor universal. In the 1960s and 1970s African economies grew. Asia seemed to be the region most likely to face disaster. Some countries in southern Africa, for example, have managed their political and economic affairs well even though they live off diamonds – usually a fuel for war and corruption in Africa. (2002)

The President of Country X, however, has underlined some very real problems facing the country. In the Foreword to the *National Development Plan* (NDP), he stated:

> There are a number of socio-economic challenges that we as a nation will have to face as we enter the twenty-first century. These include unemployment (especially among the youth), poverty, crime, HIV/AIDS, high population growth and environmental concerns, to mention but a few. (Government of Country X GoX 1997)

He continued:

> The development of a 'Vision' became imperative in order to effectively address these challenges . . . Some aspects of the 'Vision', such as national values, traditions and morals, ethics, tolerance, etc. will have to be addressed by all stakeholders, including religious organisations. . . . With rapid changes in the global economic environment, the country needs to position itself so that it does not miss out. (GoX 1997)

The 'Vision' (Government of Country X Presidential Task Group GoXPTG 1997: 28) states specifically that the 'shrinking' world and increased 'globalisation' has resulted not only in a global economic environment but also an 'increasingly intrusive global culture'. In this regard, 'Country X must provide for and respond in a pro-active way. . . . It is important that the magnitude of the challenge, and the attitudes needed to address it, are emphasized through the media, and reflected in the school syllabus'.

'*Vision 2016*' (GoXPTG 1997: 31) points to two key directions for education in Country X, namely that education must be used 'to enrich cultural diversity' and that 'gender awareness must be institutionalized throughout the education system in order to create a gender sensitive, caring and equitable society by the year 2016'.

The *NDP 8* (GoX 1997: 440) further states:

Young people in Country X find themselves in the middle of a process of transition from the traditional to modern society. The gradual breakdown of the extended family system which provides support and social guidance to the youth has compounded the problems of young people.

This final statement reflects action taken in 1994. Country X's National Policy on Education stressed the need to separate religious and moral education. Moral education gained the status of a core subject, leaving religious education as optional.

Finally, it is worthwhile noting that the *NDP 8* (GoX 1997: 435) links the concept of future economic development with culture and its preservation. The richness and complexity of that culture has been carefully documented. Following a study of 543 students in southern Africa's junior secondary schools, Mmolai (1999: 1) argues that despite current social changes, religion still significantly influences the reasoning and behaviour of young people. He (1999: 5) asserts that there is a pressing need 'to examine the role of religious education in promoting personal, social and moral development amongst secondary school pupils'.

It was in 1928 that the Catholic Church was established in Country X. Until independence from colonial rule in Malawi in 1961 and in Country X in 1966, their two school systems were modelled on that of Britain. According to Pettifer and Bradley (1992: ch 10) and Khama (2001), mission schools, even in post-independence countries, have a disproportionate influence at the secondary level because their students are more likely to gain entrance to higher education and therefore achieve senior positions in the civil service, government and the professions. Countries singled out as representative of this argument include Kenya and Lesotho. In addition, the modernizing trends of post-colonial education systems have been described by Watson (2003: 384) as 'emulating the socio-economic and technological development of the West and Japan'.

The Culture of School A in Country X

The school and its foundation

Senior secondary schools in Country X totalled twenty-seven in 2000; out of these four are run and managed by Christian churches. School A is a government-aided school, with reporting lines both to the Ministry of Education and to the bishop, who chairs the governing body. The headteacher is aided by a senior educational administrative colleague who acts as the college manager. The physical presence of the college buildings and the site itself are memorable. There is a long driveway leading up to the school with wrought iron gates at its head and an immediate awareness of space. The soil and dust on all sides are deep red. The site which is still in development is dominated by the two-storey administration block in red brick but elsewhere there are newly converted classroom buildings, well-equipped laboratories and computer rooms, and the spacious and attractive library. Varied art displays are everywhere and examples of students' crafts and design skills are to be found.

Writing in School A's magazine, whose front cover bears the school's crest and motto, the then Minister of Home Affairs, who had been one of the first students at the college argued that because it had both primary and secondary schools on the site and boarding facilities:

> People with different backgrounds, age groups, and even cultures were able to share ideas in a common meeting ground. (School A 1978: 4)

Not only therefore did the school provide such opportunities for 'difference' to be explored and lived-out in a school community, it also proved different, he argued, from other schools by providing extra-curricular activities, including motor mechanics and sports. The headteacher of that time has written:

> Over the years the college has approached education with the belief that the purpose of education is not just to impart knowledge or inculcate skills, but that it should concern itself with the total development of the whole human person. The quality of the product matters most of all and not the quantity.
>
> It is my sincere wish that each student, when he leaves the college, will be motivated by sound Christian principles and that he will prove to be a good citizen of Country X and will be prepared to sacrifice himself for the development of the country. (School A 1978: 5)

The mission from which School A grew was founded by the German Oblate Fathers. A local historian of the area, Campbell (1978: 14–17), writes that 'the early history of this place is known only from man's remains which can be found scattered both on and around the hill on which the town stands; by about a million years ago people were living there'.

The first school was opened on 25 January 1928 and consisted of one class room, one teacher and three pupils. By the end of 1930, there were thirty pupils. The manager of the school explained during the case study that in the mid-1930s the church made its first attempt at post primary education by opening a two-year agricultural school at. Although this venture later failed through lack of funding and staff, the priest-in-charge started junior secondary classes in the mid-1940s under the University of South Africa Examination Board. He added that 'this was the birth of secondary education at School A, as well as in Country X'. The church supplemented the fees to a large extent since there was no financial help from the colonial government. The policy was that education was the responsibility of tribal authorities, churches and private organizations. In this context the manager reflected, 'while the school had always opened its doors to non-Catholic students, it remained strongly Catholic in practice and ethos'. In addition the church gave financial aid to a number of students after their Junior Certificate to further their education elsewhere.

In a Foreword to the school magazine, on the anniversary of the establishment of the mission, the then Minister of Education insisted:

> The school has, from its inception, dedicated itself to the cause of uplifting Country X. From the very beginning the Missionary Fathers rightly identified education as the only meaningful and effective instrument of the development of any new country. The school has chalked up many 'firsts' in its illustrious history. It was the first to introduce the Junior Certificate Course and the first to introduce the Matriculation Course. . . . The school has indeed produced very good results in public examinations, but more than this, it has striven to provide an atmosphere in which students can develop a moral fibre to make them leaders among people . . . In its broadly based education, the school is thus preparing students to develop a sense of values, which should stand them in good stead when they meet the challenge of the modern world. (School A 1978: 3)

The first principal of the college who was a national of Country X was appointed in 1979. He has spoken of that task as 'a mammoth responsibility, socially and morally'. His recollections of this time include 'a teacher who confronted me in the office and told me in no uncertain terms that a big mistake had been made by appointing me'. Another was a parent who 'minced no words in uttering remarks tinged with tribal and ethnic connotations, in sheer contempt of this change'. In recalling his final year in the school in 1985, the challenges thrown down at the beginning of his term of office, had clearly been met:

> I recall my last days of direct association with the college that we were such a solid team; teachers and students, that it was not a question of how well the students would pass but, perhaps, which institution would dare 'beat' us in terms of final examination results.

When the case study was undertaken in 2000, both the principal and his deputy were nationals of Country X, as well as being former students of the college. The co-educational school by then had 1200 students, with approximately eighty-five teachers. In two years from 1998 these numbers had grown from 1000 and seventy-five, respectively.

One-fifth of the students are Catholics, as are a small number of staff. There are two full-time sisters in the RE department and a small number of lay staff contribute part time to RE classes. Many of the students travel into the town daily on a special train. Many live in the capital of Country X, which houses a large, very modern cathedral. During the case study, I attended Sunday morning Mass in the cathedral. The congregation was large and the altar servers were boys and girls. The Mass ended with the bishop, who had presided at the liturgy, dancing down the aisle.

Beliefs held in the school

The headteacher and the manager commented on the contribution made by the college in the country's national development. Senior politicians, including a former president, educationalists, business personnel, church ministers, medical doctors, nurses, soil scientists, lawyers, engineers and technicians of all kinds had all been educated at the college. They believed that all of these had been 'moulded into credible, honest and visionary civil servants' as a result of their education at the college.

The Principal believes the school's success is directly related to the commitment of teachers and parents' support. In discussion he stated:

> I teamed up with parents and teachers and we made sure that our students studied well. Also the management maintained a high standard of discipline at all times and it monitored performance of students by calling them individually or in groups to hear their problems. . . . The secret of the school's success is its vision which leads teachers and pupils to work extra hard.

The Vision says: by 2006 School A will be the leading institution in secondary education.

Values and attitudes

The students bustle everywhere in orderly but often noisy and cheerful groups. Examples of the students' responses to their schooling and to the social issues and concerns of their peers and their country were in evidence. Two of the students had produced poems about their understanding of education and its value to them as Africans. The first includes verses, which highlight the continuous watchfulness of the students towards imperialism and colonialism. Perhaps this is not surprising in a school in which the chronicles of 1949 record, 'the scouts and guides went to the capital today to celebrate the King's birthday' and the chronicles of 24 May, 1950 record, 'Empire Day was celebrated today. The pupils assembled at 9am. After several songs had been sung, the Director of Education gave an interesting speech appropriate to the occasion'. One poem says that;

> Without education the world would be in darkness
> Like a wise said 'EDUCATION IS THE KEY TO SUCCESS'.

The poem also captures a reflective value attached to education, which, although the key to success, is also the way 'man started to design and create his own things'. Dowden's concern, noted earlier, that Africans work out their own national identity, can be seen at work in this student's writing. The second poem reflects an understanding that education can meet needs and wants. The use of precious metals as imagery in the poem also points to the grounding of educational reflection in the precious metals which are such an essential part of the identity of Country X. Nonetheless, a former student of the school who is now a lecturer at the University of Country X, argued for a government review of the school curriculum with a view to incorporating earth sciences in schools. He argues that the country's economy is primarily dependent on revenues from the mining industry, yet that industry records the lowest number of trained citizens.

Another student wrote that:

> One approaches Country X with awe, for this is a republic that managed to stay at peace while all its neighbours were at war. To this safe haven the refugees came. . . . This is a tranquil country, after all, in which the tropics reach from the north tracking down into the salt pans. And the country's neighbours are nowadays officially at peace.

In discussion, the headteacher spoke of planning changes in the shape and culture of the college in order to meet the challenges of the new era; an era he said which will be marked by 'competition linked to globalisation'. He spoke of 'radical administrative and academic programmes being currently implemented' in order to return the school to its former position of being 'a centre for quality education'.

In addition, there is a Catholic Practices and Formation Committee. A member of the religious education department explained that:

> Since the school is government aided, the number of Catholic students as well as Catholic teachers is a drop in the ocean. Only a fifth of the students on roll are Catholics. Due to this a number of members of staff thought it necessary to mobilise Catholic youth and teachers into active participation in building the Catholic faith in the school. The committee prepares

students for baptism, first communion and confirmation. It also organises religious services in the school.

Although the committee focuses mainly on Catholic students, instruction, seminars and workshops are open to all interested non-Catholic students. With this attitude, we hope for the prevalence of the spirit of ecumenism, not only in this school but in the country as a whole.

Behaviours

The senior management team hold regular weekly meetings. The purpose of the meetings is to establish a team approach to the strategic planning of the college's development. At the meeting held during the case study, the headteacher referred to developments taking place in other senior secondary schools in the country and took advice as to how the school should respond. He also raised the possibility of the school's participation in an initiative by southern and east African Catholic schools to form an alliance to look at their particular features as Catholic schools, the needs of their students and the types of identity such schools might forge in the coming years as a result of their liaison. He spoke too of the links which had been developed with other sister Catholic secondary schools in Africa, Europe and America through the internet and e-mail. These were said to be very useful: first, in terms of understanding the potential of education in a rapidly changing world; and second, the contacts with African schools permitted discussion about pedagogies and resources which were appropriate for African schools.

The school maintains a house system within the school. In discussion, the headteacher spoke of the house system as a typical administrative innovation of the school at that time aimed at attending to, and meeting, the needs of students and teachers.

The school follows the national curriculum leading to the Cambridge General Certificate Examination and to Country X's General Certificate of Secondary Education (XGCSE). English is the medium of instruction for all subjects except for the national language. Religious education is compulsory and students study the life of Jesus, other world religions and social and moral issues. The headteacher spoke of the current school curriculum as 'one of the richest and most diverse in the country. For example, Music had been introduced as an enrichment subject'. Equally the new library (the largest in the country's secondary schools) had been planned to 'inspire our students to develop a good culture of reading and self-development in a conducive environment'.

The curriculum of the school also included agriculture, art, computer studies, design and technology, English, geography, guidance and counselling, history, home economics, the national language and science. He also spoke of the need to break into the cycle of students being unwilling to learn; once that had been achieved then support was needed. For him the new library must offer an appropriate and supportive environment for students to want to read. Often he said their homes were unable to provide such an environment. Equally counselling and guidance could move the students through particular difficulties and support them as willing participants in the learning process.

According to the Government of Country X's website, on 24 February 2004 there were 'scenes of jubilation at the school after the Examinations, Research and Testing Division released the results of the AGCSE and GCE examinations'. The report states:

> In overall performance, School A is the best school in all the government schools awarded Grade C or better in five or more subjects. The school scored 56.02 %, the highest mark since the introduction of AGCSE. Another school came second and School C came third.

School A's highest achieving student academically, who gained 'A's in English, maths, physics, commerce, history, biology, chemistry and additional mathematics and a 'B' in national language', is quoted as saying:

> I have achieved this through hardship, dedication and competition. My parents knew that I would make it, they always made sure that I had enough time for my books. (GoX website February 2004)

Most of the students belong to the many sports teams in which the school excels. Many also belong to non-academic clubs, including the PACT (Peer Approach Counselling Team) group, which is headed by a teacher from the careers and guidance department, and involves 'reaching out to our peers and talking to them about topics liked dating, rape and child abuse which are usually talked about behind closed doors'. Other clubs include a Life Skills Club, a Young English Speakers Club, a Chess club, a Traditional Dance Club, an AIDS Awareness Club and a Marimba Club.

The Culture of School B in Country X

The school and its foundation

The school was founded in 1963, using the premises of the former Catholic primary school. It is now a mixed co-educational school of over 1600 students, with its own premises adjoining the church. The church is extremely modern in design and stands starkly against the skyline. Recently the school has undergone major changes to its physical environment. At the time of the case study, extensive building work was being undertaken but already the school, which is built in a warm brick colour and has a most attractive entrance, with brick walls topped with wrought iron, had two-storey buildings housing most of its activities, a multipurpose hall, library and dining hall.

There had been an absence for five years of a religious community involved with the school. The bishop had, however, invited a community of sisters whose headquarters are in Holland to join the school. Their founding order is the same as the one from which the priests at the parish church belong. There are now five sisters in the school, some from India and south-east Asia but none from Africa. All the sisters are on permanent contract to the Government of Country X.

Unlike other aided schools in Country X where the Ministry has direct ownership, School B is overseen both by the Ministry of Education and the bishop. The headteacher is directly responsible to the Ministry and the school manager, who is the local parish priest, and to the bishop. The headteacher, the religious order which is attached to the school, the bishop and the surrounding Catholic community each influence the decision-making processes within the school. According to the headteacher, Catholic headteachers are understanding of this kind of continuum of responsibility. Nonetheless, since it is the headteacher who is responsible to government, and since the government provides 99 per cent of the school's funding, the headteacher must 'strive for financial control'.

Admission to the college is centrally controlled by the Ministry of Education. Students who have good passes in their Junior Certificate Examinations are granted admission. There are many and diverse catchment areas for the college, as is the case with all senior secondary schools in the country. In this college, though most of the students come from the villages and not the towns.

The school has twelve subject departments. The core subjects studied are religious education, English language, mathematics, science and the national language. Optional subjects include agriculture, art, business studies, design and technology, development studies, English literature, geography, history and home economics.

Beliefs held within the school

The mission statement of School B is:

> To produce a well disciplined, knowledgeable, adaptable and conscientious citizen with high moral values who thinks critically and progressively enough to face the future with confidence. (School B n.d.: 5)

At the same time, the Foreword to the School Prospectus reads:

> The high moral standard expected from members of the school community is complemented by the fact that all students do Religious Education. This is a very fulfilling subject which helps in the proper upbringing of the child. (School B n.d.: 1)

The published material about the school clearly links the development of the well-educated student specifically with 'the proper upbringing of the child' through religious education. The school motto is 'Education is a Shield'.

The use of the term 'child' in published school documents and often used by staff was the subject of comment by the head of RE, who believed that it ran contrary to the belief in the school that the students must be responsible for their own actions.

The school Prospectus sets out specific objectives which at the end of the three-year secondary course the students ought to be able to achieve. Thus in relation to the nation, the school's objectives for the students are that they ought to be able to:

1. Manifest skills in accuracy of observation and in imaginative, moral and logical thinking;
2. Contribute positively to the economic development of the country and judicious conservation of scarce natural resources;
3. Engage in worthwhile cultural and leisure time activities;
4. Acquire the necessary grades needed for admission to tertiary or otherwise appropriate levels of higher education. (School B n.d.: 6)

In relation to the Church, the students ought to be able to:

1. Manifest the true Christian spirit by living out the Gospel values.

The Prospectus also states that as a Catholic school, it adopts the Church's philosophy of education which states that:

1. A true education aims at the formation of the human person with respect to his ultimate goal and simultaneously with respect to the good of those societies of which, as a man, he is a member, and in whose responsibilities, as an adult he will share;
2. So it is that while the Catholic school fittingly adjusts itself to the circumstances of advancing times, it is educating its students to promote effectively the welfare of the earthly city, and preparing them to serve the advancement of the reign of God;
3. Above all the education of youth from every social background has to be undertaken, so that there can be produced not only men and women of refined talents, but those great-souled persons who are so desperately required for our times. (School B n.d.: 5)

In relation to the school's responsibility to the development of students as persons, the objectives state that students should:

1. Judge morally and manifest a sense of values and self-discipline;
2. Think progressively and critically;
3. Acquire appropriate knowledge and experience that is viable to face the future with confidence. (School B n.d.: 7)

The head of religious education spoke of the presence of the community of sisters as an opportunity of revitalizing the school community. With the priests in the parish, who shared their same educational psychology and spirituality, it had been possible to evangelize the school with 'gospel values' and concern and commitment to educate the 'whole student'. The sister spoke of 'primary evangelisation' as the dominant motif in missionary activity in the developing world. This was concerned to work with the person to change them, not to make them believers in Catholicism. Spirituality and morality in students is understood here as 'awareness for wider learning'. For non-Catholics, the sisters understand spirituality to be 'a deep knowledge that they are created and loved by God'. The sisters compare this with the twin tradition in African beliefs of 'faith in God and the ancestor's spirit'. The sisters and the school as a whole have pondered the question of whether Country X's society will become more secular. They answer that everything changes slowly but there is a growing belief that science has more answers than religion.

Values and attitudes

The religious community of sisters which is now based at the school described 'gospel values' as 'spreading the teachings of Christ to become better people, not to become Catholics'. The founder of the community's spirituality encouraged the community to 'go out to the marginalised and the oppressed'. At the school, Christian religious education sits alongside the other core compulsory subjects of English, mathematics, science and the national language. In non-faith schools, moral education and religious education are seen as 'enrichment subjects' rather than core. As in all other senior secondary schools in Country X, the medium of teaching, except for the national language, is English. The religious community of sisters believed that their presence had created a 'total change' in the school 'due to their dedicated service to the school' and 'personal interest in each student'.

A recurring theme in discussion with the headteacher was the change in society which was already discernible but which would be evidenced even more strongly in the next few years. He had recently presented a paper to Country X's Education Commission in which he argued that the role of schools was to develop students for a new society. As a result, his view was that only 35 per cent of his students should study the academic curriculum, and then progress to tertiary education. There should be a more vibrant skills-based curriculum and an emphasis on students achieving employment. This seemed a positive solution to the present state of society, in which, he argued, there was 'extreme poverty for the people in the midst of plenty'. Moral education should be able to respond to this situation, since, 'You can only fool the people some of the time'. Thus he reflected that as students become more mature, they 'expect more from their school'.

The head of science discussed her role in the school and that of her department. She is a non-believer but teaches in the RE department. She understood that the students had a high regard for the science department. Indeed, the department was rated the best nationally. Nonetheless, she felt it important to relate science and religion to the students' own worlds and concerns. She argued that her view of a 'good student' is one 'who is hard-working and dedicated; certainly does not have to be overly intellectual'. Instead, she and the school were concerned to develop the 'whole student'. Thus, despite the school's excellent national reputation in science education 'students know they have to struggle, and they are prepared to do this since they must get their degree first before they are accepted for professional training'.

Hand-in-hand with the focus on change, the headteacher also spoke with emphasis on the theme of 'Africanisation'. He recalled a recent Fourth Year class in which the students had become 'very excited about Africanisation – expressing themselves in their own language'. In the school this had repercussions for staff recruitment: out of seventy-eight staff, 50 per cent were from Country X. The headteacher explained that the country had insufficient senior secondary school teachers. In five years time, he argued that there would be a need for 150 ex-patriate teachers across all secondary schools. This was unhelpful to a country which had a great need for 'role-models who are African, particularly at a time when unemployment rates are so high'. Only 20 per cent of the students find employment at the end of senior secondary school.

The head of RE spoke of many students from single-parent homes; the break up of marriages has become a national problem. She also discussed elements of indigenous African religion, in which there are traditions where women are beaten. There is also a high proportion of child suicides. For the sister, the question here is, 'Is there someone who can help children with their problems; someone who can listen?' For her, the ideal student is 'God-fearing and responsible'. Lack of belief in God may become an issue in Country X as modernization and globalization take place. She referred here to what she called 'the most profound influences' on young people in the country; these, she explained, included materialism and television, rock music, computer games and internet and computer technology in general. At that time, at least 10 per cent of students had their own computer. Family life frequently meant a situation where a mother might have eight or so children, with three or four fathers. Several of the female students would have had babies before they arrived at senior secondary school. For her the best thing about the students is that they are willing to discuss problems in a group. They are supportive of each other and 'learning to cope on their own'.

Behaviours

Each Sunday the Catholic students attend the services conducted at the local parish church and for the rest of the students interdenominational services are held in the college hall. Special meetings and prayer sessions are conducted for Catholic students on Saturday mornings before morning study between 7.30 and 9.30. At the close of the academic year the bishop officiates at a Eucharistic Celebration, which is seen, according to the school prospectus, 'as a token of thanks and hope for the future'.

The college also emphasizes that 'manual work is an essential part of student's preparation and training for adult life'. Manual work may include 'cleaning the hostels and ablution blocks' as well as 'keeping the college campus clean and tidy'. The prospectus concludes, 'here the college expects staff and students to work together . . . to ensure that the college environment is a clean, healthy and happy one'.

The headteacher also conducts school disciplinary committee meetings. One was observed in which the student involved was a 16-year-old female student who had been found going into the town during the previous evening. She was severely reprimanded by the headteacher who spoke to her in a powerful and authoritarian voice and threatened expulsion. The rule which forbids students from visiting the local town is strictly enforced, since the school believes that the town offers attractions which are often new and particularly enticing to students who may have only recently arrived there from outlying villages, where the way of life is traditional and free from urban attractions. In discussion, the headteacher explained that his approach to discipline in a Catholic school is basically that of a professional teacher, with an overriding duty to look after the child as the parents would do. His treatment of the student was similar to how her misdemeanour would have been treated in a non-Catholic government school. In the matter of birth control and contraception, however, the Catholic school differed considerably from a government school. When this headteacher held the same position in a government school, he was willing to send female students to the contraceptive clinic; now in his present school, he does not permit the sending of Catholic or non-Catholic girls to such clinics.

The headteacher, however, confirmed that although corporal punishment was still permitted in the school, he was trying to steer teachers away from using it. This was because he understood corporal punishment to be part of the 'traditional' African way of disciplining children and young people, as well as it being a relic from colonial times in schools in Country X. For him it had no place in helping young people adapt and change to a new society. The head of RE also commented on the need to move away from what she called a traditional use of corporal punishment for misdemeanours in schools; the Ministry of Education, for example, still supported corporal punishment for any 'display of defiance'. She also questioned how the Christian concept of forgiveness might best be infiltrated into the current disciplinary framework in the school. Suspension as the ultimate punishment required a thorough review in the light of gospel values.

The curriculum of the school follows the senior secondary curriculum of Country X which leads to the Cambridge overseas examination. The prospectus commits the school to taking into consideration 'each student's career needs and personal skills at the end of Year 3 before they receive detailed information about their particular Cambridge curriculum before they make their final subjects choice for the Cambridge examination'. This level of advice and guidance is confirmed by the head of science, who spoke of the value of the diploma route for students. In the school, of twelve streams, only two are pure science. The diploma route encourages students to be 'realistic'; not to go straight to university but take on computer studies and engineering.

The religious education curriculum, which is compulsory, includes teaching about the life of Jesus but also covers the teaching of other religions, as well as moral education, with topics raised such as Aids and life skills. The school is situated in the town which is said to have the world's highest incidence of Aids among young people. The school buys videos for RE and ME lessons from Malawi, so that the students can relate to other African students and concerns. Videos and discussion groups are the most popular methodologies in RE. The head of religious education was educated in London and Dublin. Since the school is mainly boarding, the RE department spends much of its time involved in extra-curricular activities, so that they can become better acquainted with individual students. They also spend approximately one weekend in three leading retreats away from the campus.

One senior member of staff told of how she was unaware of the special religious status of the school until she actually joined the staff. Other new members of staff spoke of how they had been appointed to the school by the government and had not considered the religious nature of the school when they began their duties.

A particular concern raised by the head of RE was that there was no funding for continuing professional development for form tutors despite the wide-ranging and complex problems which students presented. They simply had to develop new strategies from their pre-service background.

Caribbean Country Y

Country Y is one of the smallest independent countries in the western hemisphere. It is strongly influenced by the United States as a result of family ties and emigration there, financial support received for the country's university and naval support provided by the US fleet. Meanwhile the East Caribbean states, of which Country Y is one, have formed trade alliances. Some recent data incorporated in the *Strategic Plan for Educational Enhancement and Development* reveals that:

> 32.1% of the population lives below the poverty line and 12.9% can be considered indigent. The data suggests that poverty is prevalent among youths particularly children of school age. In addition, there is the emergence of a serious drug culture and associated increase in crime among the youth population. The drug culture is contributing to the impoverishment of the human potential particularly in poor communities across the state.
> (Government of Country Y 1999: 13)

The *Strategic Development Plan* points to areas of expansion in the economy over the ten years to 1999, with particular emphasis on the services sector contribution to GDP. It (1999: 6) points to 'the impressive growth experienced since 1997 . . . due to an expanding construction sector, rapid growth in the international financial services sector, increased activity in the manufacturing sector, higher prices for nutmegs and sustained improvement in the tourism sector'. It (1999: 8) also warns that the linkage between the education system and culture is weak and calls for the expansion of 'the concept and focus of culture to enable it to make a meaningful contribution to the development of our society'. In particular, the *Strategic Plan* comments on the pressures caused by globalization on the culture of Country Y:

> Globalisation has created tremendously increasing pressures towards cultural homogenisation; the challenge therefore is to ensure that our distinctive spiritual, material, intellectual and emotional features, which characterise our society, are maintained. Country Y has an important role to play in ensuring that our Caribbean identity remains alive and to contribute to the overall development of the region. The island has produced artistes, folk groups, poets, and sports personalities of regional and international acclaim. (1999: 8)

As a result of globalization, the *Strategic Plan* argues that the overall role for education in the 'global environment' is to 'lift the poor out of their poverty by building up their educational assets'. In addition, the *Strategic Plan* adds:

> Educational development goes hand in hand with poverty alleviation, on condition however that educational policies focus on the needs and characteristics of the most deprived in society. (1999: 14)

The *Education Bill* (2000) seeks to 'promote the education of the people by establishing educational institutions which will foster the spiritual, cultural, moral, intellectual, physical, social and economic development of the community'.

Roman Catholics are in the majority in the island, being 53 per cent, Anglicans are 13.8 per cent and other Protestants, 33.2 per cent. Country Y fits Haynes' second category which he defines as 'generally religious states', which are 'guided by religious beliefs in general where the concept of civil religion is important but not tied to any specific religious tradition'.

The Culture of School C in Country Y

The school and its foundation

The school is owned and administered by a group of sisters whose religious foundation is worldwide, with its motherhouse in France. The sisters have missions in five other Caribbean islands. The sisters have their origins in the French Revolution, during which time the founder of the religious order believed she was called to 'teach the faith, defend the defenceless and bring the Word to peoples outside Europe'. She was one of the first women to establish missions in Africa. In the New World she was known as the Liberator of the Slaves, the Mother of the Colony in Mana, French Guiana. The sisters arrived in the English-speaking Caribbean from the French island of Martinique in 1836, where the first foundation was at Port of Spain, Trinidad. The sisters arrived in Country Y in 1875. There were two religious sisters in the school and six in the convent at the time of the present study. There were also 'associates' who 'embrace the paradigm' of the religious community for a year or so.

The school is of a solid appearance with the entrance based on a traditional courtyard. It is a large building on a hill sited alongside the Catholic cathedral. During the case study I attended a celebratory Eucharist in the cathedral, which was presided over by the bishop, who, at the formal act of 'the kiss of peace', greeted staff and students as colleagues and friends. Inside the school the walls are often tiled with green and blue tiles, which are very reminiscent of those of my own secondary school, which was run by sisters of Notre Dame and who originated from France. The school was founded 125 years ago, with a plaque outside the headteacher's office commemorating the event, alongside a large collection of silver cups and trophies, including examples of the school's success at the local festivals of art and sport. There are also modern and traditional religious artefacts displayed throughout the school.

The school is assisted financially by the state, that is, teachers are paid by the state and a small grant for maintenance is given. New teachers are interviewed by representatives of the Board of Governors. There are two religious sisters in the school compared with ten in 1980.

Beliefs held in the school

The mission statement of the school, which is set in stone at the main entrance of the school, is:

> To give the child a rounded education
> To promote faith in Almighty God
> Respect and love for all persons
> Self-esteem and service in a commitment
> To the total upliftment of the human situation.

The mission of the sisters is guided by 'the principle of community', according to the headteacher. In discussing what made the school special, the headteacher focused on what she called 'the natural role of the school', that is, the girls bring special things with them to the school, but the school sends good things back home. She referred to the morning's assembly where the reading had been the parable of the talents. For her the importance of this parable is the emphasis on 'stewardship of the self', which in turn was translated as 'the gifts I can share with my community'. The headteacher spoke of the 'continuous flow from one individual to the other'.

The head of RE also spoke of the school tradition of excellence based on mission as foremost in achieving the success for which the school was renowned. A contributory factor, she believed, was that 40 per cent of teachers at the school were practising Catholics. For her the mission statement committed the school to developing successful students with self-esteem, a sense of service and commitment.

According to the '*Guidelines for Teachers*' issued by the school, its philosophy is 'simple':

> It is based on the Christian philosophy of love and service. We use the word of the foundress of our congregation to summarize our gospel values:
>   Strive to do your best at all times. Strive to help others to do their best and know that all your achievements are for the greater good of the society in which you live. (School C 2000: 3)

A long-serving teacher at the school said that the majority of Catholic parents and students on the island would wish to attend the school. In terms of the students' beliefs, she pointed to the growth of Anglican students in the school, about 15 per cent, and an increase in those with evangelical beliefs and traditions. Such students tended to belong to communities whose mother church was in the United States. Among many pupils, she believed that there were residual beliefs relating to witchcraft. For her, the specialness of the school was its ability to create a community for all its members, where love and respect were uppermost.

In April 1996, the Model Education Bill for the Organisation of Eastern Caribbean States was submitted by a committee, headed by Dr Kenny Anthony of St Lucia. The bill was a project of the International Monetary Fund (IMF). The trends found in the Bill and discussed in a paper written by the headteacher of School C were in her words 'secular education for all, based on economics, statistics and population control'. Further, the Bill sought to exclude 'the denominational school category'; gave the right to the Minister of Education to appoint Boards of Management for 'private assisted schools'; and to establish the content, method and form of religious education. The headteacher wrote:

> We believe that these sections of the new draft Education Act present a serious obstacle to society in its practice of religious freedom. As such, we further believe that this Act . . . will endanger and threaten a person's constitutional rights. (Private papers by headteacher to author)

In particular, the headteacher saw education as a means of confronting the 'negativity' which was to be found in society in the Caribbean. To do this, it was important that students took responsibility for their values and action.

Values and attitudes

The school focused on 'holistic education'. The deputy head in charge of curriculum and discipline defined that as the 'development of each person in every area for the whole of life'. In turn, the headteacher defined her role as a 'champion/ advocate of children', called to 'build the Kingdom', through integrating a holistic philosophy into the organization of a school of 720 students. This the headteacher argued was to be achieved through 'the building of community' in which each person expresses love or care, thereby 'opening up the individual to growth and freedom'. She saw this of particular importance in an environment which was often hostile for the students and in which they encountered anger and abuse. The community of the school should provide them with an 'experience of love and growth'. She sought new 'leadership models' for the senior students whom she wished to be respected as older students and prefects. A 'buddy system' for students was to be initiated.

The head of religious education at the school, when speaking of the differences between the school and others on the island, spoke of the way that 'here the girls are involved with the influence of God in their lives'. To expand on this statement, she referred to a saying of the former principal of the school; namely, 'the act of doing good is a reward in itself'. The head of RE concluded that 'when the girls leave school, they will look to do good and to serve as the best they can be'. Feedback from employers of previous students to the head of RE was that the students were 'well trained', 'had good manners' and 'worked well in teams' as a result, she thought, of the school encouraging them to do projects in teams.

There is a 'Code of Education' contained in the *Education Act* and every teacher is asked to be acquainted with the 'Code of Conduct for Teachers' and to act accordingly. The *Guidelines for Teachers* at the school concludes with the following exhortation:

> We need to work with a friendly, loving and forgiving attitude. We need to work as a team. We need to strive for a distinguished professionalism in our teaching service. In this noble institution we value loyalty, initiative, creativity, simplicity and collaboration. (School C 2000: 8)

The headteacher was concerned that the school could not achieve such aims alone; rather, strong partnerships were needed with parents, past students, the Ministry of Education, benefactors and the local parishes. In relation to the role of parishes, the headteacher commented that the Caribbean lacked the vital links which were such a dominant feature of Catholic school in the United States. She reflected that the traditional administration of education and schools by religious communities had distanced the parish communities from the work of education.

Nonetheless, the Catholic church had a strong voice in Country Y, and she saw that it had a very particular mission, after September 11. That particular day of crisis had brought interfaith dialogue to the heart of everyday affairs in the Caribbean, when people of all faiths had come together to pray. For the headteacher it mattered that this coming together continued. In particular, she expressed concern that if the church was seen as a body which must always make a statement, it must not 'distance itself from the real problems of Country Y'. The example she used here was that of speaking out about children. Her concern was that if the church spoke out as an 'authority figure' it might distort its own understanding of children and increase its distance from them.

Behaviours

The school has classes of up to forty-nine pupils and is operated by a system of heads of department, deans, class teachers, assistant class teachers and subject teachers. The principal, vice-principal, heads of department, deans and other senior teachers serve on a management committee which helps formulate policy and direction for the school, thus 'the principal makes her decisions after consultation'.

There is a religious assembly every day to which 'teachers are invited'. On Monday mornings, however, when the assembly is more elaborate, 'all teachers are expected to attend'. Further, 'teachers despite their religious persuasion are expected to be reverent during prayers and to see that their charges are reverent during prayers'. Teachers are also expected to be attached to at least one extra-curricular activity. The head of RE spoke of the high level of teacher commitment in the school, giving as examples, telephones being answered at five in the afternoon and a low level of teacher turnover.

The school teaches the national curriculum leading to the Caribbean Examination Council examination and /or the General Certificate of Education and specializes in business skills as well as academic skills. There is also a firm emphasis on sport, with the school excelling in a number of areas and a heavy commitment to running sports activities and clubs outside school time. The Health and Family Education curriculum is taught in RE and the class meeting time. This differs from government schools where it is taught by non-specialist staff across the curriculum.

The head of languages described the students as being little interested in languages, although Spanish was compulsory in the first three years of secondary school. However, they had great respect for science and were very enthusiastic about sport.

The RE curriculum was based on 'doctrine, scripture and personal prayer'. In the department, there were three teachers and one counsellor. Each term the staff held two meeting to evaluate their teaching of the syllabus. School retreats, which lasted two days for sixth formers, were led by people of faith but not necessarily religious. A concern which the head of RE shared was that the RE curriculum and department were asked to integrate the religious and general mission of the school into their work but that this was not expected of the rest of the academic curriculum.

The staff actively seek partnership with other schools to develop a curriculum for 'health and family life classes'. They argued that much of the hostile environment which young adults faced had arisen because of the fragmentation of the family; in some instances, mothers had left Country Y for the UK and the USA to make money or fulfil their own potential. These 'gaps' in the family had left a vacuum about how to tackle problems. The school was therefore considering the teaching of parenting skills, which would be values oriented, in moral education classes. The headteacher also believed that concerns and issues around male underachievement in the Caribbean should be met by women taking initiatives, particularly in values formation and home making.

Country Z

Country Z is one of the largest countries in the world. Unlike the UK where it is possible to argue that religion has been privatized, Hefner (1998: 162) has contended that Islam has grown increasingly dominant in south-east Asian public life, although Muslim politics has remained 'decidedly pluricentric'. Jenkins (2002), however, puts forward the general thesis that the north, or western world, is seeing population stagnation and the decline of Christianity in the face of an overwhelming secularization. In the south, particularly, in Africa and Asia, Christianity is blooming where the population is set to rise. Jenkins, noting the missionary element within Islam, predicts likely clashes between supernaturalistic vibrant Christianity and militant conservative Islam. He suggests that where at present there is religious competition, by 2050 there may well be geopolitical power struggles or bloody wars. Although Jenkins suggests that Country Z is more likely to be quiescent, the question remains whether Christianity and Islam can coexist. Hefner, however, concludes his article on 'Secularisation and Citizenship' with a plea that conditions in society in general and in education specifically, must be organized effectively within the challenges of pluralism and multiculturalism to ensure that human beings can live cooperatively to good purpose:

> In an era when certain Western and Muslim leaders speak of an inevitable 'clash of civilzations', it is useful to remind ourselves of these shared challenges, and the fact that on all sides there are people of good will struggling to devise and defend a modern civility. (1998: 165)

Country Z's education system provides for the provision of private faith schools, both Islamic and Christian. The case study which follows sets out to examine the social reality of one such school. It is worth commenting at this stage that within three years of the case study in Country Z being completed, the government was pressing for Islam to be taught in Catholic schools. In October 1999, the Ministers of Education and Religious Affairs sent a joint letter to Catholic schools requesting that instruction in the Muslim faith be added to the school programme. The proposal was presumably motivated by the fact that 40 per cent of the pupils at Catholic schools are Muslim. The vicar-general of one of Country Z's dioceses in 2001 said to the Bishops Conference's Education Commission that in keeping with the teaching of the Second Vatican Council the local church seeks to enhance relations with, and understanding of, other religions. 'However', he said, 'if Islamic instruction is eventually taught in Catholic schools, the private schools must be guaranteed the right to appoint who teaches this religious instruction'. Further, he argued:

> What we object to is that such pressure against the Catholic schools has been politically motivated. The bishop's call to enhance religious harmony has also been twisted into demanding Islamic instruction in Catholic schools. (Catholic World News, 29 March 2000: CW News.com/Fides)

The first case study discussed here was undertaken in Country Z in 1997 in a Catholic senior high school in a city of well over three million people. It houses one of the leading national universities, as well as a Catholic university. During the case study, I attended Mass in a large suburb of the city. It was a Sunday afternoon and a large church built very much in colonial style was crowded with people. To set the place of Catholic students in the province in which the school is situated in context, figures available for the religious affiliation of school pupils in the province in academic year 2001/2 were as follows:

Muslim	116,492
Protestant	5,201
Catholic	9,948
Hindu	211
Buddhist	143
Total	131,995

The Culture of School D

The school and its foundation

The school buildings are built within the national tradition of educational institutions, that is, very solid buildings, gated from the road but opening onto a courtyard with classrooms within it over two or three levels, surrounded by a verandah. In the entrance hall and the headteacher's study, there is a picture of the president and a copy of the five-point plan adopted by the country. Within each classroom there are crucifixes or statues and a wall-mounted frame containing the five-point plan.

The school is private but works in consultation through its Board of Education with the Provincial Office of Education and the general secretary of secondary education. On Mondays, national days and days instructed by the government, the school conducts the national flag ceremony. Students wear uniforms and hats for this ceremony. It is fee-paying according to parental means, but teaches the national curriculum and the students are entered for the national senior secondary school leavers' examination.

The school was founded by a religious order of brothers whose community began in the 1920s with the sole purpose of providing education. At the time of the case study, the headteacher was a lay Catholic and there was only one brother actively employed in the school as head of spiritual affairs; the headteacher described him as 'an extension of the religious community in the school'. Teachers tend to work at the school for lengthy periods, so there is not a high staff turnover; staff receive salaries in line with government guidelines but there are also special incentives, particularly for long-serving teachers.

Beliefs held within the school

In relation to the nation and the national culture, the school *Handbook* stated that the school's graduates should:

1. Be skilled participants in development, who have a high dedication to the progress of the nation, the state and the church based on Christian spirit;
2. Have critical, creative, constructive and productive spirits and attitudes in the life of the nation-state, which has the principle of unity in diversity based on the five-point plan;
3. Have exploratory and innovative spirits which enable them to live independently, and to participate in the development of science and technology for the betterment of social welfare;
4. Have a healthy working ethos and high adaptation to new environments, that is, the higher levels of education, their working environment and society. (Summarised from School D 1996: 12)

In discussion with the headteacher, it was clear that in relation to the nation and the national culture, the school sought to develop students who would be conscious of their national identity and their particular faith identity within a society which strives for unity within diversity. The school itself is an example of the ways in which the government supports the concept of a plural society and looks to private schools (and universities) to provide levels of education which the state is not yet able to do. At the same time, the state system encourages the expression of differing religious commitments through, for example, its approach to religious education. In state schools, for example, the curriculum includes separate syllabuses for each of the recognized major faith traditions. These are taught by teachers from those faiths and the pupils receive instruction during school time; each faith syllabus is constructed to integrate the major themes and purposes of the new curriculum and thus permit genuine elements of coherence between religious and secular studies.

The school *Handbook* sets out the school's aims in relation to the Catholic Church as to:

1. make the Church present in the educational and cultural worlds in order to declare the Catholic faith and introduce transcendental purpose into human life, that is, to plant and develop a Christian mentality in society which is characterised by pluralistic cultures, materialism and pragmatism; and
2. produce a cadre of students needed to become the functionaries of an independent local church, who are well qualified, strong and able to fulfil the Church's need for a variety of service. (School D 1996: 11)

In relation to students' personal development, the *Handbook* states the school seeks:

1. To develop persons who are responsible and consistent, and therefore are able to choose freely values of life according to conscience and to develop clear attitudes in responding to life's problems;
2. To develop their potential optimally in terms of knowledge, skills, attitudes and values in life, so they will be ready to continue their studies in higher education and to live in society. (ibid: 10)

The aims of the school can be traced to a number of authoritative sources. In the first place the curriculum is seen to be 'classical', that is, academic, and grounded both in the national understanding of appropriate knowledge for educated senior high school students and in a 'Catholic' approach to curriculum discussed by, among others, Arthur and Bryk. For at least one parent, however, the curriculum and the examination system were said to impose a heavy burden on young people in the country for they made no distinction between students of differing abilities and interests. As in the rest of Country Z, students are taught in mixed-ability groups. The headteacher and the deputy head in charge of curriculum emphasized that the vision of the school sought to teach 'suitable and deeper knowledge' for 'better living', that is, 'not simply to relieve poverty and gain improved standards of living' but to incorporate it within 'religious, moral and ethical teaching', through which students gain 'solidarity with the poor'.

Values and Attitudes

All the teachers who were interviewed stressed their wish to develop the 'whole person'. For the headteacher, the ideal graduate from his school would 'have a balance between the cognitive and the emotional' and would achieve a first degree at least. For the deputy headteacher in charge of curriculum, 'morality is the priority for the curriculum'. As far as he was concerned 'for a student who has intellectual ability but not a good moral attitude, teaching has been worthless'. For the head of spiritual affairs, the mission of the school is to 'provide guidance for the young' and through its vision 'to provide brother-hood through community' and 'the option for the poor'. Most of all, 'students must be free to develop themselves' within a new kind of school organization, which he described as 'a Christ-lover for the young'.

For this vision to be achieved it was important that the school and its cur-riculum, particularly, in religious education, should 'meet the intellectual challenges of helping students know why they believe'. The head of spiritual affairs was of the opinion that some key aspects of this vision were yet to be realized in the school. He was not confident therefore that the final year students who took part in this case study would exhibit some of the charac-teristics and values for which he was working. This need for structural change within the school and curriculum would be partly accomplished by the one religious brother working with other staff 'as a useful teacher not a brother'. The principles which the head of spiritual affairs enunciated as the hoped for basis of his students lives were 'truth, justice, love and the power to encour-age and move forward', which can be said to be values emanating from the Christian gospels. He confirmed that they formed the basis for the two global and two general rules by which his community chose to live.

Behaviours

The headteacher and a newly arrived member of staff emphasized the use of an induction period lasting one semester during which the staff, led by the headteacher, involved new recruits in the principles and traditions of the school and conducted regular discussions with them. New teachers were also involved with senior teachers from outside the school through an organiza-tion of all Catholic schools in the region. Staff are also expected to attend an annual retreat of three days.

The headteacher spoke of the importance of the staff retreat and regular internal staff meetings as means of 'building partnership' and 'family'. At those meetings 'new ideas emerge' so that 'school does not become boring'. At the same time the headteacher repeated several times that each member of staff was unique and must be treated with individual respect. Staff work within the government's *Ethical Code for Teachers* (Government of Country Z 1996), which is based on the national five-point plan (security/safety, clean-liness, orderliness, beauty, familiarity), that is, 'an expression of patterns of relationship among the headmaster, teachers, clerical workers and students, which reflects feelings and attitudes of mutual assistance, openness, cooper-ation, tolerance and mutual respect in the school community' (Government of Country Z 1996: 13 my translated guide) and 'within the religious brothers' vision'.

Interviews with the headteacher, his deputy and other members of his staff identified certain individual organizational features of the school, includ-ing the 'morning meditation' in which students stay in their classrooms

accompanied by their class teacher and listen to gospel readings and medita-
tions on them, which are organized by all members of staff on a rota system,
over the school tannoy; the locking of the school gates when the morning bell
rings, thereby ensuring that students who arrive late must report to the school
counsellor; staff and students staying on the premises throughout the school
day; additional afternoon activities, including additional lessons in mathematics, language and ICT and sport.

Differences which the students encountered as a result of attending this
Catholic school, as opposed to a state school, were described as, for those
who were Catholic, attendance at the Eucharist at the beginning and end of
each semester; religious education classes held in common, unlike the state
system in which students are taught RE within their faith group; participation
in selecting readings for, and leading, 'morning congregations' and school
Eucharists; attendance at school retreats; students and parents receiving cop-
ies of the school rules, which were regularly revised, each school year; and,
every Tuesday students met with staff in a process of 'digging-out our faith',
during which time students were encouraged to express their own ideas,
opinions and uneasiness.

Included in the school rules for students are the following prohibitions:

Students are prohibited from keeping, hiding, owning and using knives,
narcotics, cigarettes, drugs, alcohol which can endanger personal safety
and all things which are contradictory and have no connection with teaching and learning activities in the school.

Students are prohibited from any destructive activity, which destroys the
norm of unity in the school environment. (School D 1996: 14)

In conclusion, the deputy headteacher spoke of the need of the school to
adapt, through its view of the curriculum and its values concerning the ideal
student, to the changing needs of Country Z's society. For society, he argued,
must modernize and the students must meet the needs of their country.

In discussion with the head of spiritual affairs, two future directions for the
school's organization and practice took priority. The first was to promote the
concept of structure-change, through which the school becomes 'an organisation for the young', 'a Christ-lover for the young'. As such an organization, its
vision would be to achieve 'brotherhood through community'. There would
be a complete acceptance of pupils as they are, and working through 'the
option for the poor' would develop in students the ability to grow and encourage their own creativity. He would wish to model the new organization on one
already working just north of the city, in which the guiding principles for the
young people's activity are 'solidarity', 'charity' and 'social action'. Thus the
ideal school graduate would become the second focus for change; namely,
that alongside the emphasis on the achievement of high academic standards,
there would be an impetus to develop students who were 'social changers'. By
giving the young students increasing responsibility, self-reliance and control

they would mature into creative adults capable of implementing social action and renewal. In terms of their faith, he would expect the students not only to have a 'feeling' for their faith but also a mature intellectual understanding.

Looking Forward to the Next Part of the Presentation of the Data

The above completes the presentation of the first part of the data collected within the present study. Analysis of the data presented from the four schools will take place when the second part of that data, which has been collected under the heading of 'The student voice', has been explored in the following chapter. This first part of the presentation has attempted to let the voices of senior managers, parents, pastoral and subject staff explain the relationship between the foundational principles of their schools and the practices which constitute the students' experience of their school communities. The documentary evidence has proved a most helpful contextual device in both the understanding the history of the foundational tradition in each school and the use of written communication in sustaining the values and practices of each culture. Only when the student voice has been heard will the full profiles of each school have been completed.

The present chapter has thus set out the first part of the data collected at four Catholic schools in three countries. The data has been presented within a framework constructed to accommodate Lawton's hierarchical plotting of the constituent parts of school cultures. Placing the highest value on the beliefs at the heart of a school culture as a means of excavating the many layers which uphold its particular understandings of the purpose of education has produced clear benefits. The first is that it presents in bold relief the kinds of educated students each school is aiming to develop. The second is that it underlines the dependence of the distinctiveness of each culture on the articulation of that culture by the headteacher, as well as its communication through the senior teachers and the approved behaviours within the whole school. The third is that in these particular schools, the religious education department stands out as being critical to the involvement of the students in the particular culture. The next chapter will complete the second half of the profile of each school through a presentation of the student voice.

Chapter 8

The Student Voice and Its Significance in the Study of School Cultures

Purpose of the Chapter

In this chapter the data collected by means of the student questionnaire (please see Appendix) will be presented under the general title of 'the student voice'. The purpose of the presentation is first to offer further data beyond that already found in Chapter 6 about the culture of each school. In the first part of the chapter, a profile of the students' beliefs, attitudes and values is established. It is hoped that the profiles will provide insight into the faith view or attitude to the world which characterizes students educated in the four Catholic schools. In the second part, the student voice records the individual student experience in each of the four school cultures. The third part will consider what can be learned specifically through the use of a student self-review or questionnaire within the present methodology for the study of school cultures.

A General Introduction to the Students Taking Part in the Survey

The students in the survey are from four schools in three countries. It is important, therefore, that we hear their voices from within the individual educational, religious and social contexts they inhabit. Nonetheless, when creating composite tables of the data from each school, it became clear that they shared some clear and common aspirations for their education in Catholic schools, as well as indicating, through the questionnaire, much common agreement with statements concerning their personal goals, values and beliefs. Apart from one school, which was private and catered mainly for Catholic students from Catholic families, but received state support and funding, the other schools were all part of the state education systems of their countries and admitted students based on their examination results and not their faith group. The emphases which become apparent across this diverse group of students, in terms of educational aspirations and perceived future identities, are, therefore, noteworthy and their commonalities are not a little unexpected.

In order to measure the students' expectations of their faith schools, they were asked to indicate the degree of importance attached to certain aims of

Catholic secondary schools. The students' responses to the statements found in questions 24–34 inclusive are presented in Table 8.1, showing their scores. Flynn (1993: 160–1) writes that expectations are 'not simply hopes or fantasies'. Instead, he argues convincingly that they are 'expressive symbols which represent deep yearnings of the human heart' and refers to Darmody (1990: 2) who draws attention to the importance of aspirations because:

> The way any group will respond to the world in which they live will be, in large measure, determined by their perceptions and expectations of the world.

The overall score in the right-hand column indicates that the following aspirations for Catholic schools found most positive agreement among this group of students:

1. Helping students discover and fulfil themselves as persons.
2. Fostering an environment in which students' faith in God can develop.
3. Supporting high standards of performance in school work.
4. Preparing students for their future careers.

All but one of the aspirations presented to the students resulted in an overall score indicating general positive agreement among them in their hopes for the nature and practices of their Catholic schools. The strong emphasis found on looking to the school to help in their personal discovery of themselves as 'persons' is most interesting to note and will lead in the final chapter to an overall examination of each school culture's commitment to, and performance in, the development of human flourishing within the lives of their students. At this point, it is worthwhile noting that Flynn's sample (1993: 164) placed no religious or social concerns amongst their highest expectations. In Mtumbuka's sample (2003: 175), on the other hand, the third highest aspiration was to have the school foster an environment in which faith in God can develop. The Malawian sample discussed by Mtumbuka (2003: 175), however, ranked the 'discovery and fulfilment of themselves as persons' seventh, with a mean of 3.7.

Equally, the lesser emphasis placed by the students, except in one school, on the role of the Catholic school in integrating religious education with other subjects where possible will be further explored later, in the light of the place of religious education within the curriculum of each school and in the attitudes of the students to it. It is helpful to note at this stage, however, that Flynn's sample (1993: 165) of students from Catholic schools in Australia also ranked the integration of religious education with other subjects lowest in their expectations. Discussion will therefore also take place later about the differing perceptions of the place of religion and religious education in the culture of each school among staff, managers and students against the background of the students' strong agreement, exhibited in the Table 8.1, with

Table 8.1 Students' expectations of Catholic schools

Expectations	Gender		Religion				School				Overall Score
	Male Score	Female Score	Catholic Score	Other Christian faith Score	Non-Christian religion Score	No religion Score	A Score	B Score	C Score	D Score	
Help students to discover and fulfil themselves as persons	4.41	4.32	4.56	4.20	4.13	4.43	4.48	4.26	4.27	4.53	4.35
Provide an environment in which students' faith in God can develop	4.23	4.42	4.42	4.35	4.00	3.86	4.35	4.09	4.61	4.43	4.34
Assist students to achieve a high standard of performance in their school work	4.22	4.37	4.23	4.40	4.00	4.14	4.29	4.41	4.71	3.65	4.31
Prepare students for their future careers	4.28	4.27	4.34	4.21	4.63	4.00	4.06	4.32	4.53	4.05	4.27
Provide an atmosphere of Christian community where people are concerned for one another	4.07	4.29	4.24	4.20	3.75	4.29	4.32	4.11	4.41	4.00	4.20
Provide students with advice on careers and further education	4.08	4.24	4.14	4.22	3.50	4.71	4.58	4.09	4.24	3.93	4.18
Prepare students for higher education (university etc)	4.01	4.21	4.22	4.06	4.00	4.29	4.16	3.98	4.39	4.05	4.13
Prepare students to become good citizens	4.03	4.09	4.11	4.05	3.38	4.57	4.06	4.08	4.16	3.92	4.06
Help students understand the society in which they live	3.84	4.15	4.08	4.00	3.88	4.00	3.94	4.09	4.12	3.88	4.03
Give all students a chance of success in some aspect of school life	4.00	4.04	4.14	4.03	3.00	3.86	4.03	3.80	4.29	4.08	4.03
Integrate religious education with other subjects where possible	3.08	3.73	3.29	3.66	3.63	3.00	3.73	3.39	4.06	2.70	3.48
Overall Score	4.02	4.19	4.16	4.13	3.81	4.10	4.18	4.06	4.34	3.93	4.13

the statement, 'the Catholic school should provide an environment in which students' faith in God can develop'.

The students' voice about the role of the school in fostering their faith in God emerges in the first table as strong and clear on this point. Perhaps it is useful to contextualize this strength of opinion among students in the global South. In Chapter 6 it was noted that each of the four schools in the study are in countries which Haynes (1998: 10–11) assigns to his second category of relationships between religion and the state. That category he defines as 'generally religious states', which are 'guided by religious beliefs in general where the concept of civil religion is important but not tied to any specific religious tradition'. It is equally interesting to speculate on students' overall satisfaction with their school in this particular respect against information contained in Table 8.2.

The overall scores recorded at the bottom of each column draw attention to some important differences in the responses to these statements between boys and girls and Catholics and other Christians. In the first place, it appears that the girls have been more exuberant in their positive assent to all the statements, except, interestingly, the first, 'Helping students to discover themselves as persons'. Second, Catholic students' scores are markedly different in all cases, except two, by at least 0.05 from the overall scores in the right-hand column. This trend is also found in the disparity between the scores resulting from the Catholic school D and the overall scores in the right-hand column.

Table 8.2 is devised from a cross-tabulation of students' responses from all four schools by gender and religious affiliation to questions 141–149, inclusive. The rubric at the head of this section of the questionnaire reads, 'the following questions refer to various influences on your religious development over the years'. It is worthwhile speculating whether the levels of responses to each possible source of influence on their religious development 'over the years' led the students to look to their senior secondary school to provide a firmer level of influence than Table 8.2 suggests that their past and present schooling has permitted.

The headline information contained in this table is clear and mirrors the findings of Flynn (1993: 290) and Mtumbuka (2003: 196). On the one hand, across boys and girls, those of a Christian affiliation and those with no religious affiliation, the examples and lives of their parents has been the strongest influence on their religious development. As a result, the section on 'beliefs' within the presentation of the data about each school below will contain background information about the religious affiliation or otherwise of the parents of the students who took part in this survey. It is not surprising to discover, however, that the students in the Catholic school rated more positively than the others the effect of school liturgies, retreats and their teachers on their religious development. It will be worthwhile, therefore, speculating about the effect of a Catholic school on the religious development of students who are on the whole Catholic and the effect of a Catholic school on students' religious development whose affiliation is primarily non-Catholic and sometimes

Table 8.2 Influences on students' religious development

Influences	Gender		Religion				School				Overall Score
	Male Score	Female Score	Catholic Score	Other Christian faith Score	Non-Christian religion Score	No religion Score	A Score	B Score	C Score	D Score	
The example and lives of your parents	4.32	4.09	4.13	4.19	4.25	4.57	4.24	4.25	3.88	4.40	4.18
The religious education provided by your school	3.67	3.58	3.81	3.51	3.25	3.29	3.66	3.78	3.31	3.70	3.62
School liturgies (Masses, prayer sessions, etc)	3.57	3.50	3.92	3.26	2.75	3.71	3.21	3.67	3.26	3.83	3.53
The influence of your Catholic school	3.49	3.53	3.85	3.32	3.25	2.71	3.17	3.52	3.52	3.75	3.51
The effect of a school retreat, Christian living camp, or similar	3.07	3.38	3.63	3.01	2.50	3.33	2.89	2.98	3.46	3.70	3.26
The influence of a youth group	3.00	3.21	3.04	3.27	2.75	2.50	3.32	2.90	3.32	3.10	3.12
The example and lives of your teachers	3.30	2.98	3.13	3.09	3.00	3.29	2.97	3.17	2.77	3.53	3.11
The influence of your friends and peers	2.97	2.89	3.05	2.91	2.25	2.43	2.66	2.67	3.00	3.43	2.92
The influence of your parish	3.07	2.78	3.12	2.72	2.43	3.17	2.92	3.07	2.29	3.35	2.90
Overall Score	3.38	3.33	3.52	3.25	2.94	3.22	3.23	3.33	3.20	3.64	3.35

non-religious as the analysis proceeds. There was a consistency of response across the schools to the level of influence of religious education on personal religious development.

The students were also asked to state the level of importance they placed on certain personal goals and aspirations. Table 8.3 contains information which makes very clear the personal goals of this particular group of students in the global South.

One headline contained in Table 8.3 is the comparatively low level of importance the students ascribe to material wealth. The overall score in the table giving guidance as to the level of importance ascribed to 'making a lot of money' shows that this goal receives the least support. Similarly, in Flynn's sample (1993: 102) and Mtumbuka's (2003: 201) 'making money' ranks lowest in importance. The four goals which receive the strongest overall rating of importance in Table 8.3 are:

- Finding God and growing in faith in Him;
- Accepting of self and person;
- Being honest;
- Living up to the example and teachings of Christ.

In Table 8.1 the students' voice registered a plea that their schools would foster an environment in which their faith in God might grow as their second most important aspiration for a Catholic school. In Table 8.3 where the students are asked to focus on their personal development, the student voice again rates the significance of developing as a person highly, but this time places it second in their 'wish-list'. Thus they hope and expect their school educationally to provide for their development as a person, as in Table 8.1. For themselves, as in Table 8.3, they seek to find God and 'grow in faith in Him'. The students' voice does not falter here. It is the school's role to develop them as people; as individuals, their hope is to find God and grow in faith. They do not see a contradiction. Caution is necessary here, though. This looks like a positive result but it may be an example of the well-known phenomenon of giving the interviewer what you think she wants to hear. On the other hand, Mtumbuka also notes the marked religiosity of the students, unlike those found in Flynn's Australian sample.

The data relating to the students' actual experience of the school and how they considered some of the issues which arose from that experience, such as satisfaction, disenchantment, worry and/or depression are provided within the data presentation framework developed for each school. The questionnaire, however, contained thirty-two statements relating to perceptions of values and beliefs and the students were asked to 'consider each carefully and indicate the degree' to which they responded to the statements. This section of the general introduction to the students from the global South is offered as a further means of examining the marked commonalities found in the values and beliefs of the students from the four schools, as well as an opportunity

Table 8.3 Personal goals

Goals	Gender		Religion				School				Overall Score
	Male Score	Female Score	Catholic Score	Other Christian faith Score	Non-Christian religion Score	No religion Score	A Score	B Score	C Score	D Score	
To find God in my life and grow in faith in Him	4.58	4.68	4.67	4.64	4.25	4.67	4.66	4.55	4.71	4.68	4.64
To accept myself as the person I am	4.31	4.65	4.57	4.55	3.63	4.67	4.59	4.30	4.78	4.50	4.52
To be honest in my dealings with others	4.37	4.54	4.38	4.57	4.25	4.50	4.52	4.60	4.49	4.22	4.47
To live up to the example and teachings of Christ	4.37	4.47	4.55	4.42	3.63	4.00	4.31	4.35	4.43	4.63	4.43
To be happily married and have a happy family life	4.30	4.32	4.16	4.44	3.88	4.83	4.41	4.15	4.35	4.45	4.31
To find personal happiness and satisfaction in life	4.10	4.17	4.12	4.17	3.88	4.50	4.52	3.89	4.53	3.80	4.15
To be important and successful in life	3.99	4.21	3.99	4.21	3.88	4.83	4.55	4.06	4.39	3.58	4.12
To serve other people	4.17	4.04	4.01	4.16	4.00	4.17	4.07	4.66	3.57	3.85	4.09
To make lifelong friendships with other people	3.94	3.99	3.84	4.09	3.50	4.50	4.07	4.26	3.86	3.60	3.97
To make a lot of money	3.08	3.07	3.07	3.10	3.25	2.67	3.03	2.68	3.57	3.13	3.08
Overall Score	4.121	4.214	4.136	4.235	3.815	4.334	4.273	4.15	4.268	4.044	4.47

to present the findings from the present study within the contexts developed by Flynn and Mtumbuka's research. The section of the questionnaire containing the thirty-two statements was headed, 'Values, beliefs and faith'. The responses which were received permits a profile to emerge of the students' views in seven value areas; namely, religious beliefs and practices, the nature and practice of the Christian/Catholic church, social and political concerns, personal development and well-being, sexual morality, the use of drugs and right and wrong.

In relation to the students' faith, Table 8.4 continues the story begun in Table 8.2, that of the student's almost unanimous belief in God, including those who belong to no religion. At the same time, these students perceive God as 'a loving father'.

Equally strongly, the students believe that their faith impacts positively on the kind of person they are. Mtumbuka (2003: 194) similarly comments that one of the most important findings of his study was that almost all the students said that they believed in God and that faith helped them to be better persons. In Flynn's sample (1993: 306) a high proportion of students, 81 per cent, say they believe in God, showing a mean of 4.37, whereas the mean relating to the impact of religious faith on their ability to be better persons is reduced to 3.53. In Table 8.4, there is also evidence that the students in this survey believe the Church to be important to them. Given their various denominational and non-religious backgrounds, this response probably indicates a personalized understanding of 'church' and not the Catholic church. With such a strong view of the church's significance in their personal lives, it will be important to enquire whether the students are able to make a formal study of religious institutions other than Catholic, in their own and others' societies.

Most importantly Table 8.4 strongly indicates that the majority of students were holding beliefs 'because of my own convictions rather than the beliefs of others'. The overall scores recorded in the table are each higher than the 3.66 achieved by Flynn's sample (1993:349) in response to the same statement. Among the students, there were a slightly higher number of Catholic students and non-religious students who hold this view, although the figures for other Christian students were very close behind. It is those who believe in a non-Christian religion who figure less positively. Perhaps, it is not surprising that it is in the school where the majority of students were Catholic that the percentage of those agreeing most strongly with this view are found. The table, therefore, provides evidence that attendance at a faith school does not necessarily induce a belief in its students that they are being indoctrinated into any one position, and that their own views and beliefs are not welcome. Perhaps, the most striking example of this is found in the Catholic school, in which all the students believe in God, and like their fellow students with varying religious backgrounds across all four schools, agree strongly in the place of prayer in daily life, yet show a very wide spread of responses to the statement, 'I accept the church's teaching on birth control'. Second, such

Table 8.4 Values, beliefs and faith

Values	Gender		Religion				School				Overall Score
	Male Score	Female Score	Catholic Score	Other Christian faith Score	Non-Christian religion Score	No religion Score	A Score	B Score	C Score	D Score	
People should be respected whatever their race, nationality or religion	4.81	4.94	4.96	4.85	4.75	4.86	4.86	4.75	5.00	5.00	4.89
I believe in God	4.75	4.83	4.88	4.77	4.25	5.00	4.86	4.57	4.90	5.00	4.80
God is a loving Father	4.72	4.84	4.89	4.74	4.38	4.86	4.86	4.53	4.92	5.00	4.79
I believe that God always forgives me	4.62	4.77	4.83	4.63	4.25	5.00	4.90	4.45	4.78	4.90	4.71
People today should respect the environment	4.58	4.64	4.78	4.57	4.63	3.57	4.45	4.54	4.73	4.72	4.62
My faith helps me be a better person	4.55	4.59	4.59	4.54	4.38	5.00	4.86	4.42	4.43	4.78	4.57
It is important for me to spend some time in prayer each day	4.28	4.57	4.57	4.38	4.00	4.67	4.48	4.27	4.56	4.60	4.45
Jesus Christ is truly God	4.15	4.60	4.70	4.33	2.63	4.57	4.48	3.84	4.67	4.97	4.42
I know that Jesus is very close to me	4.31	4.47	4.53	4.45	2.63	4.50	4.41	4.19	4.54	4.58	4.40
The trust and love of my parents influence my approach to life	4.50	4.32	4.42	4.33	4.63	4.71	4.41	4.27	4.31	4.68	4.39
The Church is very important to me	4.35	4.41	4.39	4.46	3.50	4.43	4.48	4.28	4.33	4.58	4.39

I try to be friendly and helpful to others who are rejected or lonely	4.24	4.39	4.22	4.40	4.50	4.43	4.48	4.47	4.39	3.93	4.33
Abortion is a worse evil than the birth of an unwanted child	4.43	4.26	4.38	4.26	4.38	4.57	4.17	4.47	4.06	4.55	4.33
I am coming to believe because of my own convictions rather than the beliefs of others	4.19	4.24	4.29	4.19	3.88	4.29	4.17	4.14	4.15	4.47	4.22
The Gospel of Jesus influences the way I lead my life	4.21	4.21	4.16	4.32	3.43	4.00	4.17	4.10	4.29	4.30	4.21
Euthanasia, or the mercy killing of the sick or dying, is morally wrong	4.03	4.00	3.67	4.27	4.38	4.00	4.28	4.15	4.00	3.63	4.01
Jesus Christ is truly present in the Eucharist	4.04	3.96	4.62	3.55	2.86	4.14	3.88	3.78	3.68	4.78	3.99
I have developed my own way of relating to God apart from the Church	3.60	4.02	4.08	3.71	3.13	4.00	3.79	3.56	4.27	3.85	3.85
I accept the Church's teaching on birth control	3.82	3.79	4.01	3.57	4.13	4.14	3.86	3.95	3.47	3.95	3.80
I experience times of questioning when I am uncertain and confused about my faith	3.51	3.86	4.00	3.53	2.38	4.57	3.93	3.35	3.94	3.88	3.72
I would go to Mass on Sundays even if I were free to stay away	3.57	3.72	4.3	3.32	1.86	2.71	3.50	3.40	3.38	4.50	3.66
I am disturbed at times by my lack of faith	3.27	3.74	3.86	3.37	2.13	4.14	3.14	3.19	4.06	3.80	3.55
The Church needs women priests	3.08	3.23	3.09	3.19	3.00	4.00	3.14	3.35	3.28	2.78	3.17

Continued

Table 8.4 Continued

Values	Gender		Religion				School				Overall Score
	Male Score	Female Score	Catholic Score	Other Christian faith Score	Non-Christian religion Score	No religion Score	A Score	B Score	C Score	D Score	
I try to follow the Catholic way of life without questioning it	3.00	2.55	3.25	2.39	2.00	2.29	2.34	2.56	2.60	3.46	2.73
It is all right for people who are not married to live together	2.35	2.64	2.47	2.51	3.25	2.43	2.38	2.63	3.12	1.73	2.52
I have rejected aspects of the teaching of the Church in which I once believed	2.00	2.14	1.88	2.23	2.00	2.57	2.46	2.21	2.35	1.30	2.08
I think that church services are boring	1.86	2.22	2.20	2.01	1.88	1.86	1.90	1.71	2.92	1.78	2.08
Trying out drugs is all right, as long as you don't go too far	1.89	1.55	1.62	1.77	1.50	1.57	1.41	1.97	1.53	1.63	1.69
The homeless and disadvantaged people in society don't concern me at all	1.55	1.64	1.46	1.75	1.25	1.71	1.48	1.65	1.67	1.55	1.61
It is all right to take a small item from a large department store if everyone else does it	1.61	1.60	1.46	1.69	1.50	2.14	1.86	1.95	1.29	1.27	1.60
I think that saying prayers does no good	1.35	1.26	1.26	1.30	1.63	1.14	1.38	1.42	1.18	1.18	1.30
Jesus does not mean anything to me	1.20	1.14	1.12	1.21	1.25	1.00	1.07	1.31	1.12	1.05	1.16
Overall Score	3.51	3.60	3.65	3.52	3.14	3.65	3.56	3.48	3.62	3.63	3.56

strong evidence from this data and that of Flynn regarding the fostering of individual values and beliefs among young adults prompts an examination of the whole school culture as to how each school promotes such personal development among its students.

Certain defining characteristics of this group of students emerge from the data in Table 8.4. For example, the table presents a picture of these school leavers as strongly committed to reaching out to others who are 'lonely or rejected'. The responses in this value area, however, indicate that the strength of agreement with this statement is at its lowest in the school with a majority of Catholic students. Yet by looking simultaneously at the response to the statement 'the homeless and disadvantaged people in society do not concern me at all', by the students in that same school, we see those students show almost the strongest disagreement to it. By so doing, a clear picture emerges the statement provokes almost total disagreement from the students in all four schools. The response to the statement concerning respect for others whatever their race, nationality or religion was overwhelmingly positive. Respect for others among this group of school leavers in the global South is clearly an important characteristic, as it was among Flynn's sample. An equally defining characteristic is their concern for the environment.

Attitudes towards right and wrong are highlighted in the students' responses to two statements: 'it is alright to take a small item from a large department store if everyone else does it' and 'trying out drugs is alright so long as you don't go too far'. There are two interesting patterns to note in the responses to the first statement. Girls and boys were equally in disagreement with the statement. In the two schools situated in the same country the scores were almost the same. In the two schools in countries widely differing in culture and religious composition, the strength of disagreement was virtually the same between the two schools. The response to the statement concerning the taking of drugs marks out two small differences. First the girls are marginally more disapproving than the boys. There is also a slight difference in response between students in schools A and B in the same country. The response of the students in Mtumbuka's (2003: 192) study to the appropriateness of taking drugs shows a similar unwillingness on the part of the students there to agree with the statement, 'trying out drugs is alright', giving rise to a mean of 2.1.

In respect of their responses concerning moral values and attitudes to cohabiting, abortion and euthanasia, which affect the lives of others as well as themselves, the students showed some interesting differences among themselves. In response to the statement, 'it is alright for people who are not married to live together', the girls were a little more in agreement than the boys. Overall, one country, in which it is noted that patterns of family life had often changed as a result of migration to the United States or the UK and other contributory factors such as the absence of mothers from families for long periods of time, there was a more positive trend in the responses. The statement that 'abortion is a worse evil than the birth of an unwanted child' elicited a very positive response across all the schools. It is perhaps worthwhile to note that the boys were slightly more positive than the girls. Mtumbuka's (2003: 192) mean of 4.5 to response to the statement, 'abortion is always wrong' indicates a similar level of positive response between both samples. The statement that euthanasia is morally wrong drew a slightly less overall positive response across the schools than the statement concerning abortion. Whether the difference in response can be attributed to the issue of abortion being closer to the experience of the majority of the students, or whether the attitudes to euthanasia reflected differing cultural views of death and sickness was not probed with this group. The data do show, however, that there were no substantial differences between boys and girls in their responses and that the Catholic students were less positive in their agreement than non-Catholic Christians.

Flynn (1993: 312–13) suggests that his data show 'a marked decline in the moral values of students' over the last two decades when judged in the light of the Catholic church's moral teaching. For him this involves:

1. A greater acceptance of abortion by students.
2. A greater willingness to accept that it is all right for people who are not married to live together.
3. An increasing tendency to view euthanasia as morally permissible.

Using Flynn's Australian sample as a benchmark for Western attitudes to certain moral issues among young people, it is clear that the sample of students from the global South in the present study are rather more conservative than those of Flynn but they display some similar characteristics. Used another way, it is clear that the young people in the present sample, who are of varying religious affiliations and none, despite their attendance at a Catholic school and exposure to Catholic teachers, have chosen to make up their own minds on personal, social and moral issues on which the Catholic church has very firm teaching. The question which must be probed in relation to each school culture is, 'to what extent the school explicitly seeks to develop autonomy and personal maturity in areas of personal, social, and ethical matters?'

Table 8.4, however, also offers a corrective to the view that it is simply to the school culture that the attitudes, values and beliefs of the students can be attributed. The response to the statement, 'the trust and love of my parents influence my approach to life' receives a very positive level of response within the four schools and from boys as well as girls. Thus the students perceive that their personal, social and moral values are influenced a good deal by those of their parents. At the same time, the role of the school, in partnership with parents and others, in this crucial formative personal and social development must be probed and good practice supported. As Rutter et al. (1979) pointed out, the young person spends considerable time in school and therefore away from parental and home influence. What should be the role of the school? This is a particularly worthwhile question to ask of the four schools which took part in this study since the headteachers and teachers in each of them spoke of a number of reasons why the students were often separated from their parents for long periods. For example, in the schools in Country X, the students were often from rural areas and they boarded at the school or with relatives or others in the towns where the schools were situated. In the Caribbean school, much emphasis was placed on the breakdown of traditional family life through migration and, as in the African schools, the students often lived some way from the capital city in which the school was situated.

Certain key attributes have emerged among the students with whom this general introduction has been concerned. In brief these are:

- belief in God, on the whole, and the belief that their faith impacts on their development as persons;
- beliefs held through personal conviction not the say of others;
- respect for others, whatever their religion, race or nationality and respect for the environment;
- awareness of parental influence in matters both of belief and of personal, social and moral values.

Some common aspirations for the future have also emerged:

- finding God and growing in faith in Him;
- being accepting of self;
- being honest;
- living up to the example and teachings of Christ.

When recording the life-goals and values of the Australian students, Flynn (1993: 101) describes values as 'deeply-held beliefs which persist over time and have a strong motivation towards action'. In other words, it will be such values which underpin the students' reflections on their schools, while responding to the questionnaire. This is important since some of the students' responses recorded through the questionnaire on matters such as their school, its curriculum, teachers and peers should offer an insight into the unique place of values within the culture of an individual school. On the one hand, the values of the students can be seen as a means of testing the extent to which the culture of the school, in Meissner's (1970: 124) words, 'touches and involves the individuals'. On the other, they in turn provide a test of the ability of a school culture to be shaped by the values of the student.

In the students' expectations about the schools in which they study, there have been four common emphases. Namely:

- helping students discover and fulfil themselves as persons;
- fostering an environment in which students' faith in God can develop;
- supporting high standards of performance in school work;
- preparing students for their future careers.

It is important that the data are able to record the students' response as the cultural matrix of the school touches and involves them within the loci of their personal, spiritual, moral and educated selves. The above list simply summarizes the four expectations which received the highest scores in the students' response to that particular section in the questionnaire. On almost all aspects of that section within the questionnaire the students were positive, including their hopes that the school would prepare them to be good citizens, help them to understand the society in which they lived and give all of them a chance of success in some aspect of school life. In this way, the students showed themselves very willing, active and thoughtful members of their school cultures.

The Student Experience in Four School Cultures

The following four sections, therefore, will seek to trace the students' experiences of those individual school cultures and indicate the extent to which those cultures met the students' expectations, concerns and profiles. The data will also be interrogated in order to ascertain the extent to which each school created and sustained social cohesion among sometimes diverse religious and ethnic communities of teachers and students.

The student voice telling of individual and group experiences of each of the four school cultures will be composed partly from the students' responses to both the open and the closed questions within the questionnaire and partly from records of individual and group interviews. Responses to the closed questions have provided data which indicate clear patterns in the students' experience of the beliefs, values and behaviours which create the defining structure and spirit of the individual school culture. The voice which emerges from response to the open questions which concerned the students' appreciation and valuing of their school, any changes which they would wish to make to it and their descriptions of the unique spirit which exists at the school is at times frequently confirmatory of the patterns from the closed questions. Thus within the information provided by the students' voice there also exist the small voices found at the farthest end of the five-point scale away from the majority of their peers telling a particular and individual story about living within a specific school culture.

A goodly number of students wrote individually but using some common language about the unique spirit of the religious/ family community of the school, the self-discipline promoted there, the good relations found between Catholics and non-Catholics, teachers and students, religious education and other curriculum subjects, as well as the sheer happiness of being at a particular school. One questionnaire recorded, however, that 'mission schools should be abolished' and another that 'school didn't understand the importance of drugs to youth' and another that there was a suspicion that Catholic students were treated better than non-Catholics. Equally, interviews held with individual students tended to lead to confirmation of aspects of the school's individual culture and the students' responses to them. Those held, however, with groups of five or six students generated a conversation among the group which in their character and breadth of topic yielded mature observations and reflections not only on the school but also on their perception of their lives within a whole range of diverse cultural experiences of which their school was one. The experience of such group interviews, which are recorded within the section on the Caribbean school, leads to the conclusion that this form of conversation with groups of students is rather more useful than individual interviews, within this specific framework of a study of school cultures.

School A

The sample of school leavers who responded to the questionnaire numbered thirty-one, of whom fifteen were boys and sixteen girls. The sample relating to the open-ended questions comprised (i) one Catholic male; (ii) four male and five female non-Catholic Christians; and (iii) one female of no religion.

Beliefs

In School A the students rated equally as most important in their values and beliefs that:

- People should be respected whatever their race, nationality or religion;
- I believe in God;
- God is a loving father;
- My faith helps me to be a better person.

Table 8.5 Students' religious beliefs: School A

Catholic (%)	Other Christian faith (%)	Non-Christian religion (%)	No religion (%)
25.8	61.3	–	12.9

Table 8.6 Parents' religious beliefs: School A

	Practising Catholic (%)	Non-practising Catholic (%)	Other Christian faith (%)	Non-Christian religion (%)	No religion (%)
Mother's religion	29.0	–	71.0	–	–
Father's religion?	13.8	3.4	55.2	6.9	20.7

School life and climate

The students' considered their four highest expectations of the school to be that it should:

1. Provide students with advice on careers and further education.
2. Help students to discover and fulfil themselves as persons.
3. Provide an environment in which students' faith in God can develop.
4. Provide an atmosphere of Christian community where people are concerned for one another.

There were 76.7 per cent who reported being happy at the school, with a further 13.3 per cent believing this was probably true.

Other positive findings within the table include:

- a very strong conviction that the headteacher encourages a sense of community and belonging to the school and a slightly lesser sense that he places importance on the religious nature of the school;
- a strong sense of the school's reputation in the local community;
- a very firm view that the school rules encourage self-discipline and responsibility and that adequate counselling help is available;
- a slightly less strong, though positive view, that the things that are taught are worthwhile learning, and that if students have difficulty with their school work then most teachers take time to help them. Equally positively, the students are proud to be students of the school.

A much wider spread of response is seen in relation to statements regarding relationships within the school, such as 'other students accept me as I am' and 'a good spirit of community exists among final year students'. There is, however, a more positive response to the statement 'there is a happy atmosphere here' and 'most other students are very friendly'.

On the whole, students do not believe that they are depressed at the school, although about a fifth believe they probably are. A similar response is found in relation to 'feeling worried'. Whether some of the underlying personal stresses examined above are caused partly through poor interpersonal relations between students or whether partly through the senior students ambivalence towards the religious goals of the school is not clear from the table. It is noteworthy, however, that a high proportion of the students claim not to understand or to accept the religious goals of the school. Perhaps the response to the two statements concerning their future use of Catholic schools hints at the students' own ambivalence. More positively agreed that they would send their children to a Catholic school than agreed that 'if they had to do it all over again they would attend a Catholic school', see below table 8.7.

Table 8.7 School life and climate: School A

	Certainly FALSE (%)	Probably FALSE (%)	Uncertain (%)	Probably TRUE (%)	Certainly TRUE (%)	Score
Q65 The Principal encourages a sense of community and belonging to the school	–	–	–	33.3	66.7	4.67
Q42 This school has a good name in the local community	3.2	3.2	–	25.8	67.7	4.52
Q71 School rules here encourage self-discipline and responsibility	6.7		6.7	20.0	66.7	4.40
Q48 Adequate counselling help is available to students	3.2	9.7	3.2	16.1	67.7	4.35
Q53 The things I am taught are worthwhile learning	3.2	9.7	3.2	32.3	51.6	4.19
Q63 I feel proud to be a student of this school	13.8	3.4	–	20.7	62.1	4.14
Q58 The Principal places importance on the religious nature of the school	–	3.2	19.4	38.7	38.7	4.13
Q35 The relationships between parents and staff are very friendly	–	–	19.4	51.6	29.0	4.10
Q70 If students have difficulty with school work, most teachers take time to help them	6.7	3.3	13.3	26.7	50.0	4.10
Q66 I have been happy at school	6.7	3.3	13.3	30.0	46.7	4.07
Q67 I would send my children to a Catholic school	16.7	6.7	10.0	10.0	56.7	3.83
Q39 Most teachers in this school show a good deal of school spirit	6.5	6.5	9.7	61.3	16.1	3.74
Q62 Most other students are very friendly	6.7	13.3	16.7	26.7	36.7	3.73
Q37 Most teachers are well qualified and have good teaching skills	3.2	16.1	16.1	35.5	29.0	3.71
Q52 I am treated with respect by other people at school	6.5	12.9	22.6	22.6	35.5	3.68
Q50 This school places too much emphasis on external conformity to rules and regulations	3.4	3.4	34.5	41.4	17.2	3.66
Q59 There is a happy atmosphere in the school	6.7	16.7	16.7	26.7	33.3	3.63
Q60 Catholic teachers here set an example of what it means to be a practising Catholic	10.0	16.7	10.0	26.7	36.7	3.63

Continued

Table 8.7 Continued

	Certainly FALSE (%)	Probably FALSE (%)	Uncertain (%)	Probably TRUE (%)	Certainly TRUE (%)	Score
Q55 Other students accept me as I am	12.9	9.7	9.7	38.7	29.0	3.61
Q69 If I had to do it all over again, I would attend a Catholic school	20.0	6.7	13.3	13.3	46.7	3.60
Q57 Most teachers go out of their way to help you	12.9	12.9	12.9	25.8	35.5	3.58
Q43 I can approach the Principal for advice and help	12.9	12.9	19.4	25.8	29.0	3.45
Q46 Most teachers carry out their work with energy and pleasure	3.2	25.8	19.4	25.8	25.8	3.45
Q51 Everyone tries to make you feel at home in this school	16.1	12.9	9.7	32.3	29.0	3.45
Q47 Discipline presents no real problem in this school	6.7	13.3	26.7	40.0	13.3	3.40
Q38 Students here know the standard of conduct expected of them	10.0	10.0	26.7	40.0	13.3	3.37
Q41 Most teachers know their final year students as individual persons	16.1	9.7	22.6	29.0	22.6	3.32
Q56 A good spirit of community exists among final year students	9.7	22.6	16.1	38.7	12.9	3.23
Q36 Students here think a lot of their school	16.7	3.3	36.7	30.0	13.3	3.20
Q45 Senior students understand and accept the religious goals of the school	22.6	3.2	35.5	19.4	19.4	3.10
Q40 Final year students here are not given enough real freedom	22.6	16.1	19.4	22.6	19.4	3.00
Q61 Most teachers show that people are more important than rules	16.7	16.7	20.0	43.3	3.3	3.00
Q64 There are ways to have school rules changed if most students disagree with them	26.7	6.7	30.0	23.3	13.3	2.90
Q68 Most teachers never explain why they ask you to do things around here	26.7	16.7	16.7	33.3	6.7	2.77
Q49 This school is a place where I feel lonely	48.4	19.4	3.2	12.9	16.1	2.29
Q54 This school is a place where I feel worried	48.4	16.1	3.2	22.6	9.7	2.29
Q44 I feel depressed at school	41.9	22.6	9.7	22.6	3.2	2.23

Students' attitudes and values towards the school

Agents of community spirit

In Table 8.8, students' valuing of respect as of utmost importance is presented together with their attitudes towards two other major aspects of community building.

The very high value placed on respect for people would suggest that this principle forms the basis for much of the students' moral commitments and practice. Such a finding is encouraging and reflects positively the argument made by Mmolai (1999: 1). He argues that 'a careful analysis of the roots of the various conflicts that have been raging in Africa shows the pivotal nature of social issues in the political and economic life of Africans'. He concludes that 'social issues must play a primordial role in the education curriculum'. The finding that respect for other people whatever their race, nationality or religion lies at the core of these students' attitudes and values in Country X bodes well for their interest in and commitment to the social and personal curriculum of the school. Again there is a very positive affirmation of the students' concern to befriend the rejected or lonely. Such respect and concern for others is clearly both promoted and nourished by the headteacher's encouragement of a sense of community and belonging in the school. Two comments from the students in their response to the open-ended questions support this general conclusion.

> What I can appreciate about my school is that it is a good school which supports students' ideas and the main value is trust. It is trust that is a community builder. (A non-Catholic Christian male)

> The way the school is trying to mould students into valuable citizens. The student empowerment. (A non-Catholic Christian male)

Table 8.8 Agents of community spirit: School A

	Certainly FALSE (%)	Probably FALSE (%)	Uncertain (%)	Probably TRUE (%)	Certainly TRUE (%)	Mean
Q117 People should be respected whatever their race, nationality or religion	–	–	–	13.8	86.2	4.86
Q65 The Principal encourages a sense of community and belonging to the school	–	–	–	33.3	66.7	4.67
Q113 I try to be friendly and helpful to others who are rejected or lonely	–	–	3.4	44.8	51.7	4.48

In the first, it is clear that respect for others builds trust within this particular school community. The second builds on the idea of trust as a community builder. The school community itself empowers the students and this, in turn, moves or faces the students outwards so that they begin to understand their responsibilities to others as citizens.

Students' comments

The students' comments fall predominantly into three areas. The first area is the relationship between religion and the school. On the one hand, this involves discussion of the status of the school and the role of religion in it. Thus one student writes:

> I appreciate the way teachers show the student the importance of school and religion in their lives. (A non-Catholic Christian female)

While another writes:

> My school has got nothing different from other secondary schools apart from the fact that it is a mission school. . . . The change I would make is to have Masses optional for the non-Catholic students. (A non-Catholic Christian female)

Another non-Catholic Christian male simply writes, 'Invite the different religions into the school'. While another non-Catholic Christian male expresses some of the uniqueness of the school by writing of 'the way in which little is done without involving God. Much effort has been put into making us realize the significance and importance of introducing God in our everyday lives'. Finally in this area of the relationship between religion and the school, one non-Catholic Christian female concludes that the school 'has brought change in many students' lives. It has really strengthened our beliefs and faith. I enjoy myself'.

The second area involves the perceived discipline experienced within the school. For example, one non-Catholic Christian male writes:

> The school's students have more self-discipline than the local non-Catholic schools. Cooperation amongst students is to the minimal. Despite this, it's a great school.

Three short sentences here express a seemingly diverse school experience, yet one which seems to be very satisfying. Does this particular student value the school discipline as a means of bringing together diverse groups of people, who although professing respect as their basic tenet of living, nevertheless, find being cooperative difficult. Two other students, however, write:

> There is cooperation between people and mostly there is guidance carried on people. (A female of no religion)

> All that I can say is that the students are all one group. They help each other and also the teachers support our work by guiding us on how to develop ourselves. (A non-Catholic Christian male)

The third area of comment involves the behaviours of the school as an educational institution. One comment speaks for several students and it simply asks the school to:

Abolish corporal punishment.

The headteacher had spoken of the need to replace corporal punishment with other forms of discipline, though pointing out that corporal punishment was still advocated by the Ministry of Education.

Another student pleaded, 'Build more labs', thus emphasizing the interest in the science curriculum and, at the same time, the pressure felt in the schools and the Ministry to up-grade and develop the facilities of senior secondary schools to meet the challenges of the global age.

Perhaps this final student sums up most cogently the overall character of this school as an educational institution:

> The unique spirit is hard work, excellence and perseverance. We probably are the only people who have the longest study time and our teachers are very encouraging. A lot of them have so much energy and excitement about their work. (A non-Catholic Christian female)

Behaviours

The students' expressed their most important personal goals as being to:

- find God in my life;
- accept myself as the person I am;
- be important and successful in life;
- find personal happiness.

Tables 8.9 and 8.10 are concerned with that most important behaviour of any school, curriculum, and afford some insight into the extent to which the students believe the school helps them to achieve their personal goals.

The curriculum

The statement receiving most positive agreement is 'the subjects taught offer useful knowledge and skills'. Other distribution of percentages which tend to

Table 8.9 The curriculum: School A

	Certainly FALSE (%)	Probably FALSE (%)	Uncertain (%)	Probably TRUE (%)	Certainly TRUE (%)	Mean
Q78 The subjects taught offer useful knowledge or skills	–	3.2	9.7	19.4	67.7	4.52
Q84 The school places sufficient emphasis on cultural activities (music, art, drama, etc)	–	6.9	10.3	20.7	62.1	4.38
Q75 There is a good sports programme in the school	3.2	9.7	–	25.8	61.3	4.32
Q80 The subjects taught in the school are relevant to real life and to students needs	–	3.2	9.7	38.7	48.4	4.32
Q81 The subjects taught here prepare students adequately for future employment	–	3.3	16.7	30.0	50.0	4.27
Q77 The subjects offered develop the capacity for independent and critical thinking	3.3	–	16.7	43.3	36.7	4.10
Q79 The religious education programme is an important part of the curriculum	6.5	9.7	6.5	25.8	51.6	4.06
Q82 The curriculum of the school is dominated too much by examinations	–	10.3	20.7	37.9	31.0	3.90
Q73 There are opportunities for students to get to know teachers outside the classroom	–	19.4	19.4	19.4	41.9	3.84
Q74 The out-of-school activities of the school have sufficient variety and scope	6.7	6.7	16.7	46.7	23.3	3.73
Q72 The curriculum of this school meets my present needs	10.0	16.7	6.7	33.3	33.3	3.63
Q83 A Christian way of thinking is presented in the subjects taught here	16.7	16.7	23.3	13.3	30.0	3.23
Q76 The school offers a good range of subjects to older students	25.8	6.5	22.6	25.8	19.4	3.06

Table 8.10 Religious education: School A

	Certainly FALSE (%)	Probably FALSE (%)	Uncertain (%)	Probably TRUE (%)	Certainly TRUE (%)	Mean
Q108 RE classes help me to understand the meaning of life	3.6	3.6	3.6	21.4	67.9	4.46
Q101 Christian marriage has been treated in sufficient depth in RE classes	3.6	–	25.0	28.6	42.9	4.07
Q89 RE classes are related to real life and to my needs	6.9	6.9	6.9	37.9	41.4	4.00
Q90 RE classes are not taken seriously by students	3.6	3.6	10.7	57.1	25.0	3.96
Q93 RE teachers allow sufficient time for discussion	10.7	3.6	10.7	35.7	39.3	3.89
Q86 I am enjoying RE classes this year	13.3	10.0	3.3	30.0	43.3	3.80
Q96 RE classes have helped me to understand the Gospels	17.9	7.1	7.1	28.6	39.3	3.64
Q106 RE classes have helped me understand other religious and non-religious points of view	14.3	7.1	10.7	35.7	32.1	3.64
Q100 Contemporary moral issues are given emphasis in RE classes	3.8	7.7	38.5	26.9	23.1	3.58
Q91 If RE classes were voluntary, I would still attend them	21.4	7.1	10.7	14.3	46.4	3.57
Q103 Assessment through assignments or examinations should form part of RE	3.6	25.0	14.3	25.0	32.1	3.57
Q102 RE classes help me to form my own conscience	14.3	10.7	3.6	50.0	21.4	3.54
Q87 The study of other religions has helped me appreciate my own religion	20.0	10.0	6.7	30.0	33.3	3.47
Q98 RE classes have deepened my understanding of the Catholic tradition	11.1	14.8	18.5	29.6	25.9	3.44
Q104 RE classes have helped me to pray	17.9	7.1	17.9	32.1	25.0	3.39
Q97 RE classes have shown me the place of the Eucharist in Catholic life	11.1	18.5	33.3	18.5	18.5	3.15
Q95 RE is taught at a level comparable with that of other subjects	14.8	11.1	40.7	22.2	11.1	3.04
Q99 Basic Catholic values and moral teachings are not taught in RE classes	28.6	7.1	14.3	32.1	17.9	3.04
Q105 I do not know my Catholic faith well enough	34.6	–	15.4	26.9	23.1	3.04
Q94 This school has a good RE programme for older students	29.6	7.4	33.3	25.9	3.7	2.67
Q92 RE classes are poorly prepared and taught	46.4	17.9	17.9	–	17.9	2.25
Q107 RE classes take up too much time which should be devoted to other subjects	46.4	21.4	10.7	14.3	7.1	2.14
Q88 RE classes are largely a waste of time	58.6	10.3	6.9	17.2	6.9	2.03

the very positive end of the five-point scale relate to:

- a sufficient emphasis being placed on cultural activities;
- the existence of a good sports programme;
- subjects preparing students adequately for future employment;
- subjects developing the capacity for independent and critical thinking;
- subjects taught in the school are relevant to real life.

The positive response to the statements relating to the matters above is also evident in the distribution of the majority of responses to the statement 'religious education is an important part of the programme', although a sizeable 20 per cen are uncertain or indeed believe the statement to be false. These figures move quickly towards the negative end of the scale in relation to the statement 'a Christian way of thinking is presented in the subjects taught here'. The clearly positive response to religious education might indicate that the subject in itself presents a Christian way of thinking and fits, as well, into the positive attitudes to most of the curriculum experience described above. Is it therefore the success of religious education which highlights the failure of other subjects to present a Christian way of thinking?

Religious education

The acknowledgement by the students that RE forms an important part of their overall curriculum programme is reflected in their view that RE classes are not 'a waste of time' nor are they 'poorly prepared or taught'. Three other important aspects of the RE programme of the school are highlighted very positively by the students' responses:

1. RE helps in understanding the meaning of life.
2. Christian marriage is treated in sufficient depth.
3. RE classes are related to real life and personal needs.

The very positive response to the statement that, 'RE classes help me to understand the meaning of life' indicates a highly satisfactory response (overall score 4.46) to the kind of RE being offered in the school when it is compared with the students' responses shown also by overall score to the following statements in other parts of the questionnaire and reported in Tables 8.1–8.4 at the beginning of this chapter:

- My faith helps me to be a better person (4.86 in Table 8.4).
- Catholic schools should help students discover and fulfil themselves as persons (4.48 in Table 8.1).
- To find God in my life and grow in faith in him (4.66 in Table 8.3).

One response is, however, puzzling in the context of these other responses, that is, the rather negative understanding of the statement, 'The school has a good RE programme for older students'. The rest of the tables do not help to throw light on this puzzle, nor do responses to the open-ended questions.

The students from this school consistently showed themselves to be people of religious faith. For them their school must fulfil both educational goals and personal faith goals. As the general introduction at the beginning of this chapter to the students from these three countries indicated, there are many students within the sample whose faith is religious. Such students demand that their religious faith, or attitude to life, is educated alongside their social and intellectual characteristics. Thus in understanding themselves and developing their personal meaning in life the school needs to find a way of eliciting educated growth in their faith life response. For the students in this school, there appears to be an unqualified vote of confidence in the role of RE in that process. This is a remarkable finding in a school where the majority of students are non-Catholic Christians and/or are of no religion. They clearly do not perceive that RE in a Catholic school may be unsuitable for those who are not Catholics.

Arising from this last comment, it is important to reflect on one other aspect of the data attached to the RE Table 8.10, that is, the response to question 102, 'RE classes have helped me to form my own conscience'. There is in this response, unlike in most others in this table, a very clear line drawn between the positive and the negative respondents. There is little uncertainty on the matter. Is it that there is a group of students who had already developed their consciences to their own satisfaction without RE or does the content and pedagogy of the RE confirm the bases of individual consciences, thus leaving little room for critical discussion and evaluation in RE classes? As has been noted in Table 8.9, 'The curriculum', one of the four most positive responses to statements about the school's curriculum related to the statement, 'Subjects develop the capacity for independent and critical thinking'.

Against the background, too, of the positive response made by the students to the statement that 'RE is relevant to real life and personal needs', Mmolai's (1999) comments on the significance of RE in the political and social development of southern Africa are important. For him neither political nor economic stability can be achieved without some workable harmony amongst the uniquely diversified ethnic components of nation-states in Africa. Indeed, he is of the view that RE perhaps more than any other discipline can help to achieve 'Social Harmony', 'particularly at the secondary school level', where 'the ripple effect of social harmony could eventually lead to viable and sustained economic development'. Mmolai has written about a matter of great importance. He has acknowledged that Country X's national strategic planning, which is rooted in the concept of 'Social Harmony', has little chance of succeeding, unless the concept of social harmony is broken down into viable elements within the national curriculum of the schools. His argument is that social harmony cannot be decreed; rather, it must be fostered and sustained. The students in this school give evidence of their commitment to others and respect for others.

The question arises starkly, therefore, how best to foster and sustain those values and attitudes which lead to social harmony, once the rudimentary value of respect for others has been evoked within a school culture? To begin to find answers to this it would be important to examine aspects of the school culture as they form a learning organization and support a sense of community among staff and students. Freire's concept of 'conscientization' has already been proposed within this present study as one potential model for a pedagogy for learning about plurality. It is therefore instructive to enquire of the whole culture of this school whether it can sustain the students' present modes of valuing, perhaps through promoting the students' cooperation with each other, as well as with their peers outside the school.

The discussion above arose from hearing within the students' voice twin aspirations for learning at the school. Their voice demanded that education fitted them for their future roles in the world of work and learning and simultaneously helped them discover themselves as people and develop their faith in God. Within the framework of this present study, the student voice adds an urgency to the argument that the faith or world view of the individual student in complex pluralities should constitute a part of the core business of schools. These students also welcomed faiths and world views as part of the content for becoming educated in, and reflecting, on pluralism.

School B

There were 36 boys and 30 girls who responded to the questionnaire at School B. The sample taken relating to the open-ended questions comprised (i) four male and three female Catholics; (ii) five male and five female non-Catholic Christians; (iii) three males from a non-Christian religion; and (iv) one female of no religion.

Beliefs

In School B, the students' highest values and beliefs were:

- People should be respected whatever their race, nationality or religion;
- I believe in God;
- God is a loving father; and jointly;
- I try to be friendly and helpful to others who are rejected or lonely;
- Abortion is a worse evil than the birth of an unwanted child.

Table 8.11   Students' religious beliefs: School B

Catholic (%)	Other Christian faith (%)	Non-Christian religion (%)	No religion (%)
18.2	69.7	9.1	3.0

Table 8.12 Parents' religious beliefs: School B

	Practising Catholic (%)	Non-practising Catholic (%)	Other Christian faith (%)	Non-Christian religion (%)	No religion (%)
Mother's religion	12.1	–	81.8	3.0	3.0
Father's religion	10.6	3.0	56.1	15.2	15.2

School life and climate

In School B, the students' four highest expectations of their school were for it to:

- assist students to achieve a high standard of performance in their school work;
- prepare students for their future careers;
- help students to discover and fulfil themselves as persons;
- provide an atmosphere of Christian community.

There were 82.8 per cent of students who reported they were happy at the school and a further 9.4 per cent thought this was probably true.

The students at the school affirm very positively that they have been happy there. Two comments from the students perhaps help to identify reasons for their happiness in and with the school:

> It's like teachers actually care whether or not you live or die unlike other schools I've been to . . . The sense of community and belonging that is encouraged by at least some teachers (RE teachers) and the headteacher. The acceptance and respect of individuals no matter what their creed, colour, religion. (A Catholic male)

> They helped me to understand a lot about internal life and how to live long and understand my community. (A non-Christian female)

Other important findings in this table include:

- students recognize the high regard in which the school is held and are very proud to belong to it;
- there is equal high regard for the things that are taught and the belief that the school rules encourage self-discipline and responsibility;
- there is a positive belief among the students that the teachers are well qualified and show a good deal of school spirit and at the same time, an

equally strong view that Catholic teachers set an example of what it means to be a practising Catholic;

- the students credit the headteacher equally for both encouraging a sense of community and belonging to the school and for placing importance on the religious nature of the school;
- although the students say that they have been happy at the school, and that other students are very friendly, an equal number (71.9 per cent) express the view that the school places too much emphasis on external conformity to rules and regulations. On the other hand, 86 per cent believe that school rules encourage self-discipline and responsibility. Flynn (1993: 203) found that over an 18-year period, students' concern with too much emphasis on external conformity moved away from 62 per cent in 1972 to 39 per cent in 1982 and increased slightly again in 1990 to 42 per cent.

Further, with regard to regulation and conduct, the students at the positive end of the five-point scale divide equally with 36.9 per cent and 35.4 per cent, respectively, saying that it is certainly or probably true that they know the standard of conduct expected of them. There are another 18.5 per cent who are uncertain and 6.2 per cent and 3.1 per cent claim this to be probably or certainly false. Allied to this uncertainty is possibly the strong belief that their teachers place more emphasis on rules than people. In response to the statement, 'most teachers show that people are more important than rules', 29 per cent and 17.7 per cent, respectively, claimed this was certainly or probably false and 17.7 per cent said they were uncertain. Nonetheless, equal percentages said that it was probably or certainly true that most teachers show a good deal of school spirit and equal percentages of the students also expressed the view that 'they were treated with respect by other people at the school' but 21.5 per cent were uncertain and 12.3 per cent said this was probably false.

The highly positive response to the statement concerning the friendliness of other students has already been noted above. Among, however, the very positive messages of there being a happy atmosphere at the school, with, for example, 40.6 per cent and 35.9 per cent, agreeing respectively that this is probably or certainly true and similar percentages agreeing that other students accept them as they are, there is evidence of a hard core of uncertainty about these matters, or even of disaffection. There is, for example, a reluctance on the part of about 20 per cent of the students to be certain about agreeing with any of these statements. The table does, also, show that the percentages are very similarly distributed in response to the two statements relating to whether the students would send their own children to a Catholic school and whether, if they had to do it all again, they would attend a Catholic school. To the first question, 20.3 per cent and 46.9 per cent, respectively, agreed this was probably or certainly true. To the second, 25 per cent and 37.5 per cent, respectively, agreed they probably or most certainly would, leaving many who were not sure or who did not.

Table 8.13 School life and climate: School B

	Certainly FALSE (%)	Probably FALSE (%)	Uncertain (%)	Probably TRUE (%)	Certainly TRUE (%)	Mean
Q42 This school has a good name in the local community	4.6	–	–	15.4	80.0	4.66
Q63 I feel proud to be a student of this school	6.3	1.6	3.1	23.4	65.6	4.41
Q71 School rules here encourage self-discipline and responsibility	6.3	–	7.8	26.6	59.4	4.33
Q53 The things I am taught are worthwhile learning	3.1	4.7	10.9	20.3	60.9	4.31
Q70 If students have difficulty with school work, most teachers take time to help them	1.6	1.6	10.9	35.9	50.0	4.31
Q60 Catholic teachers here set an example of what it means to be a practising Catholic	3.1	7.8	4.7	31.3	53.1	4.23
Q62 Most other students are very friendly	1.6	6.3	6.3	40.6	45.3	4.22
Q37 Most teachers are well qualified and have good teaching skills	9.2	9.2	9.2	40.0	41.5	4.14
Q66 I have been happy at school	6.3	1.6	9.4	37.5	45.3	4.14
Q50 This school places too much emphasis on external conformity to rules and regulations	4.7	–	23.4	25.0	46.9	4.09
Q58 The Principal places importance on the religious nature of the school	7.8	4.7	10.9	28.1	48.4	4.05
Q65 The Principal encourages a sense of community and belonging to the school	6.3	3.1	10.9	40.6	39.1	4.03
Q55 Other students accept me as I am	3.1	1.5	23.1	38.5	33.8	3.98
Q38 Students here know the standard of conduct expected of them	3.1	6.2	18.5	35.4	36.9	3.97
Q48 Adequate counselling help is available to students	9.4	4.7	10.9	31.3	43.8	3.95
Q56 A good spirit of community exists among final year students	4.6	6.2	20.0	29.2	40.0	3.94

Continued

Table 8.13 Continued

	Certainly FALSE (%)	Probably FALSE (%)	Uncertain (%)	Probably TRUE (%)	Certainly TRUE (%)	Mean
Q59 There is a happy atmosphere in the school	6.3	7.8	9.4	40.6	35.9	3.92
Q39 Most teachers in this school show a good deal of school spirit	7.7	6.2	15.4	35.4	35.4	3.85
Q46 Most teachers carry out their work with energy and pleasure	7.7	7.7	10.8	43.1	30.8	3.82
Q67 I would send my children to a Catholic school	15.6	3.1	14.1	20.3	46.9	3.80
Q35 The relationships between parents and staff are very friendly	1.5	6.2	30.8	36.9	24.6	3.77
Q52 I am treated with respect by other people at school	4.6	12.3	21.5	30.8	30.8	3.71
Q43 I can approach the Principal for advice and help	9.2	12.3	13.8	29.2	35.4	3.69
Q69 If I had to do it all over again, I would attend a Catholic school	15.6	6.3	15.6	25.0	37.5	3.63
Q47 Discipline presents no real problem in this school	10.9	12.5	18.8	29.7	28.1	3.52
Q51 Everyone tries to make you feel at home in this school	13.8	7.7	18.5	33.8	26.2	3.51
Q57 Most teachers go out of their way to help you	9.2	9.2	26.2	33.8	21.5	3.49
Q36 Students here think a lot of their school	3.1	13.8	29.2	40.0	13.8	3.48
Q45 Senior students understand and accept the religious goals of the school	10.9	17.2	23.4	23.4	25.0	3.34
Q40 Final year students here are not given enough real freedom	21.5	21.5	12.3	16.9	27.7	3.08
Q68 Most teachers never explain why they ask you to do things around here	18.8	15.6	29.7	21.9	14.1	2.97
Q41 Most teachers know their final year students as individual persons	18.5	18.5	32.3	15.4	15.4	2.91
Q61 Most teachers show that people are more important than rules	29.0	17.7	17.7	16.1	19.4	2.79
Q64 There are ways to have school rules changed if most students disagree with them	29.7	18.8	20.3	14.1	17.2	2.70
Q44 I feel depressed at school	44.6	21.5	15.4	7.7	10.8	2.18
Q54 This school is a place where I feel worried	59.4	17.2	7.8	4.7	10.9	1.91
Q49 This school is a place where I feel lonely	63.1	16.9	10.8	4.6	4.6	1.71

Students' attitudes and values towards the school

Agents of community spirit

In the table below, students' valuing of respect as of utmost importance is presented together with their attitudes towards two other major aspects of community building.

The students responded very positively to the core value of respect for other people, no matter what their race, nationality or religion. This would suggest that as individuals they are ready to place respect at the heart of their valuing of, and their positive attitudes to, others. Such a personal basis for their attitude to other people would suggest their 'readiness' for the kinds of social learning envisaged by Mmolai as the basis for taking forward the educational agenda required in southern Africa if political and economic sustainability is to be achieved. Equally, they affirm that they try to be friendly and helpful to others who are rejected or lonely. Such evidence of personal valuing of, and respect for, others is highlighted against a background of a lived experience of community within the school, according to the understanding which students show of their headteacher's role in fostering a sense of community and belonging in the school.

Students' comments

The students' comments address three main areas of school experience. The first relates to the genus loci. Below are a number of their comments.

> We have been taught that we are in a mission school so we have to care, love, accept others as they are, support others in life, showing each other faith and respect of human life. (A Catholic male)

> Unique: this is the spirit of hope, respect and good will. . . . Everyone has their own understanding of things and certainly help other students.
>   Everybody respects each other as persons. (A non-Christian female)

> The unique spirit in the school is that the students do well in their school work and they do respect and love one another as human beings. (A female of no religion)

> Catholics and non-Catholics finding themselves able to live together. (A non-Christian male)

The emphases throughout these comments are on the positive attitudes towards others, found among the students, who themselves are seen as 'persons' and the ability of the school community to live well together, including experiencing a common faith environment, not a specifically denominational one. Perhaps the *genus loci* can be summed up in the comment, 'I have learnt how to live as a person'.

Table 8.14   Agents of community spirit: School B

	Certainly FALSE (%)	Probably FALSE (%)	Uncertain (%)	Probably TRUE (%)	Certainly TRUE (%)	Mean
Q117 People should be respected whatever their race, nationality or religion	–	–	3.1	18.8	78.1	4.75
Q113 I try to be friendly and helpful to others who are rejected or lonely	1.6	1.6	3.1	35.9	57.8	4.47
Q65 The Principal encourages a sense of community and belonging to the school	6.3	3.1	10.9	40.6	39.1	4.03

A second area which the students' comments addressed was that of religious education and other areas of the curriculum and the attitude of teachers. For example, one student talks of religious education in the following way:

> I appreciate the RE department because my RE has helped me to be what I am now: to respect others, to love each other and care for one another as I do myself. (A female of no religion)

A similar outcome for another male student who is a non-Catholic Christian in terms of his faith development is summarized as, 'I appreciate and value the school because I have to try to develop my attitude to God our Father'. Another said, 'it teaches us how to behave and how to understand life'. One non-Catholic Christian female student comments on the content of RE, saying, 'I appreciate the way the Gospel is taught to us during RE lessons. They are really interesting in the sense that a good explanation is given to us in everything we are taught'. Finally, a student talks about the balance between RE and the rest of the curriculum:

> Emphasis is placed on RE but other subjects are treated very well. There is plenty of time for sports and clubs. The teachers and sisters are always willing to help. (A non-Catholic Christian female)

The third area which receives comment is the outcome of the teaching and learning process:

> Good behaviour, seriousness in school work, self-motivated. (A non-Catholic Christian male)

> I'm going to appreciate the way the teachers taught us to be tomorrow's people. (A non-Catholic Christian female)

Finally, the students spoke of changes they would like to make in the school. These mainly were concerned with:

- the abolition of corporal punishment: 'Stop active punishment to students, walloping with sticks';
- school rules: 'Change all the silly regulations';
- the place of religion in non-religious students' lives: 'Not forcing non-Christians to pray'.

But one spoke of wishing to make changes so that they could 'learn even more about change'.

Behaviours

In School B, the students' highest personal goals were to:

- serve other people;
- be honest;
- find God in my life;
- live up to the example and teachings of Jesus.

The curriculum

In this table the most positive measure of agreement among the students was with the statement 'the subjects taught offer useful knowledge and skills'. Other statements to which the percentage of responses tended clearly to the positive end of the five-point scale were:

1. the subjects taught are relevant to real life;
2. religious education is an important part of the curriculum;
3. the subjects taught offer an adequate preparation for future employment.

Two other statements show a definite emphasis within the positive end of the five-point scale. The first is 'the subjects offered develop the capacity for independent and critical thinking'; and the second 'there is a good sports programme in the school'. Despite the positive response to the importance of religious education in the curriculum, the students are not clear that a Christian way of thinking is shown in the subjects taught. At the same time, despite the positive view of the relevance of the curriculum to real life and its preparation for future employment, there is a less positive view of the curriculum meeting the students' present needs. Perhaps this is a result of the gaps in the students' overall curriculum experience seen for example in a rather negative response to the statement concerning sufficient emphasis being placed on cultural activities.

Table 8.15 The curriculum: School B

	Certainly FALSE (%)	Probably FALSE (%)	Uncertain (%)	Probably TRUE (%)	Certainly TRUE (%)	Mean
Q78 The subjects taught offer useful knowledge or skills	–	3.1	–	40.0	56.9	4.51
Q80 The subjects taught in the school are relevant to real life and to students needs	4.6	–	3.1	36.9	55.4	4.38
Q79 The religious education programme is an important part of the curriculum	4.6	1.5	13.8	12.3	67.7	4.37
Q81 The subjects taught here prepare students adequately for future employment	3.1	3.1	7.8	28.1	57.8	4.34
Q77 The subjects offered develop the capacity for independent and critical thinking	4.6	1.5	16.9	35.4	41.5	4.08
Q75 There is a good sports programme in the school	7.7	4.6	6.2	40.0	41.5	4.03
Q72 The curriculum of this school meets my present needs	4.6	12.3	15.4	36.9	30.8	3.77
Q84 The school places sufficient emphasis on cultural activities (music, art, drama, etc)	6.3	7.9	15.9	42.9	27.0	3.76
Q82 The curriculum of the school is dominated too much by examinations	4.7	10.9	25.0	32.8	26.6	3.66
Q83 A Christian way of thinking is presented in the subjects taught here	6.3	9.4	28.1	29.7	26.6	3.61
Q74 The out-of-school activities of the school have sufficient variety and scope	4.6	10.8	32.3	26.2	26.2	3.58
Q73 There are opportunities for students to get to know teachers outside the classroom	7.7	15.4	20.0	33.8	23.1	3.49
Q76 The school offers a good range of subjects to older students	13.8	12.3	20.0	21.5	32.3	3.46

Religious education

The responses to the closed questions were very positive to a wide range of statements about RE at the school. RE classes were valued for being well prepared, comparable with other subjects and helping students understand meaning in their lives. They were enjoyed and were not thought to constitute a waste of time. Key areas of interest in the subject focused on:

- their ability to help students understand the meaning of life;
- teachers allowing sufficient time for discussion;
- classes relating to real life and personal needs;
- their ability to help students form their own conscience;
- teaching an understanding of the Gospels;
- teaching about Christian marriage at a suitable depth.

There was a mainly positive view that RE classes helped the students to understand other religious and non-religious points of view. It is important to note that the students in both schools in Country X gave first priority to RE helping them to understand the meaning of life. Equally they placed a very positive value on the relationship between RE classes and real life, together putting this focus into third place. The notable difference between the two tables from each school is that in School B, the students rated the time allocated to discussion in class to second place. Equally their enjoyment of RE was in fifth and sixth place on the two tables, though there was slightly more enjoyment in School B. Interestingly, the students at School B chose to write more extensively about religious education when discussing the *genus loci* (see their comments above in the section, 'Students' attitudes and values towards the school').

It is worthwhile speculating about the reason for the students writing so extensively about RE, and indeed talking so much about the RE department during one-to-one interviews, when discussing the unique spirit of the school. In Table 8.1 showing their expectations of the school, the students recorded their most positive responses to statements concerned with a) being supported in achieving a high standard in their school work, with a score of 4.41 and b) preparation for their future careers, with a score of 4.32. Was their perception of the significance of RE within the *genus loci* simply a response, therefore, to a highly visible RE department and teaching base? Or did they, in fact, find that, since RE was taught at a level comparable with other subjects and was as demanding in terms of skills, knowledge and understanding as other subjects, it formed part of an integrated curriculum offering which was indeed preparing them for their future careers.

Within the table charting the students' expectations of their school, the statement which came third in their response was that it should 'help students to discover and fulfil themselves as persons'. Presumably they believed

Table 8.16 Religious education: School B

	Certainly FALSE (%)	Probably FALSE (%)	Uncertain (%)	Probably TRUE (%)	Certainly TRUE (%)	Mean
Q108 RE classes help me to understand the meaning of life	7.8	3.1	6.3	18.8	64.1	4.28
Q93 RE teachers allow sufficient time for discussion	1.6	9.4	4.7	29.7	54.7	4.27
Q89 RE classes are related to real life and to my needs	9.4	1.6	6.3	23.4	59.4	4.22
Q102 RE classes help me to form my own conscience	3.1	4.7	10.9	32.8	48.4	4.19
Q86 I am enjoying RE classes this year	9.4	1.6	12.5	25.0	51.6	4.08
Q96 RE classes have helped me to understand the Gospels	9.5	3.2	9.5	25.4	52.4	4.08
Q95 RE is taught at a level comparable with that of other subjects	4.7	4.7	12.5	39.1	39.1	4.03
Q101 Christian marriage has been treated in sufficient depth in RE classes	4.7	3.1	20.3	31.3	40.6	4.00
Q106 RE classes have helped me understand other religious and non-religious points of view	9.5	9.5	7.9	33.3	39.7	3.84
Q94 This school has a good RE programme for older students	6.3	4.8	25.4	27.0	36.5	3.83
Q103 Assessment through assignments or examinations should form part of RE	4.8	1.6	25.4	42.9	25.4	3.83
Q91 If RE classes were voluntary, I would still attend them	17.2	3.1	10.9	25.0	43.8	3.75
Q104 RE classes have helped me to pray	10.9	7.8	12.5	34.4	34.4	3.73
Q87 The study of other religions has helped me appreciate my own religion	6.3	9.4	15.6	43.8	25.0	3.72
Q100 Contemporary moral issues are given emphasis in RE classes	3.3	6.6	39.3	31.1	19.7	3.57
Q98 RE classes have deepened my understanding of the Catholic tradition	17.2	9.4	10.9	37.5	25.0	3.44
Q97 RE classes have shown me the place of the Eucharist in Catholic life	14.5	9.7	25.8	29.0	21.0	3.32
Q90 RE classes are not taken seriously by students	17.2	14.1	23.4	29.7	15.6	3.13
Q105 I do not know my Catholic faith well enough	13.3	23.3	23.3	23.3	16.7	3.07
Q99 Basic Catholic values and moral teachings are not taught in RE classes	28.6	23.8	27.0	14.3	6.3	2.46
Q107 RE classes take up too much time which should be devoted to other subjects	56.3	18.8	12.5	6.3	6.3	1.87
Q88 RE classes are largely a waste of time	64.1	20.3	7.8	1.6	6.3	1.66
Q92 RE classes are poorly prepared and taught	68.8	17.2	4.7	1.6	7.8	1.63

their expectations were indeed fulfilled in RE since they agreed very strongly that it helped them to understand the meaning of life, as well as relating to their real-life and personal needs. Perhaps the comment made by one of the non-Catholic Christian female students, 'I have learnt how to live as a person' exemplifies the student view that the school caters for the whole person. In that case, it is important to examine the curriculum offering and the school culture in the light of the students' own statements about how they perceive and understand themselves.

School C

The school is the only single sex category school in the survey. There were forty-nine girls who responded to the questionnaire. The sample relating to the open-ended questions comprised (i) three Catholics and twelve non-Catholic Christians.

Beliefs

In School C, the students' most important values and beliefs matched the highest overall scores derived from the cross-tabulation of gender, religion and school and were:

- People should be respected whatever their race, nationality or religion;
- God is a loving Father;
- I believe in God;
- I believe that God always forgives me.

Table 8.17 Students' religious beliefs: School C

Catholic (%)	Other Christian faith (%)	Non-Christian religion (%)	No religion (%)
40.8	55.1	2.0	2.0

Table 8.18 Parents' religious beliefs: School C

	Practising Catholic (%)	Non-practising Catholic (%)	Other Christian faith (%)	Non-Christian religion (%)	No religion (%)
Mother's religion	36.7	10.2	44.9	4.1	4.1
Father's religion	24.5	12.2	40.8	4.1	18.4

School life and climate

The students' highest expectations of their school were to:

- assist students to achieve a high standard of performance in their school work;
- provide an environment in which students' faith in God can develop;
- prepare students for their future careers;
- provide an atmosphere of Christian community.

There were 79.5 per cent of the students who reported that they have been happy at the school, with a further 8.2 per cent thinking this was probably so true.

Other important findings in this table include:

- there was an overwhelming positive agreement found with the statement that school rules encourage self-discipline and responsibility and very positive agreement that students know the standard of conduct expected of them;
- the girls positively identified the high reputation of the school in the local community and their sense of pride in being a student at the school;
- there is positive recognition that the headteacher places importance on the religious nature of the school and, at the same time, encourages a sense of community and belonging to the school;
- there is agreement that the things they are taught are worthwhile learning; there is also considerable agreement that if they have difficulty with school work, most teachers take time to help them.

There is a certain ambivalence shown by the girls in their response to the statement 'everyone tries to make you feel at home in the school', with a distribution of percentages, showing disagreement at 22 per cent, 16 per cent uncertain and 38 per cent thinking they agree but 22 per cent strongly agreeing. A similar distribution of percentages can be found in response to the statement, 'a good spirit of community exists among final year students'. Within this spread of responses to statements concerning their personal experience of community, the students' response to the statement about the respect they have been shown by other people at the school is illuminating. Individual identity, personal experience, and possibly social or religious background might begin to explain such a distribution.

Finally it is noteworthy that the percentage responses of students to the statements, 'I would send my children to a Catholic school' and 'If I had to do it all over again, I would attend a Catholic school' indicate a strong tendency to agree with the statements very positively. At this school, where the students recognized clearly that the headteacher laid emphasis on the

Table 8.19 School life and climate: School C

	Certainly FALSE (%)	Probably FALSE (%)	Uncertain (%)	Probably TRUE (%)	Certainly TRUE (%)	Mean
Q71 School rules here encourage self-discipline and responsibility	–	2.0	–	2.0	95.9	4.92
Q63 I feel proud to be a student of this school	–	–	2.0	8.2	89.8	4.88
Q65 The Principal encourages a sense of community and belonging to the school	–	–	4.1	8.2	87.8	4.84
Q42 This school has a good name in the local community	–	2.0	4.1	4.1	89.8	4.82
Q58 The Principal places importance on the religious nature of the school	–	–	8.2	6.1	85.7	4.78
Q53 The things I am taught are worthwhile learning	4.1	–	2.0	6.1	87.8	4.73
Q70 If students have difficulty with school work, most teachers take time to help them	–	2.0	2.0	22.4	73.5	4.67
Q38 Students here know the standard of conduct expected of them	–	2.0	6.1	22.4	69.4	4.59
Q57 Most teachers go out of their way to help you	4.1	4.1	6.1	28.6	57.1	4.31
Q69 If I had to do it all over again, I would attend a Catholic school	4.1	–	14.3	24.5	57.1	4.31
Q59 There is a happy atmosphere in the school	2.0	–	14.3	34.7	49.0	4.29
Q66 I have been happy at school	2.0	10.2	8.2	22.4	57.1	4.22
Q67 I would send my children to a Catholic school	2.0	2.0	22.4	18.4	55.1	4.22
Q37 Most teachers are well qualified and have good teaching skills	6.1	2.0	6.1	36.7	49.0	4.20
Q62 Most other students are very friendly	2.0	2.0	10.2	46.9	38.8	4.18
Q39 Most teachers in this school show a good deal of school spirit	6.1	4.1	4.1	38.8	46.9	4.16
Q55 Other students accept me as I am	6.1	6.1	10.2	26.5	51.0	4.10
Q41 Most teachers know their final year students as individual persons	–	4.1	26.5	32.7	36.7	4.02
Q60 Catholic teachers here set an example of what it means to be a practising Catholic	2.0	8.2	20.4	24.5	44.9	4.02
Q52 I am treated with respect by other people at school	4.1	10.2	10.2	34.7	40.8	3.98
Q36 Students here think a lot of their school	4.1	4.1	12.2	51.0	28.6	3.96

Continued

Table 8.19 Continued

	Certainly FALSE (%)	Probably FALSE (%)	Uncertain (%)	Probably TRUE (%)	Certainly TRUE (%)	Mean
Q46 Most teachers carry out their work with energy and pleasure	6.1	6.1	18.4	36.7	32.7	3.84
Q56 A good spirit of community exists among final year students	6.1	6.1	24.5	26.5	36.7	3.82
Q48 Adequate counselling help is available to students	10.6	6.4	21.3	19.1	42.6	3.77
Q45 Senior students understand and accept the religious goals of the school	4.1	6.1	34.7	32.7	22.4	3.63
Q43 I can approach the Principal for advice and help	12.5	8.3	27.1	12.5	39.6	3.58
Q51 Everyone tries to make you feel at home in this school	10.2	12.2	16.3	38.8	22.4	3.51
Q35 The relationships between parents and staff are very friendly	4.1	14.3	36.7	30.6	14.3	3.37
Q47 Discipline presents no real problem in this school	6.1	18.4	28.6	26.5	20.4	3.37
Q61 Most teachers show that people are more important than rules	6.1	10.2	46.9	22.4	14.3	3.29
Q40 Final year students here are not given enough real freedom	22.4	14.3	20.4	20.4	22.4	3.06
Q68 Most teachers never explain why they ask you to do things around here	24.5	18.4	32.7	12.2	12.2	2.69
Q50 This school places too much emphasis on external conformity to rules and regulations	32.7	20.4	20.4	12.2	14.3	2.55
Q64 There are ways to have school rules changed if most students disagree with them	38.8	12.2	38.8	2.0	8.2	2.29
Q44 I feel depressed at school	49.0	14.3	12.2	18.4	6.1	2.18
Q54 This school is a place where I feel worried	69.4	18.4	2.0	10.2	–	1.53
Q49 This school is a place where I feel lonely	77.6	4.1	8.2	10.2	–	1.51

religious nature of the school and they knew what standard of conduct was expected of them, the students were in agreement with the statements concerning their desire to re-live the experience of the school and to send their children to a Catholic school. This level of agreement may be evidence of a number of students' belief that they had enjoyed a quality education at the school and would therefore wish to send their own children to a Catholic school. On the other hand, the overall positive response may have included a number of Catholic students, who, though not enjoying their own experience at this particular school, may have felt an obligation to send their own children to Catholic schools.

Students' attitudes and values towards the school

Agents of community spirit

In Table 8.20, students' valuing of respect as of utmost importance is presented together with their attitudes towards two other major aspects of community building.

The absolute value placed on respect for persons indicates that students within the school register this value as the basis for their attitudes and responses to other people, whether fellow students or people in their community in general. Comment must also be made about the overwhelmingly positive view of the headteacher's role in encouraging a sense of community and belonging. It appears that the headteacher is seen by the students as both the leader of the school and the definer of the school's core values. The high value placed on being outgoing to the lonely and rejected suggests that the students also have a 'consciousness' of the needs of others and the role they might play in relating to them.

Table 8.20   Agents of community spirit: School C

	Certainly FALSE (%)	Probably FALSE (%)	Uncertain (%)	Probably TRUE (%)	Certainly TRUE (%)	Mean
Q117 People should be respected whatever their race, nationality or religion	–	–	–	–	100.0	5.00
Q65 The Principal encourages a sense of community and belonging to the school	–	–	4.1	8.2	87.8	4.84
Q113 I try to be friendly and helpful to others who are rejected or lonely	–	4.1	6.1	36.7	53.1	4.39

Students' comments

The comments are taken from the students' response to the three open-ended questions in the questionnaire and also from group interviews. The students addressed a variety of matters, which can be divided into three major areas of their experience. The first was the *genus loci*. Here comments included;

> Being a member of the school means belonging to a family. Sometimes I see my teachers more often than my parents. There is a great sense of belonging. (A non-Catholic Christian)

> I appreciate everything at this school because I used to attend another school which is non-Catholic where the discipline and academic standards are well below average. Compared to this situation which has great discipline and a great academic programme, all because of the principal and the entire staff including the cleaners and the gardeners dedication to this school. The school has helped me to better myself as a person. (A non-Catholic Christian)

Perhaps the following statement sums up the *genus loci,* both in its method of presentation and in the personal confidence it displays:

> The unique spirit is of togetherness and support. We are encouraged to be true, kind, respectful, loving, committed, determined, thankful and it DARES us to be DIFFERENT. It encourages us to be our very best and to acknowledge God at all times. (A non-Catholic Christian)

In discussion, the students agreed that their experiences of the school had been positive and all would recommend that their siblings attended too. They each spoke of the school as successful and different from others on the island. First they mentioned the 'discipline of the school'. One favoured the way that the school had high standards in regard to the ability to express themselves, and taught excellent grammar and language skills. Another spoke of the support the school gave when you chose to 'give 100% to a sport or project'.

They recognized too that one of the differences about attending a Catholic school is the 'ability to define yourselves as religious people'. One spoke of her hope that faith as part of the human condition might 'remain part of who I am'. In a similar vein, they saw the school retreats as 'wake-up calls – to help you see what kind of person you are'.

The second area about which comments were offered is that of the students' own sense of their personal development. Comments here included:

> In my school everyone works hard . . . and it does not matter if you are placed first or last but it matters if you try to the best of your ability. (A Catholic)

In discussion the students spoke of the main reasons for staying on at the school, rather than attending the local sixth-form college. They emphasized the 'high standards' which they and the school set for them; standards they argued emanated from their home backgrounds as well as from the school. They also argued that they had chosen the school rather than the general sixth form college because they believed that in college, 'you are left to your own devices'; in school, 'you have privileges as sixth-formers but you are also looked after'. They elaborated further their choice of attending the school rather than the college by explaining that the school 'offers both commercial skills and insights and preparation for commercial college' and 'personal maturity, while they still feel young; therefore they are not rushed into specific career choices'.

At the same time the students explained how the school offered the opportunity to work in a small enterprise development unit, which was sponsored by local banks and businesses. The local Chamber of Commerce sponsored students from different schools to run small companies. The companies must offer a product or solution which would assist and support either the poor or the elderly. As a result of their experiences in this development unit, five out of six of the students favoured setting up their own company. In this way they argued that they could increase local employment opportunities and improve the economy.

After school, the student's expectations differed. Two wished to leave the island to 'make money', then to 'come back and give something back to Country Y'. Two wished to go overseas to have 'real experiences'. Two wished to go to the United States or Europe for their further education, then return home to work in the professions.

All the students in the group discussed the approach which the school takes to 'measuring success'. The students are taught not to measure their success against each other but to look at themselves: 'what you judge is from inside you'. As a result, they argued, 'you just know how to do things well'.

The third area the students addressed was their engagement with the wider island community and their present and future roles in it. First they spoke of their enjoyment of the wide variety of sports and extra-curricular activities at the school, of which they must choose at least one. They were proud of their steel band and its success in local competitions, as well as their participation in major sporting events. The students also spoke of their awareness of the dependency of their island on other countries for basic resources but aligned themselves with other young people on the island who were no longer interested in agriculture as a way of life but instead favoured the opportunities offered by ICT.

Despite this enthusiasm and optimism, the students spoke of difficulties in acting out their ambitions. First they acknowledged that although there is a general friendliness on the island and that the events of 9/11 brought people together, there is a tendency that everyone fights for themselves as they perceive life getting harder. Second, they were beginning to understand that 'people just talk about what should be done'. They believed that 'we must get to solutions faster'. Equally they spoke of the 'breakdown of family life'; children were offered televisions and the internet but they were not monitored and the parents seemed to have little time for their children.

They summed up the methodology which the school employed in relating to and joining in with their community as:

> From the home they [the students] brought 'respect for people and charity' and the school taught them to take those values back into society.

When discussing changes they would like to see in the school, the students referred to two curriculum matters. The first refers to the religious foundation of the school and is, interestingly, made by a non-Catholic Christian:

> The change I would make is basically to create a curriculum in such a way that it would accommodate all students of other faiths in order that we all receive a well-rounded education.

The other developed the theme of the need for vocational education within the school, perhaps building on what was already provided, rather than emphasizing the distinction between the academic and the vocational in the school:

> I would change the curriculum to provide an even wider range of subjects to appeal to every student, for example, Technical Drawing, Accounts and Office Procedures. (A Catholic)

Behaviours

The students' highest personal goals were to:

- accept myself as the person I am;
- find God in my life;
- find personal happiness;
- live up to the example and teachings of Jesus.

The curriculum

The response to the majority of statements in Table 8.21 is very positive. Two statements received jointly the highest positive levels of agreement. These are 'the subjects offer useful knowledge and skills' and 'the subjects prepare students adequately for future employment'. A much more varied pattern of responses is seen in relation to the statement regarding there being too much emphasis in the curriculum on examinations.

Table 8.21 The curriculum: School C

	Certainly FALSE (%)	Probably FALSE (%)	Uncertain (%)	Probably TRUE (%)	Certainly TRUE (%)	Mean
Q78 The subjects taught offer useful knowledge or skills	–	–	–	18.4	81.6	4.82
Q81 The subjects taught here prepare students adequately for future employment	–	–	–	18.4	81.6	4.82
Q84 The school places sufficient emphasis on cultural activities (music, art, drama, etc)	2.0	–	4.1	10.2	83.7	4.73
Q80 The subjects taught in the school are relevant to real life and to students needs	–	4.1	2.0	22.4	71.4	4.61
Q75 There is a good sports programme in the school	–	–	12.2	16.3	71.4	4.59
Q77 The subjects offered develop the capacity for independent and critical thinking	2.0	2.0	4.1	22.4	69.4	4.55
Q79 The religious education programme is an important part of the curriculum	–	4.1	8.2	18.4	69.4	4.53
Q72 The curriculum of this school meets my present needs	4.1	4.1	4.1	32.7	55.1	4.31
Q76 The school offers a good range of subjects to older students	2.0	8.2	12.2	18.4	59.2	4.24
Q74 The out-of-school activities of the school have sufficient variety and scope	2.0	6.1	24.5	26.5	40.8	3.98
Q73 There are opportunities for students to get to know teachers outside the classroom	6.1	6.1	14.3	36.7	36.7	3.92
Q83 A Christian way of thinking is presented in the subjects taught here	2.0	12.2	38.8	26.5	20.4	3.51
Q82 The curriculum of the school is dominated too much by examinations	32.7	22.4	14.3	22.4	8.2	2.51

Again there is diversity in the responses to the statement regarding a Christian way of thinking being taught in all the subjects in the curriculum. Such a wide range of responses shown in the table might indicate either (a) that in some parts of the curriculum there is an explicit model of integrating a Christian way of thinking with a particular subject, for example, in religious education, and/or (b) that students perceive differing pedagogies, containing a variety of attitudes and values, in different ways. For example, if a religious sister teaches a particular subject and uses discussion and questioning techniques to elicit individual responses from each student and the student responds positively, then that student might connect such a pedagogy with the sister's overall lifestyle and not her professional bias towards a particular methodology.

Religious education

The response to the closed questions indicates some very positive levels of agreement among this group of students who expressed their belief in Table 8.21 above that RE is an important part of the school curriculum. In Table 8.22 it is clear that RE classes are not seen as a waste of time, nor should the time they do take be occupied by other subjects. Nearly 70 per cnet of the students did not believe either that RE classes were poorly prepared or taught. Other key areas of very high agreement were that:

- RE relates to real-life and personal needs;
- teachers allow sufficient time for discussion;
- RE helps students understand the meaning of life;
- the study of other religions helps students appreciate their own religion;
- RE helps individuals to form their own consciences.

The students jointly rated highly two aspects of RE in terms of their personal development; namely, the teaching of contemporary moral issues and the teaching of other religious and non-religious points of view. The table from this school makes very clear that the pedagogy favoured by this group of students includes discussion, presumably since it allowed time for an exploration of personal attitudes and values towards important areas of contemporary moral and social concern. The students' response also indicates that the methods employed to teach about other religions and non-religious positions, in some way, engages the students sufficiently so that they not only begin to appreciate aspects of their own religion but also are conscious that they are responsible for forming their own consciences.

The data indicate, too, that the school, at least partially through its religious education programme, has responded successfully to two major aspirations of the students. They have indicated that they hoped the school would assist them in achieving a high standard in their school work (score: 4.71) and second, that it would provide an environment in which students' faith in God can develop (score: 4.61). According to Table 8.22, the students believe very

Table 8.22 Religious education: School C

	Certainly FALSE (%)	Probably FALSE (%)	Uncertain (%)	Probably TRUE (%)	Certainly TRUE (%)	Mean
Q89 RE classes are related to real life and to my needs	6.1	–	8.2	22.4	63.3	4.37
Q93 RE teachers allow sufficient time for discussion	2.0	8.2	6.1	30.6	53.1	4.24
Q108 RE classes help me to understand the meaning of life	10.4	2.1	4.2	27.1	56.3	4.17
Q87 The study of other religions has helped me appreciate my own religion	6.1	4.1	18.4	20.4	51.0	4.06
Q102 RE classes help me to form my own conscience	6.1	8.2	10.2	28.6	46.9	4.02
Q100 Contemporary moral issues are given emphasis in RE classes	2.1	6.3	20.8	33.3	37.5	3.98
Q106 RE classes have helped me understand other religious and non-religious points of view	10.2	6.1	12.2	28.6	42.9	3.88
Q98 RE classes have deepened my understanding of the Catholic tradition	10.4	10.4	8.3	25.0	45.8	3.85
Q86 I am enjoying RE classes this year	14.3	10.2	8.2	20.4	46.9	3.76
Q90 RE classes are not taken seriously by students	8.2	10.2	14.3	34.7	32.7	3.73
Q94 This school has a good RE programme for older students	2.0	18.4	26.5	14.3	38.8	3.69
Q96 RE classes have helped me to understand the Gospels	14.3	10.2	12.2	26.5	36.7	3.61
Q91 If RE classes were voluntary, I would still attend them	14.3	8.2	20.4	22.4	34.7	3.55
Q104 RE classes have helped me to pray	20.8	10.4	2.1	27.1	39.6	3.54
Q97 RE classes have shown me the place of the Eucharist in Catholic life	21.3	8.5	27.7	12.8	29.8	3.21
Q105 I do not know my Catholic faith well enough	22.0	7.3	29.3	12.2	29.3	3.20
Q103 Assessment through assignments or examinations should form part of RE	24.5	8.2	20.4	20.4	26.5	3.16
Q95 RE is taught at a level comparable with that of other subjects	18.4	12.2	28.6	18.4	22.4	3.14
Q101 Christian marriage has been treated in sufficient depth in RE classes	25.0	12.5	25.0	16.7	20.8	2.96
Q99 Basic Catholic values and moral teachings are not taught in RE classes	43.8	25.0	12.5	6.3	12.5	2.19
Q92 RE classes are poorly prepared and taught	46.9	22.4	16.3	8.2	6.1	2.04
Q107 RE classes take up too much time which should be devoted to other subjects	67.3	10.2	8.2	6.1	8.2	1.78
Q88 RE classes are largely a waste of time	69.4	12.2	4.1	10.2	4.1	1.67

strongly that their RE classes are related to real-life and personal needs and they help them understand the meaning of life. This would suggest that the content and pedagogy of those classes is able to touch their faith, commitments and personal concerns.

During the extraordinarily intensive period of global concern with religion which formed the backdrop to the case study at this school, being only two months after the events of 9/11, it is noteworthy that such a high proportion of the students believed that the study of other religions in RE succeeded in helping them appreciate their own. They emphasized too that RE had caused them to understand other religious and non-religious points of view. The data indicating that RE also contributed to the students' developing individual consciences might suggest that the students use both the content of their RE programme and the elements of its pedagogy to reflect on the values and attitudes which form the kernel of their individual consciences. If this is the case, then it would be important in a further study to examine those characteristics of teaching an epistemology of values for living in a complex plurality which are to be found within some faith-based schools. For the present it is only possible to ask the question whether a student is given more or less assistance in becoming aware of his/her values, and being conscious of where they come from, and what actions might result from them, within an RE programme that is 'tethered' to a particular faith tradition.

School D

There were twenty-three boys and seventeen girls who responded to the questionnaire. The sample relating to the open-ended questions comprised (i) ten Catholics; (ii) two non-Catholic Christian females; and (iii) one non-Christian religious male.

Beliefs

In School D, in which the majority of the student sample were Catholic, the students' highest values and beliefs were expressed in scores of three lots of 5 and the fourth, 4.97 and were:

- People should be respected whatever their race, nationality or religion;
- I believe in God;
- God is a loving Father;
- Jesus Christ is truly God.

Table 8.23   Students' religious beliefs: School D

Catholic (%)	Other Christian faith (%)	Non-Christian religion (%)
92.5	5.0	2.5

Table 8.24   Parents' religious beliefs: School D

	Practising Catholic (%)	Non-practising Catholic (%)	Other Christian faith (%)	Non-Christian religion (%)	No Religion (%)
Mother's religion	92.5	–	5.0	2.5	–
Father's religion	87.5	–	2.5	10.0	–

School life and climate

Students' highest expectations of their school were for it to:

- help students to discover and fulfil themselves as persons;
- provide and environment in which students' faith in God can develop;
- give all students a chance of success in some aspect of school life;
- prepare students for their future careers.

Some 90 per cent of the students say they are happy at the school, with a further 7.5 per cent thinking this is probably true. This very positive finding is reflected in the words of one Catholic male student who wrote that 'there is a spirit of being one family and togetherness as well as good relationships between teachers and students and among students'.

Other important findings in this table include:

- students' high esteem for the school and its staff and their 'feeling of pride' in belonging there;
- students' absolute sense that the things they are taught are worthwhile;
- students' strong sense that the school rules encourage self-discipline and responsibility;
- students' very clear perception that the headteacher encourages a sense of community and belonging to the school and a less clear but still strong view that a good spirit of community exists among final year students.

It is also important to note that, although a high proportion of the students speak of a happy atmosphere at the school, there is a less clear commitment to wanting to attend a Catholic school, if they 'had to do it all again'. Responses to two questions raise a challenging issue. Although 30 per cent say it is probably true, and 30 per cent say it is certainly true that the headteacher places importance on the religious nature of the school, an even higher proportion, that is, 37 per cent and 32.5 per cent, respectively, agree they would send their children to a Catholic school. The data would seem to suggest some kind of ambivalence, perhaps, among the students about the religious nature of the school. So, although 97.5 per cent speak very positively indeed of the headteacher's encouragement of a sense of community, it is unclear whether they perceive the basis of that community spirit as religious, educational or

Table 8.25 School life and climate: School D

	Certainly FALSE (%)	Probably FALSE (%)	Uncertain (%)	Probably TRUE (%)	Certainly TRUE (%)	Mean
Q53 The things I am taught are worthwhile learning	–	–	–	15.0	85.0	4.85
Q65 The Principal encourages a sense of community and belonging to the school	–	–	2.5	12.5	85.0	4.83
Q71 School rules here encourage self-discipline and responsibility	–	–	10.0	12.5	77.5	4.68
Q63 I feel proud to be a student of this school	–	–	7.5	17.5	75.0	4.67
Q66 I have been happy at school	–	2.5	7.5	17.5	72.5	4.60
Q59 There is a happy atmosphere in the school	–	–	12.5	20.0	67.5	4.55
Q48 Adequate counselling help is available to students	–	–	12.5	25.0	62.5	4.50
Q42 This school has a good name in the local community	–	–	5.0	42.5	52.5	4.47
Q37 Most teachers are well qualified and have good teaching skills	–	2.5	5.0	42.5	50.0	4.40
Q56 A good spirit of community exists among final year students	2.5	2.5	7.5	32.5	55.0	4.35
Q39 Most teachers in this school show a good deal of school spirit	2.5	–	15.0	27.5	55.0	4.32
Q43 I can approach the Principal for advice and help	–	5.0	15.0	25.0	55.0	4.30
Q57 Most teachers go out of their way to help you	–	2.5	10.0	42.5	45.0	4.30
Q60 Catholic teachers here set an example of what it means to be a practising Catholic	–	2.5	12.5	37.5	47.5	4.30
Q62 Most other students are very friendly	–	2.5	12.5	37.5	47.5	4.30
Q55 Other students accept me as I am	–	2.5	17.5	30.0	50.0	4.27
Q36 Students here think a lot of their school	2.5	5.0	10.0	32.5	50.0	4.22
Q46 Most teachers carry out their work with energy and pleasure	2.5	7.5	7.5	37.5	45.0	4.15

Question						Mean
Q35 The relationships between parents and staff are very friendly	–	2.5	32.5	25.0	40.0	4.03
Q70 If students have difficulty with school work, most teachers take time to help them	2.5	5.0	15.0	42.5	35.0	4.03
Q38 Students here know the standard of conduct expected of them	–	2.5	42.5	12.5	42.5	3.95
Q45 Senior students understand and accept the religious goals of the school	–	5.1	28.2	33.3	33.3	3.95
Q67 I would send my children to a Catholic school	2.5	2.5	25.0	37.5	32.5	3.95
Q69 If I had to do it all over again, I would attend a Catholic school	2.5	2.5	37.5	25.0	32.5	3.83
Q52 I am treated with respect by other people at school	2.5	5.0	27.5	37.5	27.5	3.82
Q47 Discipline presents no real problem in this school	7.5	5.0	27.5	22.5	37.5	3.77
Q51 Everyone tries to make you feel at home in this school	2.6	10.3	30.8	33.3	23.1	3.64
Q41 Most teachers know their final year students as individual persons	–	5.0	47.5	30.0	17.5	3.60
Q58 The Principal places importance on the religious nature of the school	7.5	15.0	17.5	30.0	30.0	3.60
Q61 Most teachers show that people are more important than rules	7.5	15.0	47.5	22.5	7.5	3.07
Q64 There are ways to have school rules changed if most students disagree with them	12.5	30.0	30.0	17.5	10.0	2.83
Q40 Final year students here are not given enough real freedom	27.5	20.0	22.5	27.5	2.5	2.58
Q68 Most teachers never explain why they ask you to do things around here	27.5	30.0	17.5	20.0	5.0	2.45
Q50 This school places too much emphasis on external conformity to rules and regulations	42.5	22.5	15.0	12.5	7.5	2.20
Q44 I feel depressed at school	72.5	15.0	2.5	10.0	–	1.50
Q49 This school is a place where I feel lonely	75.0	17.5	2.5	–	5.0	1.43
Q54 This school is a place where I feel worried	67.5	30.0	–	2.5	–	1.38

personal. On the other hand, in this group of students where the overwhelming majority are Catholic, 85 per cent think it is probably or certainly true that the Catholic teachers in the school set an example of what it means to be a Catholic. A question arises whether there is any dichotomy in the students' experience between the religious and educational culture of the school. In this respect it is interesting to speculate on the distribution of percentages among the students agreeing or not with the statement, 'senior students understand and accept the religious goals of the school'. Although two-thirds believe this to be certainly or probably true, a further third are uncertain or believe it to be probably false.

Finally, the even distribution of percentages which can be seen in response to the statement, 'I am treated with respect by other people at school' can perhaps be related to the responses to two other statements; namely, 'other students accept me as I am' and 'students here know the standard of conduct expected of them'. A high percentage of students believe that other students accept them as they are, whereas 42.5 per cent are uncertain about the standard of conduct expected of them and yet a further 42.5 per cent think it is certainly true that they know the standard of conduct expected of them. The matter of perception of standards of conduct must surely be tied to each student's developing and maturing identity as they prepare to leave school. A frustration can be sensed from the distribution of percentages of students who disagree that they are 'not given enough real freedom'. Nonetheless, a positive picture emerges of the adequacy of counselling arrangements.

Students' attitudes and values towards the school

Agents of community spirit

In Table 8.26, students' valuing of respect as of utmost importance is presented together with their attitudes towards two other major aspects of community building.

Table 8.26   Agents of community spirit: School D

	Certainly FALSE (%)	Probably FALSE (%)	Uncertain (%)	Probably TRUE (%)	Certainly TRUE (%)	Mean
Q117 People should be respected whatever their race, nationality or religion	–	–	–	–	100.0	5.00
Q65 The Principal encourages a sense of community and belonging to the school	–	–	2.5	12.5	85.0	4.83
Q113 I try to be friendly and helpful to others who are rejected or lonely	–	–	27.5	52.5	20.0	3.92

The absolute value placed on respect for persons indicates that students within the school register this value as the basis for their attitudes and responses to other people, whether fellow students or people in their community in general. In this school, the students' high level of commitment to this value must surely reflect in part the national tradition in the five-point plan of respect for people whatever their race, nationality or religion.

The high value placed on the role of the principal in fostering the 'sense of community' experienced within the school is also noteworthy. The distribution of certainty among the students to their personal attitude to those who are rejected or lonely raises certain issues. For example, has the emphasis on the 'I' in this statement as opposed to 'people' in the first statement elicited an act of reflection on the part of the students about their personal conduct in differing situations. This latter statement might therefore appear to be about a general principle or value in action which is worth holding as a human being, as distinct from a testament to their personal conduct at all times. Nonetheless, there was still a high degree of assent to the statement concerning their attitude to others who are lonely or rejected. In this regard, a personal comment made by a student from this school about the poor and rejected among his/her own age group showed a real concern for others and a suggestion for bringing about some kind of justice in the matter:

> Provide grants (to attend this school) to the have-nots who are brilliant.
> (A Catholic female)

The response to the statement (Q110) from the students in this school reflects a deep commitment to the homeless and disadvantaged in society. It might also provide further evidence of their positive attitude to a value concerned with social and moral relations in general as distinct from a statement which asks them to reflect on their individual actions in the moral sphere.

Students' comments

The students' comments in the open-ended questions reflect their commitment to values of respect and concern for others. One Catholic male student wrote that their school 'respects others, there is no discrimination and there is honesty'. It was also noted by a non-Christian religious female that the school works with a 'spirit of implementing high discipline and educating students to become successful persons'. Thus the students value the school's twin foci on respect and commitment to others while helping its students to become successful persons. Several other students, including Catholics, non-Catholic Christians and non-Christian religious, referred to 'the school having its own characteristics, such as promoting discipline in school life' and so they argued 'the students are trained to be self-disciplined and responsible persons'. Another student spoke of the school's 'attempt to shape the good personality of the students which is in accordance with Christian values'. Despite such a positive claim to value the school because of its emphasis on discipline and the development of certain kinds of human being, one Catholic male student called for a change in emphasis on discipline because, 'It has got to be realized that human beings are more important than regulations. Discipline must be implemented but a Catholic school should see the human dimension'.

Noteworthy, too, among the comments was one which spoke about the mission of a Catholic school to foster good Catholic students, when writing, 'I appreciate the school because it lays stress on religious education which is useful for my future in order to become a real Catholic'. Another Catholic female speculated on the changes which would be most important in the school. Perhaps her comment related to the paucity of resources which private schools might accept in order to stay educationally viable:

> Change would be for more extracurricular activities. I don't have chance to grow my youth spirit – that is through activities such as camping, hiking, red cross.

Certainly the student's words echoed a note made during the interview with the headteacher when he spoke of the continuing need for vigilance to ensure that the school developed adequate IT, sports and cultural resources in order to compete with other private schools in the area. Perhaps too the headteacher would have agreed with the following extract from a Catholic male student:

> The school is actively concerned with its development, either to improve its achievement or its reputation. Even though the product is not always satisfactory, I find the process more important.

Overall, the students' comments and valuing about the uniqueness of their school might best be summarized in this extract from a Catholic male:

> The way the school educates and trains the students to obey the school rules; the encouraging of a sense of responsibility; the education of how to live in society according to religious practice; and how to solve a problem without hurting other people; and lessons on vocational guidance.

Behaviours

Students' highest personal goals were to:

- find God in my life;
- live up to the examples and teachings of Jesus;

- accept myself as the person I am;
- be happily married.

The curriculum

The majority of responses to the statements concerning the school curriculum are positive. The two statements receiving the most positive agreement are, 'the subjects offered develop the capacity for independent and critical thinking' and 'the subjects taught offer useful knowledge and skills'. Other distributions of percentages which tend towards the very positive end of the five-point scale refer to:

- religious education as an important part of the curriculum;
- the curriculum meeting the students' present needs;
- the good range of the subject offer and the subjects taught being relevant to real life;
- opportunities for students to get to know teachers outside the classroom.

There is a positive response to the idea that a Christian way of thinking is presented in the subjects taught at the school. Nonetheless, a specific form of Christian pedagogy does not emerge from Table 8.27 as the key element within the overall curriculum experience of the students. This might suggest that the higher ranking of religious education as an important part of the curriculum fulfils students' expectations of meeting up with a Christian way of thinking within the curriculum.

Those responses whose direction on the five-point scale indicate a less positive direction underline a major characteristic of the group who responded to the questionnaires; namely, a real diversity of thinking on two critical matters. First, the statement suggesting that the curriculum is over dominated by examinations draws a diverse range of responses. Whether the students responded in terms of their own successes or failures in terms of examinations, or whether they reflected on the high stakes involved in the national system of examinations for school leavers is, of course, uncertain. At this point it is helpful, perhaps, to note the less positive response to the question of whether subjects prepare the students for future employment. The students might rightly reflect on the present division in the upper secondary schools between the academic in which they are studying and the vocational schools which the government is seeking to develop and enhance. The identities, interests and backgrounds of the individual students must surely, too, have influenced their response to the statement concerning the level of emphasis on cultural activities in the school. Responses are distributed reasonably evenly.

Religious education

The students' responses to the closed questions concerning religious education show an overwhelmingly positive response. The students not only value

Table 8.27 The curriculum: School D

	Certainly FALSE (%)	Probably FALSE (%)	Uncertain (%)	Probably TRUE (%)	Certainly TRUE (%)	Mean
Q77 The subjects offered develop the capacity for independent and critical thinking	–	–	7.5	25.0	67.5	4.60
Q78 The subjects taught offer useful knowledge or skills	–	–	10.0	25.0	65.0	4.55
Q76 The school offers a good range of subjects to older students	2.5	2.5	2.5	35.0	57.5	4.43
Q79 The religious education programme is an important part of the curriculum	–	2.5	7.5	45.0	45.0	4.33
Q72 The curriculum of this school meets my present needs	–	2.5	12.5	40.0	45.0	4.27
Q80 The subjects taught in the school are relevant to real life and to students needs	–	2.5	15.0	42.5	40.0	4.20
Q73 There are opportunities for students to get to know teachers outside the classroom	–	–	25.0	37.5	37.5	4.13
Q83 A Christian way of thinking is presented in the subjects taught here	–	10.0	12.5	45.0	32.5	4.00
Q75 There is a good sports programme in the school	–	7.5	22.5	37.5	32.5	3.95
Q81 The subjects taught here prepare students adequately for future employment	–	2.5	20.0	60.0	17.5	3.93
Q74 The out-of-school activities of the school have sufficient variety and scope	2.5	15.0	25.0	40.0	17.5	3.55
Q84 The school places sufficient emphasis on cultural activities (music, art, drama, etc)	7.5	27.5	25.0	30.0	10.0	3.08
Q82 The curriculum of the school is dominated too much by examinations	12.5	25.0	15.0	40.0	7.5	3.05

the content of the subject and the care teachers take in their preparation but also its relevance to their immediate lives. They also affirm their view that they welcome RE as part of the whole curriculum, rate its teaching on a par with other subjects and do not perceive it as a waste of time.

Dominating the students' understanding of the place of RE in their lives and the curriculum of the school are four key areas:

1. The formation of their own conscience.
2. Their relationship to real life and to their needs.
3. Their ability to help them to understand the meaning of life.
4. The place of the Eucharist in Catholic life.

In relation to the first point, it is worth speculating about three matters which arise. First, the students have already shown a sensitivity when reflecting on their personal commitment to certain key values. The level of their positive response to statements beginning with 'I' was lower than those which began 'people', giving rise to speculation that the students were indeed searching their own conscience as to whether they had fully put into practice a key moral value. In Table 8.28 relating to religious education, the students affirm that the development of conscience is a major concern for them and for religious education in the school. Second, the conviction attached to the level of response about the formation of conscience prompts an external researcher to wish to explore the nature of the RE curriculum and its pedagogy in order to ascertain how such personal security in autonomy is achieved among the students within the confines of a Catholic curriculum taught chiefly to Catholic students. Third, there is among the students' responses in general throughout the questionnaire a sense of 'conscientization' among them.

This has been captured, for example, in their awareness of, and commitment to, the needs of the homeless and the poor, in the midst of whom many of the students live. Perhaps, the very positive response among these students to several other key statements within this RE section of the questionnaire points to elements of the curriculum which foster such 'conscientization'. They speak very positively of RE classes 'helping them understand the meaning of life', 'the place of the Eucharist in Catholic life', the 'understanding of the Gospels' they have received, and the emphasis given to 'contemporary moral issues'.

Aligned to this curriculum which is rich in both Catholic and Christian teaching and commitment, there is evidence from the students that their values and attitudes are also formed by 'religious and non-religious points of view' and that 'the study of religions other than my own have helped me appreciate my own religion'. Equally, it is important to note that 80 per cent of the students said that they had 'enjoyed their RE classes this year'.

Table 8.28 Religious education: School D

	Certainly FALSE (%)	Probably FALSE (%)	Uncertain (%)	Probably TRUE (%)	Certainly TRUE (%)	Mean
Q102 RE classes help me to form my own conscience	–	–	7.5	17.5	75.0	4.67
Q89 RE classes are related to real life and to my needs	–	2.5	5.0	17.5	75.0	4.65
Q108 RE classes help me to understand the meaning of life	–	–	5.0	30.0	65.0	4.60
Q97 RE classes have shown me the place of the Eucharist in Catholic life	–	–	7.5	27.5	65.0	4.58
Q98 RE classes have deepened my understanding of the Catholic tradition	–	–	12.5	22.5	65.0	4.53
Q96 RE classes have helped me to understand the Gospels	–	–	7.5	32.5	60.0	4.52
Q101 Christian marriage has been treated in sufficient depth in RE classes	–	–	5.0	45.0	50.0	4.45
Q106 RE classes have helped me understand other religious and non-religious points of view	–	5.0	5.0	30.0	60.0	4.45
Q91 If RE classes were voluntary, I would still attend them	–	2.5	12.5	25.0	60.0	4.43
Q95 RE is taught at a level comparable with that of other subjects	–	2.5	10.0	30.0	57.5	4.43
Q104 RE classes have helped me to pray	–	2.5	12.5	27.5	57.5	4.40
Q94 This school has a good RE programme for older students	–	2.5	10.0	37.5	50.0	4.35
Q87 The study of other religions has helped me appreciate my own religion	–	2.5	12.5	40.0	45.0	4.27
Q86 I am enjoying RE classes this year	5.0	7.5	7.5	37.5	42.5	4.05
Q100 Contemporary moral issues are given emphasis in RE classes	2.5	7.5	7.5	47.5	35.0	4.05
Q93 RE teachers allow sufficient time for discussion	2.5	12.5	27.5	25.0	32.5	3.73
Q103 Assessment through assignments or examinations should form part of RE	5.0	12.5	27.5	42.5	12.5	3.45
Q90 RE classes are not taken seriously by students	22.5	27.5	20.0	25.0	5.0	2.62
Q105 I do not know my Catholic faith well enough	32.5	27.5	15.0	25.0	–	2.32
Q92 RE classes are poorly prepared and taught	60.0	22.5	10.0	7.5	–	1.65
Q99 Basic Catholic values and moral teachings are not taught in RE classes	62.5	32.5	2.5	2.5	–	1.45
Q88 RE classes are largely a waste of time	75.0	15.0	2.5	7.5	–	1.43
Q107 RE classes take up too much time which should be devoted to other subjects	72.5	17.5	5.0	5.0	–	1.42

Lessons Learnt from the Four Schools about the Significance of the Student Voice in a Study of School Cultures

Listening to the student voice permits an insight into the personal understanding of individuals and groups of students as they reflect on their relationship with themselves, their peers, teachers, parents and others in the communities they inhabit. Their voices draw attention to the need for further examination of aspects of their living, learning and valuing within their school cultures, particularly in two areas. First, there is a need to look at those which embed the individual into their school culture so that they respond positively to their learning environment. Second, more understanding is required of those aspects of a school culture which permit the individual to learn and make meaning about themselves as people, and the cultures which they inhabit, in a way that is both satisfying and personally crafted, and achieved without undue intellectual or cultural pressure on their autonomy.

A previous chapter proposed with Roberts (2000: 1) that Freire 'theorized an intimate connection between education and the process of becoming more fully human'. The students in this study widely indicated that one of their most pressing goals was to 'accept myself as the person I am'. Here was a signal of intentionality in the students' voice. The human persons that they were or aspired to become must find acceptance within each student's self. Their wider profiles in terms of their values, attitudes and beliefs showed the kinds of human beings they were or wished to be. For example, they widely committed themselves to the respect of others, whatever their race, nationality or religion and they recognized the significance of their parents' trust and love in their lives. Importantly, too, they saw a link between their faith and the kind of people they were. Finally, the great majority of this group of students claimed that their beliefs were increasingly based on their own convictions rather than those of others.

The analysis of the data presented from individual schools experimented with finding connections between the students expressed agreement with, or liking for, aspects of the school's life, climate and curriculum and the kind of aspirations they held for their time at the school, their personal goals and religious education. Such analysis was a means of excavating the manner in which differing aspects of a school culture touched, and sometimes permeated, an individual's search for knowledge and meaning.

The discovery of the ways different schools and different students achieved this focus on human development is made apparent partly through the tables of data, partly through individual students' comments and partly through the commentary offered on responses to statements about religious education in each school. Those commentaries were offered from three perspectives already discussed in earlier chapters: the national, sociointellectual and cultural contexts of the countries in which each school was situated; the attitudes of the students towards the religious and non-religious traditions or world views that they encountered in their lessons;

and the impact which the study of religion or faith might have on individual human growth.

The kind of educated person who emerges from each of the school cultures can be gleaned from the data contained in 'the student voice'. This chapter has also recorded whether the students in each school believed themselves to be happy in the school. On the one hand, this information provides an important insight into the nature and practice of the school culture and its impact on each student. On the other, it acts as a predictor of the student's lifelong attitude to continuing education and development. The data also provide evidence of the student's concern that religious education should, on the whole, be related to real-life and personal needs. If the evidence can also show that the students believed that RE was meeting their concerns and needs, then it might be anticipated that at least some of the attitudes and values which the students were developing during their time in school will be deployed by them when as mature citizens they approach certain social, personal, religious and cultural situations. Similarly, there is evidence from the data that the students have learnt about religious and non-religious ideas which differ from their own. They say that they have used this knowledge as a means of appreciating their own point of view and to form their own consciences. It might, therefore, be predicted that such students will be willing and able to meet up with many differing world views and commitments as mature citizens and find their own way of responding in an educated manner. All of this is in some ways a matter of speculation.

The reason, however, for letting the students speak for themselves within a separate chapter is so that the value of such a major part of the research/audit methodology might become more apparent. On the one hand, the empirical study stands as a means of introducing evidence-based discussion into policy making in relation to the kinds of educated students who emerge from certain schools. It permits an in-depth study into the kinds of cultures and practices which faith communities contribute to the overall educational endeavour of a country. On the other, it acts as a prompt to a plural society to put on its agenda a debate based on the evidence from empirical studies about the place of religion in education. The future of individual communal and personal identities is to some important extent dependent on this debate.

The extent to which students have experienced communities with a real sense of belonging and cohesion as part of their formal education is currently understood in England to be critical to a good education. The time is therefore propitious to evaluate the potential for searching out examples of good practice in schools which provide an enhanced sense of inclusion and community for their students, while at the same time offering a successful academic and vocational education. In this way, schools offering a community in which their students can learn, and develop in, those fundamental aspects of being human might be said to be taking a positive role in community-wide development for as Chodorkoff (1990: 71) has argued:

> True community development from the perspective of social ecology must be a holistic process, which integrates all facets of a community's life. Social, political, economic, artistic, ethical and spiritual dimensions must all be seen as part of a whole. For this reason, the development process must proceed from a self-conscious understanding of their relationships.

The questionnaire and interview process described here has provided a means by which a number of future citizens of plural societies have been able to reflect upon their 'self-conscious understanding of their relationships' within their individual schools. The extent to which their reflection permits a sufficient view of the school culture to make an evaluation of each school as a sustainable epistemic community for learning in, and about, living and being human in a complex plurality will be discussed in the next chapter. It is possible to argue, however, that the richness of the student voice found here positively indicates that it is worthwhile to evaluate the effectiveness of a school culture in meeting the faith and educational aspirations of its students through the use of self-completion surveys and interviews.

The information contained in this chapter, together with that in Chapter 7, completes the profiles of the four Catholic schools. In the next chapter a composite profile of this particular group of schools will be developed in order to evaluate which factors within a school culture contribute to its distinctiveness.

Chapter 9

Building a Meta-Narrative of School Cultures from a Composite Profile of Four Faith Schools

Purpose of the Chapter

The profiles of each school developed in Chapters 7 and 8 provide a means of testing the climate of their cultures. This chapter will therefore critically examine the means by which the faith and world views of the students were met and included in each school's culture; the extent to which students were taught to be critical and educated about their own and other people's world views; and the extent to which each culture sustained, and was sustained by, an effective epistemic community for being educated in a plural society. The examination takes the form of interrogating the meta-knowledge gained from the study of the four Catholic schools, asking what can be learnt about (a) the *genus loci* of each of these schools; (b) the schools as mediating institutions; (c) the attitudes and values of students preparing to graduate from those schools; (d) these schools as epistemic communities of the human condition; and (e) faith as the foundation of the four schools. Resulting from this examination a summative statement will be made about the purposes of education inherent in the four cultures.

The chapter concludes that empirical studies of faith schools which can tell an informed story about how a faith foundation impinges on the way a school sets about educating its students are particularly urgent. If some faith schools are seen as educating effectively and distinctively both for the common good and for individual personal flourishing, then a meta-narrative of the particulars of such school cultures might enhance such discussion.

Perspectives from the Four Schools: Cooperating in a Study of How Best to Meet the Human and Economic Needs of Young People in Late Modern Times

One of the most striking features of the data presented in the previous chapter was the similarity in the responses from the students across the four schools. When I set out to enquire into the cultures of the schools set as they were in widely varied geographical and political contexts, I had expected to find not only differences in their organization and management but also in the students' expectations, concerns and attitudes towards them. I had also expected to find marked differences between the personal beliefs, values and attitudes within the student cohorts taking part in the study. In the light of the similarities, it will be important to try to discover whether there are common building blocks to be found in the construction and educational environment provided by each school. Second, it will be worthwhile to explore the relationship between the overall purpose of education which emerges from this study of school cultures with the attitudes and values espoused by the students.

One of the most privileged features of this study has been the opportunity to ask questions about what kind of human beings educators are hoping young people will become at the beginning of the twenty-first century. The process of engaging in a structured enquiry through collaboration with colleagues in these four very different schools encouraged a feeling of mutual discovery and shared concern about the key elements of being an educated human being in these complex, plural and global times. The shared mapping of concepts, values and behaviours underlying education in and for faith in turn raised questions about the fitness for purpose of all schools in plural societies.

A most important benefit of a comparative educational study is that participation in such a study encourages the growth of a meta-knowledge. Lankshear (1997: 72) defines such meta-knowledge as 'knowing about the nature of that practice, its constitutive values and beliefs, its meaning and significance and how it relates to other practices'. In one school the headteacher invited me to join a regular senior management team meeting. An item on its agenda as to whether the school should join a collaborative venture of Catholic schools through east and southern Africa prompted a most important discussion. It focused on the value of reflection on the nature and practice of Catholic schools which the team considered this present study had generated among the staff. A review of the practices of the school which related to its Catholic foundation was then added to the regular senior team meetings on a termly basis and the team made the decision to join the collaborative programme of Catholic schools.

The enhanced understanding which arises from a developing meta-knowledge has arisen here from a keen awareness of the importance of context in the study of faith school cultures; the observation of a number of alternative school cultures in practice; and critical reflection on the nature and practice of school cultures among practitioners and between practitioners within an empirical research methodology. Such was indeed the value of this partnership approach to re-thinking this particular concept map of faith in education that it underlined the need for continuing international cooperation, at both local and national levels, for human development through education in general. In particular, it pointed to the value of follow-up studies concerning new paradigms for policy development concerned with how best to develop schools which serve both the economic and the human development needs of the young people in both the North and the South. Similar studies of faith schools in different countries could prove a most valuable catalyst to such discussion.

Learning from the Meta-Knowledge: What Can We Know about the *Genus Loci* of Individual School Cultures?

The distinctive nature of each school culture was made apparent through a number of the research strategies within the study. These strategies included an examination of school prospectuses and handbooks; discussion with the headteacher and senior teachers about their policies and behaviours; analysis of the students' self-review and their comments during interview; the nature of the curriculum and understanding of whether it included vocational guidance and teaching among its academic programme and, particularly, the purpose and practice of religious education.

In discussion with the head of religious education in a school in Country X, for example, her concern for the safety and security of young people in school was a priority. She spoke of many students from single-parent homes; the break up of marriages had become a national problem. She also discussed elements of indigenous African religion, in which there are traditions where women are beaten. There was also a high proportion of child suicides. For the sister, the question here is, 'Is there someone who can help children with their problems; someone who can listen?' One headteacher defined her role as a 'champion/ advocate of children', called to 'build the Kingdom', through integrating a holistic philosophy into the organization of a school of 720 students. This, the headteacher argued, was to be achieved through 'the building of community' in which each person expresses love or care, thereby 'opening up the individual to growth and freedom'. She saw this of particular importance in an environment which was often hostile for the students and in which they encountered anger and abuse. The community of the school should provide them with an 'experience of love and growth'.

The *genus loci* found in each of the schools in the study suggests that their cultures provided a happy environment, a place where students were comfortable and ready to learn. Most of all the students felt they belonged to a community, much of which owed its spirit and conduct to the leadership of the headteacher. This indeed appears to be the case in terms of the positive learning outcomes which were recorded by the students and their very positive agreement with the statement, 'I have been happy at the school'. Notwithstanding these particular findings, there remains the question of the place of corporal punishment in two of these school cultures, partly as a result of Ministry of Education guidelines.

Enquiring what might constitute the *genus loci* of each culture prompted a significant finding that each of the schools had a very strong sense of place within its local town or city and within its nation. Asking questions about the nature of the town or city helped to locate the school in its nested ecology. Asking the school about its role in the town or the country prompted some illuminating conversations about their very particular understandings of that role.

One school promoted a significant view of the role of the home in personal and community development. It believed that the students brought values and talents from their home: it was then the duty of the school to teach the students to take those same values and talents back out into the community through their education. A former student of one of the schools in Country X had written that the school provided for 'people with different backgrounds, age groups, and even cultures to share ideas in a common meeting ground'.

This comment is most instructive about the particular sense of place experienced in the school within a country that continues to be the scene of a plurality of ethnic divisions and tensions. It is therefore significant to find that the students in the two schools from that country, under the section in the questionnaire on personal goals, made a very positive and strong response to the statement that their personal goal was 'to make lifelong friendships with other people'. At the same time, all the students made clear that they were aware of their school's esteem in the local and national community and were proud to belong.

Learning from the Meta-Knowledge: What Can We Learn about Schools as Mediating Institutions?

There were many examples provided of the schools acting as mediating institutions within their often fraught and sometimes violent societies. There was a sense that each of the schools believed its task was to explain what education contributed to their students and their country. At a policy level, the headteachers built partnerships across towns, cities, schools and communities because they believed that they could not achieve on their own a good education for their students. They clearly and patiently explained the purposes and values of education to their partners, the students and their parents. Frequently, too, the students wrote about the importance of education and about the *genus loci* of their school. One of their poems used the imagery of precious metals to great effect in a country whose mineral resources are the key to much human development, stability and educational provision.

The student voice made clear that the secure and purposeful learning environment which each of the schools provided was the base for an education which did indeed meet their needs and wants. A headteacher spoke also of planning changes in the shape and culture of the school in order to meet the challenges of the new era; an era he said which will be marked by 'competition linked to globalization'. He spoke of 'radical administrative and academic programmes being currently implemented' in order to return the school to its former position of being 'a centre for quality education'.

Learning from the Meta-Knowledge: What Can We Know about the Students' Attitudes and Values?

The sense of responsibility found in the student voice to their peers, their fellow citizens, to their God, to their environment and to themselves was also very clear. They wished to be honest in their dealings with others, to accept themselves as they are, to find God in their lives and to live up to the examples and teachings of Jesus. The highest values to which they were committed were 'respect for others whatever their race, nationality or religion' and respect for the environment. Significantly Flynn obtained the same results. Carr (2004: 29) argues that values are not 'primarily beliefs but rather rational dispositions or principle preferences which are plumbed into practical human affairs'. As such he believes that 'they are apt for appraisal in terms of the practical rather than the theoretical aspects of human life'. Each school offered examples of the practical consequences of their beliefs.

The student voice provided insights into how these values were influential in the students' present understanding of the kinds of learning in which they engaged as a community. Primarily the students wished to have knowledge, skills and understanding which were useful and prepared them for future employment and which fostered in them the capacity for independent and critical thinking. Their strong views on the state of cultural education in their schools, including music, art and drama suggested that they believed their curriculum experience was gravely deficient if their school was not offering an adequate experience of these. There were similar strong views about sport, with one student bemoaning his inability to 'grow his youth spirit' because of the lack of extra-curricular activities such as camping, hiking and the Red Cross.

The call by the students for a curriculum which is practical, related to the real world and to their personal needs suggests that these four schools have enrolled students who are active, or prepared to be active, in the principles and practice of their learning. Such evidence suggests that each of the four schools met the conditions laid down by Pendlebury for creating an epistemic community. It suggests that the schools form identifiable communities which have sufficient financial and educational resources to teach a curriculum which conforms to national guidelines and national examination standards. The curriculum offers a variety of discourses and epistemological methods for an exploration of a wide number of areas of experience or discrete disciplines. The schools have spoken of their modes of engaging the students with experience. For example, two schools cited the students' particular interest in science, with one seeking to maintain its lead in national quality in science education. At the other, comment was made that the traditional view that African people had an innate religious spirituality may well be overtaken in not too many years by the great interest in science and technology. The student voice affirmed very positively that they were conscious that their developing beliefs were being formed increasingly from their own convictions rather than those of others, thereby acknowledging that they had been exposed to procedures for qualifying and disqualifying evidence.

Overall the students' concern for knowing themselves and their world and accepting who they might become reflected strongly an innate sense of the spiritual as part of the human condition.

Learning from the Meta-Knowledge: Schools as Epistemic Communities of the Human Condition in Late Modern Times?

The schools most certainly include a sufficient critical mass of learners to form an epistemic community. All the teachers and school managers showed a great concern for continuously interpreting the global, national and local situation. It was from such reflection and speculation that they achieved their sense of place as a school culture. Moreover, their ongoing critical reflection led them to learning more about the needs and situation of their students. In turn the students spoke of how their learning touched their 'real' lives and personal needs. The overwhelming impression of each school culture, and its strong resemblance to Pendlebury's epistemic community, can perhaps be most succinctly summarized in the words of the National Curriculum Council (NCC) (1993). In a paper which sets out to discuss the nature of 'spiritual development', the NCC argued that the term applied to 'something fundamental in the human condition'. Those school cultures all presented themselves as epistemic communities concerned with learning that was fundamental to the human condition. The NCC's further elaboration of the term applies aptly to the four cultures:

> It has to do with relationships with other people and, for believers, with God. It has to do with the universal search for individual identity – with our responses to challenging experiences, such as death, suffering, beauty and encounters of good and evil. It has to do with the search for meaning and purpose in life and for values by which to live. (NCC 1993: 3)

Additionally, Pendlebury (1998: 186) has noted the similarity of her thinking about a community's ability to maintain its definitive practices with MacIntyre (1984) who argued that to enter a practice is to enter into a relationship with its practitioners, present and past, especially those who have 'extended the reach of the practice through their achievements'. Finally, therefore, in this context of the study of faith-based schools and the cultures of four of them within the concept of epistemic communities, it is important that some consideration is given to the defining practice of integrating a faith or religious tradition into the core business of epistemic communities.

Each of the schools spelled out the Catholic basis of their beliefs, attitudes and values and behaviours in both their prospectuses and their handbooks and during interviews for this study. In one of the schools in Country X, for example, the prospectus states that as a Catholic school, the college adopts the Church's philosophy of education which includes 'the formation of the human person with respect to his ultimate goal and simultaneously with respect to the good of those societies of which, as a man, he is a member'. In this manner the school explained its particular religious identity within a much larger identity, or cultural tradition; namely, a Catholic philosophy of education. Thus it called upon a long-established tradition of educational endeavour within a faith tradition and drew attention to some specific dimensions of the nature and practice of that tradition in education.

Unequivocally it states that the school adopts that philosophy of education and it finds no hindrance in setting this philosophy alongside, or indeed perceiving of it as the determining ingredient, of the culture of the school. In this way, the school sets out its aims in relation to the nation and national education policy for its students who should be able to:

1. Manifest skills in accuracy of observation and in imaginative, moral and logical thinking.
2. Contribute positively to the economic development of the country and judicious conservation of scarce natural resources.
3. Engage in worthwhile cultural and leisure time activities.
4. Acquire the necessary grades needed for admission to tertiary education.

The Catholic philosophy in this situation is partly illustrative of Bartelt's concept of 'nested ecologies of education':

As we examine macro-ecologies we unearth a second or a third ecological system at work, much like the nested Russian doll. (1995: 161–2)

For this purpose the concept of nested ecologies illuminates a particular kind of understanding for that which takes place in schools is not only directly affected by the definitive practices of the school and the character of the communities from which the students are drawn but also by the macro-ecology of the civic society. The interdependence of the school and society or the state can be examined from many perspectives, of course, such as policy making; curriculum thinking and development; values development and citizenship; school admissions; and assessment. In these schools the aims outlined above establish very clearly the interconnectedness between the faith foundation, the nation-state and the concept of education in providing the sources of the humanistic, civic, educational and religious values of each school's culture.

Learning from the Meta-Knowledge: Faith and the Establishment of Educational Communities?

This study has illustrated the complex and varied nature of the interplay between faith and religion and school ecologies. For example, the data points to the students' satisfaction with receiving an education which catered for their twin needs: that of achieving high standards in school work and becoming accepting of the people that they are. The data show a wide set of contributors to the success of the students in achieving high standards; for example, one school has put great energy and resources into achieving an outstanding science education for its students. The students also speak highly of the sense of community, belonging and safety which the schools provide. They profess themselves happy at their schools. All students identify the headteacher's contribution to the overall feeling of community. Each of the headteachers in turn spoke of their perception of their role emanating from their beliefs as educators, their Catholic beliefs and values and their consciousness of national and local needs and challenges to young people trying to get to grips with their world. They also stressed the vital role of the RE team in developing a particular school. For example, the headteacher who developed the handbook referred to above, where he establishes the provenance of the school's approach to education by placing it firmly within the long-established Catholic doctrines on education, also firmly supported the move by his government to invite a community of religious sisters to set up a base at his school.

In Country Z's school the head of spiritual affairs, when discussing the mission of the school, referred to the philosophy of his religious order of brothers as the inspiration for the belief that the school was there to 'provide guidance for the young' and through its vision 'to provide brotherhood through community' and 'the option for the poor'. Most of all, 'students must be free to develop themselves' within a new kind of school organization, which he described as 'a Christ-lover for the young'. For this vision to be achieved it was important that the school and its curriculum, particularly, in religious education, should 'meet the intellectual challenges of helping students know why they believe'. From here a central tenet arises of these school cultures; namely, that the teaching of and about religion in each of the schools is there to contribute to the overall education of the students. Education in this definition is about providing an intellectual climate in which people have reasons for believing and understanding. This finding reflects Bryk et al.'s argument that Neo-Scholasticism made two important contributions to the thinking of the Catholic church:

> A belief in the capacity of human reason to arrive at ethical truth and an affirmation of the place of moral norms and principles in public and personal life. (1993: 51)

Most certainly in Country Z's school in which the majority of the student sample were Catholics, all the students affirmed very positively that they were coming to believe 'because of their own convictions rather than the beliefs of others'. There was also a very positive response to this same statement by students in the other three schools who came from rather more varied religious backgrounds than those in Country Z's school. These responses also lend credence to the students' definite view that they are respected as people who are self-disciplined and personally responsible for their development. Significantly, the students, except for those in Country Z's school, also record that they are ambivalent as to whether they have had their understanding of the Eucharist in Catholic life deepened as a result of their RE and equally they are uncertain as to whether they have deepened their understanding of the Catholic tradition.

There appears therefore to be a deliberate screening process at work by the students and perhaps by some of the staff of these schools in that they affirm positively their happiness at being in the school but appear to learn little formally, if they are disinclined to do so, about the religious tradition which forms a living ecology for their school experience. Perhaps the data can point to some particular reason for this. Each of the schools puts a heavy priority on defining the kind of students they wish to emerge as a result of belonging to the school. Thus teachers are enjoined in one school to follow a philosophy of education which is 'based on the Christian philosophy of love and service'. The emphasis in the handbook is clear: Christian values are to be the impetus towards a philosophy and pedagogy of education. The content and values of Christianity are to be integrated into the educational work which the institution deems significant. For example, in this same school, the headteacher saw her work as to 'build the Kingdom' through 'integrating a holistic philosophy into the organisation of the school'. Her ultimate work was to be a 'champion of children'.

Thus religious values and personal faith infuse the ecologies at work sustaining the school culture but, perhaps, the teaching of doctrine and specifically Catholic beliefs receive a lower priority in the defining practices of the school. Such an interpretation finds support from the students' voice who welcomed RE for meeting their needs, developing their personal faith, helping to learn about other religions and leaving space for them to shape their consciences autonomously. Second, it finds support in the discussions held both in the Country Y and Country X's schools. There the heads of RE spoke of the concentration in the Global South on 'primary evangelization', in which the Christian communities were setting out afresh, finally free of their colonial associations, to preach Gospel values. In that kind of ecology, there is little room for the teaching of second-order doctrines and examples of world views and lifestyles which do not appear authentic in the contexts in which they are being lived out.

If this interpretation of the defining practice of Catholicism is right within the four school cultures in this study, then it is possible to evaluate the schools' understanding of religion and faith with the aid of Flanagan. He speaks of his perspective on the place of religion within the intellectual, political and social cultures which presently form the ecologies within which those four schools operate in the following manner:

As an issue religion seems disconnected from society, a corpse of modernity buried with a tombstone called secularisation. But now comes a resurrection, the seeds of which can be denoted in the issues which have come to signify postmodernity. A searching, and escaping, a rootlessness of image and affiliation, the effects of technology and globalisation, mark an unsecured self, now forced to ask questions of metaphysical identity inconceivable on the agenda . . . two decades ago. (1999: 1)

Developing a Meta-Narrative of Faith-School Cultures from the Meta-Knowledge Generated by a Particular Study

The schools in this study where religion is a significant defining practice in their support of viable learning communities exhibit remarkably similar characteristics. The first, that religion forms the basis for much of their epistemology of education and educational practice but their ultimate concern is with developing educational institutions that work. The second characteristic is that their headteachers and senior management teams spend significant time in reflecting on the state of their nations and their students. They see the effects of globalization and technological developments in communication on the development of their curricula, their goals and the lives of their communities and their students. Third, they examine ways in which their teaching and learning can meet with the many worlds and identities of their students. Fourth, they allow space in the curriculum for students to find ways of developing their personal faith, while at the same time stimulating learning which encourages the students to make up their own minds about the evidence for belief. Finally, they commit much of their time, energy and resources to the establishment of communities in which the students flourish as learners and identify with pride.

The nested ecologies found in each of the four schools, through examination, can tell a distinctive story about each one. Yet together they reflect a definition of culture provided by Heelas. This definition appears to support their ability to form epistemic communities in the twenty-first century because their organized cultures contain:

> sustained voices of moral authority (which) serve to differentiate values, to distinguish between what is important and what is not, and to facilitate coherent, purposeful identities, life-plans or habits of the heart. (1999: 64)

In many ways, that definition of culture above would also serve as a succinct summary of those four schools' understanding of the purpose of education.

The student voice and the many voices of the headteachers, senior managers and teachers at each school give adequate testament to the culture of the school providing a rich ecology for those who seek to find purposeful identities, life-plans or habits of the heart.

There can be no question that religion has played a not insignificant part in the formation and sustenance of these particular epistemic communities. In some striking and innovative ways, these schools have shown themselves mindful of the view put forward by Sutherland (1985: 140) that beliefs and values are 'matters of deep-seated conviction, which involve emotion as well as intellect, soul as well as mind'. Despite their pressured national examination systems and accompanying rigid curricula, as well as the students' commitment to succeed academically, the schools gave authority to teachers and students together, in the words of Country Z's headteacher to 'dig out their faith'. To use Carr's phrase, matters of beliefs and values were 'plumbed into their system'. In another phrase borrowed from Lewis' (2006) for these cultures, there could be no 'excellence without a soul'.

Towards a Re-Assessment of the Meta-Narrative of School Cultures

During the recent period in education, when the effective school discourse was dominant, research into school cultures began from the need to map out those elements in a school which could be transformed through external initiatives and internal management activities. Transformation was necessary in order to import those mechanisms agreed by researchers and the DfES into each school that were thought to ensure the successful achievement of indicators of effectiveness or standards. Formulae based on the relationship between a headteacher's effectiveness as a manager and leader, curricular rigidity and continuous testing of students resulted from that particular mapping of school cultures. Relationships between teachers and students, individual students and national targets and individual schools and their local communities and catchment areas found little space on school effectiveness maps.

The maps or profiles of each school culture developed here are very different. Their purpose is to clarify the relationship of beliefs and faith with the values and practices through which each school builds its distinct educational culture. This mapping of beliefs, values and behaviours of individual schools provides the ground-plan from which to build, interrogate and evaluate a knowledge base of faith-school cultures in general. This knowledge base is the foundation of the meta-narrative which could play a crucial part in any informed deliberative engagement with faith schools. The form which this meta-narrative takes is directly tied to the purpose of such deliberative engagement. That purpose is to expose the extent to which one particular faith or set of beliefs can shape the culture of a school so that its educational endeavour is distinct from that in any other school. With the result a meta-narrative of school cultures must assist in explaining how and why a distinct culture creates a particular kind of learning and teaching community; the particularities of the *genus loci* of those cultures; the porosity of a school culture in taking in its sources of educational, social, civic and religious values and in giving out its commitment to share in the wider community's development; and the means by which it has sought to contribute to the students' attitudes, values and faith.

This study has contextualized its examination of faith schools within three prevailing socio-intellectual modes: the modern, the postmodern and the global late modern. It has described how the grand narrative of modernity privatized faith and belief and consequently sustained an educational discourse which saw no place for faith schools. The postmodern through its abandonment of the grand narrative has instead encouraged the study of the microculture. It is among those very microcultures which were once abandoned, or at least marginalized, by the grand narrative that minorities within pluralism are finding their voice. If this is indeed the case then minorities such as faith schools can once more participate legitimately in debate about civic education. If the proposed meta-narrative of school cultures were to find acceptance in educational debate in these global late modern times, then there would be the opportunity for an appropriate educational discourse to hold in tension the democratic principles of modernity in debate with a new late modern narrative of school cultures. This would not be a narrative concerned solely with the economic imperative of these present times but rather one concerned with the personal, spiritual, ethical and civic sources of successful schools.

This chapter has thus been concerned to analyse the information collected about the four Catholic school cultures by interrogating what it has to say about the particularities of faith schools, such as their *genus loci*, their understanding and teaching of the human condition and the attitudes and values of their students and the relationship of these to the faith foundation of each school. From these it has provided a succinct statement of the purpose of education articulated by each school. It has proposed that the meta-knowledge generated by empirical studies in turn creates a meta-narrative of distinctive school cultures. Its acceptance into educational discourse might help to ensure that the study of school cultures receives a new impetus and direction. Rather than there being studies concerned only with describing effective management structures whose achievement can be measured by external performance indicators, a new form of school culture studies might develop. These would be undertaken partly to understand the ways in which a school's faith/values foundation impinges on the education it offers and partly to discern the distinctive epistemological and communal bases found in successful schools for learning about the human condition in plural societies.

Chapter 10

Practice Informing Policy:
The Case for Evidence-Based Policy
Concerning Faith-Based Schools

Purpose of the Chapter

This final chapter is concerned to tackle the lacunae in the evidence currently available about the nature and practices of distinctive faith schools and their effects on the students who study in them. It is also concerned to examine afresh the purpose of education in the light of the evidence provided by profiling four faith schools.

The first part of the chapter examines the problems which arise for effective policy development concerning faith schools in the absence of appropriate evidence to illuminate Ofsted findings and league table results, following the publication of the White Paper, *Schools Achieving Success*. The second part provides summative statements arising from the empirical studies of four Catholic schools and suggests that the methodology used has three important outcomes for the present discussion: a base for data modelling; a means of deciding indicators of successful school cultures; and a need to examine the culture fit between macro-education policies and micro-school cultures. The third part calls for a civic conversation about faith schools within a wider debate about the purpose and practice of education in plural late modern times. The final part signals to government and policy makers the benefits of developing educational policies whose origins lie in school practice. Most particularly it is argued that in the matter of faith schools, if comprehensive evidence is weighed before policy is made, education itself might become the catalyst for a newly emerging democratic, inclusive and normative culture of pluralism.

A Critical Lack of Evidence-Based Policy Concerning
Faith Schools in Plural Civic Societies

The publication by the DfES (2001) of the White Paper *Schools Achieving Success* in England was the catalyst for the organization and development of this book. Contained in it was the policy to support a substantial increase in faith schools. This study has previously commented that educational policy often consists at present of a series of measures bolted on to existing, rather old and often fragile, education systems. This seems indeed to have been the case in 2001 in England. The need to resolve the tensions found in some plural communities was met by a call for inclusion of all children into schools whose concerns were tolerance and respect for others. The Cantle Report (2001) asserted that faith schools were inherently divisive. At the same time, the White Paper supported the expansion of faith schools. The Church of England's (2001) response to the White Paper called for the development of schools which were inclusive and had a religious character. There seemed to be little attempt at joined-up policy.

The Press Notice (5 September 2001) which accompanied the publication of the White Paper spoke of it as 'a blueprint that will give every secondary school the freedom to develop its own unique ethos and centre of excellence'. At the same time, a Schools Innovation Unit was to be established to help 'stimulate new ideas, spread best practice and cater significantly better to the diverse requirements and aspirations of pupils'. There was widespread and heated discussion about the content of the White Paper. In particular, questions were raised as to whether faith schools were a help or a hindrance in shaping the present plural society into an inclusive and tolerant culture.

The then schools Minister, Stephen Timms (2002), asserted that the evidence is clear that faith schools are doing very good jobs, and are doing them, in particular, in disadvantaged communities. Schagen and Schagen (2005), though, disputed presumably this same evidence used by the Minister, arguing that any improvement in test scores by students is better explained by faith schools' selection criteria, not by their distinct ethos. Neither the Minister nor the Schagens seemed prepared to dig deeper into the statistics about schools which were available to them. Was there something different going on educationally inside each of these faith schools which assured the success and achievement of their students? In what ways did they judge that the students emerging from existing faith schools contributed to the development of a tolerant and inclusive plural society? By what means was the DfES to establish the relationship between the 'unique ethos' which each school was invited to create and the 'centre of excellence' which the DfES believed would follow?

Several years on, the debate still rages. Indeed as this study reached its conclusion the intense and often uninformed and misinformed discussion surrounding the place of faith schools showed no sign of abating. The Schools Innovation Unit has published some case studies of faith schools on its website designed to show evidence of tolerance and inclusion. These rely mainly on information about sharing resources between faith and non-faith schools. This barely begins to provide insights into the relationship in faith schools between their distinctiveness as educational cultures and their faith foundation. Without such evidence how might the DfES know whether a school's foundation in faith directly impinges on its educational practice? Without evidence concerning the effect of one school's social, moral, spiritual and cultural education on its students' attitudes and values to themselves, others, and their society, how might the DfES compare different schools' contribution to the development of good citizens of the future? The work of Osler (2007) with the Runnymede Trust in investigating faith schools and social cohesion does contain real potential now, however, for some worthwhile evidence becoming available.

In the absence of any widespread appropriate data at present to respond to these critical concerns about faith schools in plural societies, this chapter seeks to underline the kinds of knowledge which might become available through examination of individual or groups of schools using a methodology similar to that employed in the present study. Since education in a plural democracy must be concerned with both the common good of society and the ability of each student to live well, this study has set itself the challenge of solving the educational question: 'What should be the balance between all schools contributing to a politically driven understanding of the common good or civic culture and each school's contribution to a particular understanding of what constitutes the most effective culture for the development of flourishing individuals?' Indeed, to what extent might further studies of school cultures, such as those suggested above by Slee and Weiner (1998: 111) in which there is 'explicit discussion of values and the types of society to which schools articulate/adhere' contribute some illumination to a civic discussion about the need to return to a 'common schooling' for all?

Certainly such a conversation would have as its focus school cultures, not simply as vehicles for importing national school effectiveness projects into individual schools but as living ecologies of human, civic and educational values. A desirable outcome of such discussion would be a return to Wrigley's (2003: 7) 'unavoidable question': To what end is all this? Where is the vision? A return to a sense of needing to find a common purpose in education might well in turn spawn means of establishing the value or otherwise of different kinds of schooling which bring about the learning with which education is associated.

The need for a civic education has arisen simultaneously with the breakdown of common assumptions about the purpose of education. Just as parents and religious authorities demanded the right to educate the characters of their children within the cultural tradition of their beliefs at the beginning of the twentieth century, so now the state at a time of disculture, or a-cultural pluralism, believes it must take responsibility to shape the civic dispositions of the young. Education standing between the state and its citizens must therefore seek guidance from its host democratic society as to how best to reintroduce virtue as a major focus of its core business. Civic virtue has been defined in this study through two methods. The first sought a theoretical analysis of the nature of principled living at a time of pluralism, with key values derived from the concepts of respect for persons, democratic government and social and political engagement through deliberative respect. The second set out definitions of civic virtue found in (i) government-sponsored reports, such as those of Swann and Cantle; (ii) national educational policies, such as those found in Countries X, Y and Z and the UK; and (iii) school handbooks and curriculum policies. The Cantle Report argues that community cohesion can be found in social and civic commitments which bind individuals together. Civic virtue would therefore be, at least, partially expressed in community cohesion. On the other hand, Forrest and Kearns questioning of whether cohesion is virtuous and a positive attribute in every context, receives support in the Cantle Report:

> Individuals may be well integrated into their local ethnic or religious-based communities, which then creates divisions between these communities and others. (2000: 9)

The difficulty with such an assertion is that individuals who belong to ethnic or religious groups generally cohere not out of an autonomous choice but as a result of their inheritance of this ethnicity or that religion. It would be alarming to consider government or civic society interfering with the right of individuals who 'inherit' particular identities to associate freely. It is an entirely different matter, however, for government or local communities to engage with faith schools to ensure that the cohesion which results from a faith's ability to establish a welcoming and inclusive learning community should be of an outward-looking and educational character.

Sutherland (1996: 47) issued an important warning when he argued that education for pluralism in democracies is only as successful as the (economic) strength of all the constituents of that pluralism. The previous chapters have also been concerned with another kind of strength which is necessary if a fair, inclusive and just pluralism is to be achieved through education. It is the democratic strength of a civic society to engage with all voices of pluralism found within it. Gutmann both summarizes the strengths and hints at the processes through which democracies arrive at ethical policies:

> democracy is a political ideal – of a society whose adult members are, and continue to be, equipped by their education and authorized by political structures to share in ruling. Democratic societies must therefore prevent majorities (as well as minorities) from repressing critical enquiry or restricting political access. (1987: xi)

The remainder of this concluding chapter will be concerned with ways in which educators and government, also as part of the moral matrix, might be engaged in principled policy making regarding both the fostering of civic virtue in all schools and the place of faith schools in civic societies. Any conclusions which might be reached will be proposed within the secure knowledge of participating in educational research in a democracy. Once again

Gutmann articulates so clearly the researcher's position together with the likely outcome of any of her conclusions:

> the most distinctive feature of a democratic theory of education is that it makes a democratic virtue out of our inevitable disagreement over educational problems. (1987: 11)

The Value of Empirical Studies in Faith Schools: Some Lessons Learnt from the Present Study

This section of the chapter attempts to make a case for further and wider examinations and audits of school cultures. Their study is worthwhile in terms both of learning more about the nature and behaviours of particular kinds of school culture and of furnishing examples of how micro-cultures engage with human philosophies and macro-educational policies. The increasing aims, targets and expected outcomes to which schools have been asked to respond have been evidenced throughout this study. One view of this increasing expectation is that schools and, indeed, the governments which maintain them have lost oversight of the purpose of education. The schools in this study in articulating their values and beliefs about education spoke, inter alia, of intense social pressures on their students; expansion of academic curricula in order to manage increased national and global demands; and, at the same time, they delineated their own educational identities such as being 'children's champions', 'someone who can listen to students' problems' and 'radical administrative programme implementers to meet competition linked to globalisation'. Perhaps the most important contribution which further study of school cultures might make would be to set out 'the values and the types of society to which different schools articulate/adhere' and thereby raise collectively the need for a revisiting of the overall purpose of education in plural societies, described by Jackson (2004: 8) as being a fragmented diversity, 'with various groups having competing and often contradictory rationalities'.

The research process presented here included empirical studies in four schools in three different countries set within a theoretical framework designed to examine the role, nature and purpose of faith schools at present in plural civic societies. The study was very small and therefore unable to uncover, for example, broader national data relating to a number of faith schools in one country. There are many issues arising therefore in relation to designing other larger research projects, such as the content of the questionnaire, the quality of large data management and specific packages to support computer-generated analysis. As a result the means suggested below for solving concerns about the place of faith schools through methodological enquiry are offered with humility and a sense of the inevitability of value disagreement. Bassey (1999: 47), however, has argued that an essential feature of case studies is that sufficient data are collected for researchers to be able to explore significant features of the case and to put forward interpretations of what is observed. Another essential feature is that the study is conducted mainly in its natural context. If these conditions are met, then a study may put forward 'fuzzy generalisations'. These are a kind of prediction, arising from empirical enquiry, that says 'something may happen, but without any measure of its probability. It is a qualified generalization, carrying the idea of possibility but no certainty'.

On those terms then the engagement with individual school cultures as social realities described here might be judged to have worked, insofar as:

1. Each complex culture seems to have proved susceptible to exposure in the matters of beliefs, attitudes and values and behaviours through an externally moderated process.
2. The continuous inter-play between the three constituents of a school culture have been demonstrated to inform both school policy and behaviours, including that of the senior managers and teachers, the students and the culture as a whole.
3. Distinctive values and beliefs on the part of the school managers have been able to be evaluated against the students' own satisfaction and happiness with belonging to a particular school culture.
4. A distinctive perspective on each culture has been gained through eliciting a separate self-review from among the student body.
5. A database has been developed of cohorts of school leavers who were about to enter their own societies as full citizens from Catholic senior secondary schools in three countries. Interrogation of the database proved worthwhile in terms of establishing a profile of the students' developing attitudes, values and beliefs.
6. Each school culture has been profiled within a historical, educational, sociological, and religion-state perspective.

Examining schools in this way also gave rise to data which supported some comparative perspectives on the kinds of distinct school cultures which are currently sustained by a faith group, in this case, the Catholic Church and the response of the students to those cultures, whether they were Catholic, non-Catholic Christian, from other faiths or from none. Perhaps the most important comparison that the data facilitates is that between the attitudes and values of the students within each school and between different schools and across the schools. From this particular data derived from four schools, a strikingly similar profile of the school leavers from all four emerged. Most notably the students shared, or thought they shared, the following values, attitudes and beliefs:

- belonging to their school as a community;
- being happy at school;
- purpose in their learning and a desire to do well in their school work;

- acceptance of themselves as they are;
- respect for other people, whatever their race, nationality or religion;
- respect for the environment;
- recognition of the influence of their parents in their religious development and attitude formation;
- honesty in their dealings with other people;
- commitment to the disadvantaged in society;
- believing based on their own convictions and not the beliefs of others.

As with all human beings, the students might have chosen other values and developed other attitudes. The holding of one set of values over another always has a cost. For these students the prospect of making a great deal of money did not figure highly in their value systems. For them being a human being who is knowledgeable about their world and themselves and actively concerned with their fellow human beings, through respect and concern, emerges as the basis of their valuing and their attitudes as learners, citizens and individuals in relationship. In many ways the students' values and attitudes reflected the feminine ethic of care, responsibility and love, articulated by Gilligan (1982).

This profile of the young school leavers has been susceptible to further elaboration as a consequence of the students' written and spoken comments about their schools. One, for example, indicates that although discipline is important, 'It has got to be realized that human beings are more important than regulations. Discipline must be implemented but a Catholic school should see the human dimension'. Another says, 'What I can appreciate about my school is that it is a good school which supports students' ideas and the main value is trust. It is trust that is a community builder.' Yet another appreciated, 'the way the school is trying to mould students into valuable citizens. The student empowerment.'

Further studies of faith schools might therefore be considered as worthwhile by a variety of researchers. There might be those undertaken by groups of faith schools in one area, for example, or some conducted by national religious bodies in conjunction with external researchers/critical friends to encourage specific forms of supported school self-evaluation. In England there might be a proposal among a group of schools to engage in research which distinguished between the outcomes of individual schools as reported through Ofsted and the processes in which those same schools engaged in order to achieve their specific mission and purpose. The profiles from a significant number of distinct schools might also generate generalizable examples of good practice in personal, social and civic education which could be made available across all sectors of state-supported education. The profiles might also be used to focus public/civic discussion about the attributes of a good citizen in plural societies as well as to furnish examples of micro-cultures living well in the wider macro-cultures of late modern times.

The Outcomes of the Present Research/Audit Process for Further Enquiry into Faith Schools: (1) Data Modelling

The present study appears to indicate that there were seven sustaining constituents at work in each of the four school cultures. Given that each of the four schools was situated in a plural society, these seven constituents can be built into a model which might provide a possible template for the development or evaluation of other faith schools in plural societies. The constituents will be grouped below under the same headings of belief, attitudes and values, and behaviours which have been used throughout the methodological enquiry.

Belief

1. Staff and students' belief that faith impacts on the kind of people they are and the significance of religious education in that process.

Attitudes and values

2. The students' dominant (spiritual) concern to learn about themselves and their world, so that they can become particular kinds of people.
3. The headteacher's commitment to building a community to which all could feel a sense of belonging.
4. Senior management's concern individually and collectively to reflect on their school's place in the life of the nation and the local community and offer a critique as Catholic educators of what they encountered in the nation and the local community.
5. Students' universal commitment to respect for themselves, other people and their environment.

Behaviours

6. Attendance at the Eucharist at points in the school year.
7. Religious education as a distinct curriculum experience.

Taking these in order, the educational belief which is shared by staff and students at the four schools is that faith impacts on the kind of people they are and that religious education has a part to play in that shaping of people and their attitude to the world. Common attitudes and values prevail; in particular, the emphasis on respect for others and the environment and, equally, the importance of a school culture forming a community to which all feel a sense of belonging. There was also clear evidence of students being happy at their schools. Religious education as a defining practice of the schools was acknowledged as significant by the students for their knowledge both of themselves and others and of their world, as, for example, through the study of other religions. Thus Jackson (1997: 129) would be able to observe debates in those schools about the nature of religions and cultures. At the same time, Hulmes (1979: 17) would be able to see curriculum thinking based on the Catholic theory that 'religion lays claim to the whole person and at the same time refuses to be classified as just one of many possible ways of apprehending reality'. Perhaps he (1994: 4) would also recognize among the students' values those which he listed as characterizing a Catholic perception of wholeness such as autonomy, belief, choice, community, conscience, discernment, enjoyment, pluralism, responsibility, self-control, success, tolerance, tradition, truth, uncertainty and unity.

The behaviour of whole-school attendance at a compulsory Eucharist was common to all four schools and in all four it drew criticism from Catholic and non-Catholic students alike. Therefore its practical and symbolic strength within the culture of each of the four schools must be examined. Practically, the whole community of the school is present at these termly, or otherwise, Eucharistic events. For the rest of the time, the school functions as an educational community, whose behaviours are concerned with curricular and pastoral matters. The schools function efficiently in introducing the students to modes of learning concerning academic and vocational knowledge. The students believe that their educational and personal needs are being met well. However, they speak of other needs. Some of these are about who they are, or wish to be, some are about meeting with and responding to change, some want to know how to be 'tomorrow's people'. For these students the desire for academic success goes hand-in-hand with personal development. They want to know where they are going and why. They want to know how to respond as individuals with their own consciences to differing situations. The personal sense of growing their own consciences emerges.

One of the major characteristics of many of the students in this sample is the wish or ability to apply their principles and attitudes to specific situations. Perhaps it is possible to say that the defining attitude found in each of the schools, both among senior management and students, was 'praxis', a synthesis of reflection and action. This defining attitude can be contextualized also in wider studies on young people's spirituality. Hay and Nye (1998: 62) place 'heightened awareness' within one of three categories or themes of 'spiritual sensitivity or awareness'.

Hay and Nye (1998: 63) also characterize a second category as 'value-sensing'. They suggest that it is important to examine young people's 'ideas of worth or value in the intensity of their everyday experience of delight and despair'. The values and attitudes of the students in these four schools are seemingly reflected in the words of Flynn and Mok when describing their own visits to Catholic schools in New South Wales:

> We felt the depths of their searching regarding life and God as they reflected on their experience of Catholic schools and the place of God in their lives. (1999: 1)

There was evidence from both senior managers in the schools and the students themselves that they used imagination to develop new ways of understanding the world through their experience of faith schools. The boy who spoke of wanting to develop his 'youth spirit' and the headteacher who described her role as 'a champion of children' were giving evidence of their deep spiritual questioning of the meaning of existence. Ofsted would indeed be able to recognize such questioning as evidence of spiritual development for they have, in the words of one HMI, David Trainor (1995: 8–9), described 'spiritual development as discovering the self'. As Priestley (2005: 211) has argued, 'the spiritual is connected with being – with what we are – not with what we know or what we can do'. These four schools seem to have provided an environment which encouraged a spiritual development which could be discerned outside of its particular religious or faith foundation.

Herein lies the importance of reflecting on the finding that the behaviour found in common in each school was the attendance by all at the Eucharist. The students themselves were from diverse religious, and sometimes ethnic, backgrounds in the four schools. The headteacher in each school was Catholic and many of the senior management team; the rest of the teaching staff, however, were simply allocated to the schools, as were the students, through central government direction. For the senior staff in each country, there was a great consciousness of leading a Catholic school. For every other member of the school, such belonging to a Catholic institution seemed of little significance. What mattered was the school's competence in education: for the students this meant an education for the world ahead and its ability to respond to their personal and social needs.

The presence of the Eucharist within each school culture as a distinguishing behaviour held in common within these four very particular kinds of school merits further comment. In the first place, it is important to evaluate the place of the Eucharist in Catholic Christian thought, just as it would be equally important to evaluate the place of a specific distinguishing behaviour in Hindu, Jewish, Muslim or Sikh schools. The Eucharist, as an institution or practice, was seen in the very early Christian communities, such as at Ephesus, as the identifying mark of a united community. In more recent times, the success of Catholic schools was, and still is, partly measured by the continuing presence of students at the Eucharist years after they have left Catholic schools. A dwindling Sunday Mass congregation has been used to signal the failure of Catholic schools in many countries.

The four schools in this study did not see their role as guarantors of their students' future attendance at Sunday Mass, however. Rather, they each saw themselves as in some way carrying forward the tradition of the Catholic Church in education in the country where they were situated. Second, they each spoke of a need for primary evangelization within their schools, that is, drawing attention to the primary Gospel values, through their focus on 'the option for the poor' and 'relationship within community'. Theirs was not a mission to convert to Catholicism but, rather, to infuse, or 'plumb in' gospel values into their structuring of an educational community. The evidence of the students appears to confirm that these schools in different ways offered the kind of dual perspective in spiritual education advocated by Tacey (2005: 176) when he called for 'respect for religious traditions, along with a constructive critique of traditions'.

The study suggests that each of the four school cultures was sustained by an intermixing of faith, educational values and attitudes. In mapping the beliefs, values and attitudes, and behaviours of each of the schools through this study it is apparent that faith, both as a specifically Catholic world view and as an individual attitude to the world, has infused the educational mission and practice of each school community.

These four schools, grounded in faith and education, have provided evidence that, in general, they educate in order to develop particular kinds of human beings who will learn and use their knowledge in a way consistent with their personal faith, beliefs and values. They have also shown that they are capable of creating and sustaining viable communities of learners concerned with themselves, others and their world. In that sense these four schools suggest that the cultures of faith schools, by combining educational and faith values can be, at their best, cultures of praxis in which human development and human values and practice form their core business.

The individual students in this study showed that they were in the process of developing the capability to respond to and evaluate the complexities of living in the twenty-first century and take decisions about what they needed to do. The self-review by students through the questionnaire in this study permits a profile both of individual students and of cohorts in the same school, city and country or in different schools, cities or countries. Those profiles might be usefully analysed in relation to Pring's (1984) personal domain of values or within the kind of grid developed by the Assessment of Performance Unit (1982), *Personal and Social Development: a map of the territory*. The purpose of such analysis would be to explore where the students recognized their learning had taken place, whether at home or in school, in separate curricular areas or in the whole community of the school. The methodology might also support an investigation of students' perceived response to civic virtue alongside their competence in their outlook on the world or faith. A profile of student capability, a combination of beliefs, attitudes and values, and behaviours, might, thereby, form the basis of testing the competence of any school to operate in plural societies at this time.

This study has attempted to set out a means by which faith school cultures can be examined in order to expose their defining beliefs, values and behaviours. The study has produced a statement about faith schools on which it might be possible to arrive at some judgement as to the validity of supporting such schools in the education systems of complex pluralities. Judgements in this study are rooted in Aristotelian 'practical wisdom', elaborated so valuably by Sherman (1997: 39) above. They are formed by building the understandings learnt from one school culture on to those found in the next and so

forth. The cumulative narrative about all four schools has provided a potential model of a particular group of faith schools which could be evaluated and
discussed within the theoretical framework set out in the first four chapters
of this study.

(2) The Development of Indicators of Successful School Cultures

The case-by-case study presents an opportunity to examine both very general
and very particular relationships between faith and education in schools and
the overall purpose of education. This is critically important if Peters' (1966:
25) particular standards are to be defined 'in virtue of which activities are
thought to be of value and what grounds there might be for claiming that
these are the correct ones'. From the findings gained in the four Catholic
schools, it is possible to develop five indicators of the value of such schools
within macro-educational policies and their individual approaches to educational and faith matters. Set out below are those indicators, derived both from
the beliefs, values and behaviours which contributed to three main areas in
which each school operated and from the theoretical discussion which formed
the first part of this study:

- the school's ability to function as a cohesive educational community for its
  students within a plural society;
- the school's capacity to understand the relationship between its beliefs and
  values and its understanding of what constitutes an educated student;
- the school's expression of the spiritual as understanding their students as
  whole beings and responding to them with its own sense of wholeness;
- the students' capability to reflect on, understand and act for themselves in
  their 'worlds', from principled positions for the common good;
- the school's position in the moral matrix of society.

(3) The Need to Evaluate the Culture-Fit between Macro-Policies and Micro-Cultures

The study outlined here combined an intellectual exploration of the issues
raised by the existence of faith schools with the empirical studies discussed
above. As such the presentation and shape of the book is central to the process of answering the question as to whether faith schools have a distinctive
and valuable role in a plural society. The book has set out the theoretical
dimensions of the problem and employed case studies to illuminate both the
nature of the question and its possible solution. Theory and practice together
provide the framework for discussion and evaluation of this important social
and educational matter.

Theoretically it has been shown that the recent stripping of educational
evaluation of an ethical dimension has touched the core of the problem

facing educators. Resources in education have been mainly concentrated on developing skills and enterprise in young people so that they might achieve economic competence. Through such policy decisions education has taught that economic values are the most important principles of human action and performativity the most important goal of schools. Yet their citizens have other expectations of education. This study indicates that policy needs to articulate much more clearly that the core business of education combines an education for human and economic flourishing. Without such clarity an emerging 'citizens' culture' might begin to act as a de-stabilizer, and ultimately falsifier, of state education systems. Education systems have been at work in all the countries characterized by complex cultural situations for a very long time. As a result, different needs, tensions and global concerns have been incorporated into some rather elderly and fragile education systems, whose foundations lie in very different landscapes from the present. The kernel of the educational and cultural problem with which such societies today live, which is set out below in the form of a question, has the potential to be both constructive and destructive:

To what extent can plural societies which comprise a spectrum of world views and cultural perspectives sustain a common schooling for all?

The possible contribution of this study of four faith schools to a much wider debate about this question has been explained by Simons when arguing that 'paradox is the point of case study'. She continues:

Living with paradox is crucial to understanding. The tension between the study of the unique and the need to generalise is necessary to reveal both the unique and the universal and the unity of that understanding. To live with ambiguity, to challenge certainty, to creatively encounter, is to arrive, eventually, at 'seeing' anew. (1996: 237–8)

'Seeing anew' has been a dominant motif within this theoretical, empirical and evaluative study. For example, the attraction of Hobsbawm's (1994: 15) argument was acknowledged that the intellectual and cultural landscape within which human beings now lived afforded no visible means of supporting their particular or collective journeys. His conclusion that within this bleak landscape, there was 'an inability of both public institutions and the collective behaviour of human beings to come to terms with it' had resonance. Yet that same landscape, as evidenced within this book, has supported a 'moral matrix' of concern for others and for the common good; given rise to the sociological phenomenon of 'social capital'; and the opinion, represented by Flanagan (1999: 7), that precisely because communities share this 'fragmented, variegated range of beliefs and values . . . spirituality has unexpectedly entered'.

Divisions and faultlines within the present global late modern landscape will continue for the foreseeable future and Sutherland's (2004: 216) warning that 'superficial bridges over faultlines will not do' must be heeded carefully. There are indications, however, that the volcanic rumblings and seismic shifts associated with the faultlines are stirring human reflection and understanding of the present problem. In particular, the theoretical part of this book noted the developing concept of social capital, described by Gamarnikow and Green (2000: 96–7) as 'the rediscovery of community and of the idea that social relations are an essential resource for people'. They (2000: 99) also raised the significance of 'trust' within the 'social capital' framework, which they argued can be found in 'generalized cultural norms of reliability, reciprocity and accountability; dense social networks; and civic engagement'. The concept of principled trust at the heart of the moral matrix in society emphasizes that morality is a consequence of living together.

Perhaps the important concept, and experience, of social capital arises from the conscious need to understand the potential for living well with and in plurality. Some of the characteristics of this emerging form of culture seem to be an intense interest in the self and ways of connecting with other selves; a concern to experiment with new visions of community; and a search for, and dependence on, trust. Participation in a personal search for meaning and purpose, the capacity to recognize worthwhile forms of community in plurality and the exercise of trust in social networks and civic engagement represent a real participation in the moral matrix of living in complex plurality. No doubt indications of individual participation would present wide variations along the moral matrix of each plural society. Nonetheless, the sum total of activity characterized by norms of reliability, reciprocity and accountability within this matrix could be said to be a major contribution to a shifting paradigm of culture.

The emergence of a new incipient culture from within pluralism marks out a very important role for educational policy making 'to see anew' within the surrounding landscape. Up to now there has been an assumption that the cultures of schools were susceptible to receiving new directions in policy. These might result from a global economic situation as much as from the arrival in large numbers of children from many diverse countries and cultures or from the need to teach skills appropriate to new forms of human knowledge or to technological developments. That assumption of a 'culture fit' between school cultures and new policy initiatives can no longer be taken for granted. Examination of the 'culture fit' between macro-education policies and micro-school cultures in the four schools suggests the need for an intense reappraisal of the purpose of education if individual schools are to reach their potential to educate for human and economic flourishing within the overall system. If such a reappraisal were to contribute to the development of this incipient culture, it should involve:

- an overall re-assessment of the purpose of education by engaging the concerns and desires of citizens in the exercise;

- a consultation based on a new 'social interaction order' characterized by norms of reliability, reciprocity and accountability;
- policy making which is fit for purpose in a newly emerging culture of pluralism, rooted in praxis where comprehensive evidence is weighed before policy is made.

A reappraisal of the nature and purpose of education would involve a considerable amount of learning, by both government and citizens, at such times of cultural instability and fragility. It is only through learning from the specifics of a situation that real praxis can occur. The learning stretches from and back to government, between citizens, and across the constitutive communities which form the backbone of the emerging culture.

The empirical investigations described here indicate, inter alia, that:

- the interplay of beliefs, values, knowledge and behaviours found in some faith schools suggests that school cultures can be porous, flexible and responsive;
- the added value of some faith schools appears to result from a carefully crafted relationship between the knowledge, attitudes and values required to achieve national educational standards with the knowledge, attitudes and values necessary to become a particular kind of deliberative, reflective human being.

In other words, it appears that it is schools themselves which are finding ways of accommodating pluralism within the educational cultures which they both inherit, as a result of national educational policies, and create, as a result of their particular beliefs and values.

If illuminating evidence about faith schools were able to enter into a wider educational debate about what kinds of school cultures were most capable of meeting the needs of education in plural societies, then a suitable point might have been reached in which a plural society might be able to answer the question:

Should plural societies operate common schools which will ensure the full educational entitlement of all students, from whatever social, cultural, ethnic or religious background or a plurality of schools, in which religious groups are accorded the right to their own schools?

That discussion would also provide an opportunity to assess the viability of responding to citizens' faith or attitudes to the world within distinct contexts rather than in a one-size-fits-all type of school. Such a discussion based on deliberative engagement with all cultural, ethnic and religious groups would signal that pluralism itself is seeking a new form of culture which is sustainable within plurality.

Further strategic research might thereby contribute to the development of a corporate comprehensive imagination within a particular plurality which, in Kearney and Sanders's (1988: 107) words, both 'resides between the faculties of sensation and reason' and acts as 'a window on the world and a mirror in the mind'. Such a fostering of a common imagination might lead to new and sustainable ways of embedding faith, difference, learning and plurality into the schools of complex societies. The success of further strategically conceived research or audit, with the purpose of 'seeing anew' might then be judged on its ability to initiate a culture of praxis among both the politicians and the citizens of those same pluralities. In that way, politicians and citizens could reflect on the nature of their pluralism and take steps to transform their plural cultures in ways which owed not a little to the school cultures of distinct but inclusive sites of learning in their societies.

Practice Informing Policy: A Solution to the Problem?

A reassessment and statement of the purpose of education within the framework set out above would have as its main task the steering of a primary focus for educational endeavour within a society deeply conscious of plurality in its ethnic, religious, social and intellectual life. Part of its task would be to encourage ways of thinking about achievement in schools through an examination of their cultures rather than an examination of their outcomes, as in the present Ofsted process. Part of its task would be to decide whether government-sponsored education could be the sole provider of a new educational ground-plan fit for purpose or whether government would need to work in partnership with other creative modes. In England, The White Paper *Schools Achieving Success* (DfES 2001) has laid the foundations for such a model of educational partnership. Indeed the White Paper might be said to have had as its primary purpose the abolition of the comprehensive ideal of a common worthwhile education for all. If governments are to invite partners to shoulder the maintenance of state education, which authorizing practices would they confirm within religious, secular, humanistic or scientific modes as ethically and educationally fit to provide schools? In particular, how might governments define the quality and standards of personal, social, civic and economic formation at secondary level for which it is seeking partners? On what basis would they make their decisions?

Government might adopt guidelines developed earlier in this study from a) Wittgenstein (1953: 143) when he argued that the presentation and exposition of the religious world view must come across as a moral challenge and b) Biesta (2003: 62) who pointed out that for Kant *Bildung* was more than an educational ideal: it was primarily an answer to the question about the role of a person in the emerging civil society, that is, subjects who can think for themselves and who are capable of making their own judgements. Thus the starting point for government authorizing any mode as a partner in the foundation of an epistemic community would be that the particular mode would

(i) act as a moral challenge in the cultivation of the person's humanity for all who learn and teach in that particular school and (ii) foster independent and critical thinking in future citizens. For the time being the concern remains about how to achieve a balance between all schools being required to contribute to the common good and each school's contribution to the development of flourishing individuals.

A solution to the problem might also result, however, from a civic conversation concerned with how best to provide an adequate education for all within a society in which pluralism has not yet established a normative base for religious and secular philosophies to live in common. Its aims might include the broadening of evaluative discourse in education from the narrow perspective of economics to one infused also by humanitarian and ethical concerns. An educational discourse which defined the ends of education as both economic viability and sustenance of virtuous citizens might well constitute the beginning of a new practice in political leadership. This new practice would be the fostering of a deliberative discussion between politicians and citizens about what they considered essential to the conduct of a satisfying civic life. If together they were to recognize some shared meanings about the conduct of human life in pluralities, then the common good would have been defined not by avoiding citizen's own beliefs and values but rather by engaging them in the pursuit of the political good in civic life. Whether that would be the case is speculation.

If, however, decisions are taken within that conversation which have resulted from both a top–down specification of general ends of education and a bottom–up narrative of circumstances which prevail in individual schools, then the concern which has formed the central motif of this book will have been solved by the device of practice informing policy. Empirical research processes and theoretical reflection in this study have been necessary in order to assist policy makers and citizens to see a very taxing and complex problem anew. In turn, a process of practice informing policy might itself generate a re-definition of policy in global late modern plural societies. This re-definition would be served well by the *Oxford English Dictionary* when it suggests that 'policy' is 'a principled proposal of action' designed 'to polish or refine a culture'. How worthwhile such an exercise in both theoretical reflection and empirical studies might be if educational policy itself were to foster a new normative culture of inclusive and tolerant pluralism. Indeed, supported by such a new culture's beliefs and values there might perhaps grow a rich educational ecology, capable of sustaining a variety of school communities, whether they were distinctive yet inclusive or communal yet tolerant. Only subsequent civic conversations will tell.

Appendix

The Student Questionnaire

CATHOLIC SCHOOLS NOW

Dear Student in a Catholic School,

Quite a lot of research is being carried out into Catholic Schools in the year 2000. I have decided to do a study with an international flavour. Among other things, it will involve doing 'case studies' of Catholic Secondary (High) Schools in several countries. In each of these schools I will be inviting a typical group of final-year students to help me by filling in this questionnaire.

It attempts to discover what you think about certain issues and to explore your experience of your Catholic School and its influence on your life. **I would really like to hear from you about your hopes, aspirations, uncertainties, beliefs.** In the questions that follow, therefore, the best answers your honest personal opinion – which we will value whatever it is.

The replies which you make will be treated as **strictly confidential**. No attempt will be made at any stage to identify individual students. **So, please do not sign your name anywhere.** I will not be showing your replies to any of your teachers, or indeed to anyone else.

Thank you sincerely for your cooperation.

Yours sincerely,
Jo Cairns

London University Institute of Education
20 Bedford Way
London WC1H 0AL

SECTION 1 – Background

1. Please indicate whether you are:
   A. Male
   B. Female
2. Are you a day student or a boarder?
   A. Day student
   B. Boarder
3. What is your religion?
   A. Catholic
   B. Other Christian faith
   C. Non-Christian religion
   D. No religion
4. What is your mother's religion?
   A. Practising Catholic
   B. Non-practising Catholic
   C. Other Christian faith
   D. Non-Christian faith
   E. No religion
5. What is your father's religion?
   A. Practising Catholic
   B. Non-practising Catholic
   C. Other Christian faith
   D. Non-Christian faith
   E. No religion
6. What is the final level of your father's formal education?
   A. Attended primary school
   B. Completed some secondary education
   C. Finished secondary education
   D. Completed a degree or diploma
7. What is the final level of your mother's formal education?
   A. Attended primary school
   B. Completed some secondary education
   C. Finished secondary education
   D. Completed a degree or diploma
8. With regard to your parents:
   A. One of my parents has died
   B. Both of my parents have died
   C. Both my parents are living at home
   D. My parents are divorced
   E. My parents have separated
9. Are there any religious pictures or objects (e.g. Cross, holy picture, book) displayed at home?
   A. Yes
   B. No

10. Are your parents interested in your progress at school this year?
    A. No
    B. Uncertain
    C. Yes
11. Compared with the majority of students in your Year level, how well are you doing in your school work?
    A. Very poorly
    B. Not very well
    C. About average
    D. Better than average
    E. Very well
12. What do you intend to do next year after leaving school?
    A. Take a year off
    B. Take up an apprenticeship
    C. Get a full-time job
    D. Commence a technical course in further education
    E. Go to full-tme university
13. How important would you say religion is in your life?
    A. Not important at all
    B. Not very important
    C. Of some importance
    D. Fairly important
    E. Very important

SECTION 2 – Staying at School

HOW IMPORTANT WERE THE FOLLOWING REASONS IN YOUR DECISION TO STAY ON AT SCHOOL UNTIL THIS FINAL YEAR:

Please read each answer carefully and decide on the degree of importance of each. Put the letter that indicates your answer in the left hand column.

A. No importance
B. Little importance
C. Some importance
D. Very important
E. Most important

14. I do well in my school work
15. My parents wanted me to stay at school
16. I enjoy school
17. My teachers thought I should stay at school
18. Most of my friends decided to stay at school
19. I want to go on to higher education

20. I like the subjects I am studying at school
21. I feel at home in this school
22. I would get a better job later
23. I had no other plans

SECTION 3 – Expectations

THIS SECTION REFERS TO THE GOALS WHICH YOU CONSIDER
CATHOLIC SCHOOLS SHOULD HAVE. EACH QUESTION BEGINS:
'CATHOLIC SCHOOLS SHOULD . . .'

Please record the degree of importance which you consider should be given
to each:

| A. No importance |
| B. Little importance |
| C. Some importance |
| D. Very important |
| E. Most important |

CATHOLIC SCHOOLS SHOULD:

24. Help students to discover and fulfil themselves as persons
25. Prepare students for their future careers
26. Help students understand the society in which they live
27. Provide an atmosphere of Christian community where people are concerned for one another
28. Prepare students fo higher education (university, etc.)
29. Provide students with advice on careers and further education
30. Give all students a chance of success in some aspect of school life
31. Integrate Religious Education with other subjects where possible
32. Assist students to achieve a high standard of performance in their school work
33. Prepare students to become good citizens
34. Provide an environment in which students' faith in God can develop

SECTION 4 – School Life and Climate

THIS SECTION CONTAINS STATEMENTS ABOUT ASPECTS OF THE
CATHOLIC SCHOOL YOU ARE ATTENDING THIS YEAR.

Please indicate the extent to which you agree, or disagree, with each statement as follows:

> A. Certainly false
> B. Probably false
> C. Uncertain
> D. Probably true
> E. Certainly true

35. The relationships between parents and staff are very friendly
36. Students here think a lot of their school
37. Most teachers are well qualified and have good teaching skills
38. Students here know the standard of conduct expected of them
39. Most teachers in this school show a good deal of school spirit
40. Final year students here are not given enough real freedom
41. Most teachers know their final year students as individual persons
42. This school had a good name in the local community
43. I can approach the Principal for advice and help
44. I feel depressed at school
45. Senior students understand and accept the religious goals of the school
46. Most teachers carry out their work with energy and pleasure
47. Discipline presents no real problem in this school
48. Adequate counselling help is available to students
49. This school is a place where I feel lonely
50. This school places too much emphasis on external conformity to rules and regulations
51. Everyone tries to make you feel at home in this school
52. I am treated with respect by other people at school
53. The things I am taught are worthwhile learning
54. This school is a place where I feel worried
55. Other students accept me as I am
56. A good spirit of community exists among final year students
57. Most teachers go out of their way to help you
58. The Principle places importance on the religious nature of the school
59. There is a happy atmosphere in the school
60. Catholic teachers here set an example of what it means to be a practising Catholic
61. Most teachers show that people are more important than rules
62. Most other students are very friendly
63. I feel proud to be a student of this school

64. There are ways to have school rules changed if most students disagree   with them
65. The Principal encourages a sense of community and belonging to the school
66. I have been happy at school
67. I would send my children to a Catholic school
68. Most teachers never explain why they ask you to do things around here
69. If I had to do it all over again, I would attend a Catholic School
70. If students have difficulty with school work, most teachers take time to help them
71. School rules here encourage self-discipline and responsibility

SECTION 5 – Curriculum

THIS SECTION REFERS TO VARIOUS ISSUES RELATED TO THE CURRICULUM i.e. ALL THE SUBJECTS, ACTIVITIES AND OPPORTUNITIES FOR LEARNING PROVIDED BY YOUR SCHOOL.

For each statement please indicate how strongly you agree, or disagree, as follows:

| A. Certainly false |
| B. Probably false |
| C. Uncertain |
| D. Probably true |
| E. Certainly true |

72. The curriculum of this school meets my present needs
73. There are opportunites for students to get to know teachers outside the classroom
74. The out-of-school activities of the school have sufficient variety and scope
75. There is a good sports programme in the school
76. The school offers a good range of subjects to older students
77. The subjects offered develop the capacity for independent and critical thinking
78. The subjects taught offer useful knowledge or skills
79. The Religious Education programme is an important part of the curriculum
80. The subjects taught in the school are relevant to real life and to students' needs
81. The subjects taught here prepare students adequately for future employment

82. The curriculum of the school is dominated too much by examinations

83. A Christian way of thinking is presented in the subjects taught here

84. The school places sufficient emphasis on cultural activities (music, art, drama, etc.)

85. Have you found that what you learnt in school subjects other than R.E. has had any influence on your Christian beliefs? Select ONE of the following answers only;

A. What I have learned in my other school subjects has contradicted my Christian beliefs

B. What I have learned in my other school subjects has weakened my Christian beliefs

C. What I have learned in my other school subjects has not affected my Christian beliefs

D. What I have learned in my other school subjects has supported my Christian beliefs

E. What I have learned in my other school subjects has strengthened my Christian beliefs

SECTION 6 – Religious Education

THIS SECTION REFERS TO YOUR EXPERIENCE OF RELIGIOUS EDUCATION AT THIS SCHOOL IN THE PRESENT AND THE PREVIOUS YEARS.

For each statement please indicate how strongly you agree, or disagree, as follows:

| A. Certainly false |
| B. Probably false |
| C. Uncertain |
| D. Probably true |
| E. Certainly true |

86. I am enjoying R.E. classes this year

87. The study of other religions has helped me appreciate my own religion

88. R.E. classes are largely a waste of time

89. R.E. classes arerelated to real life and to my needs

90. R.E. classes are not taken seriously by students

91. If R.E. classes were voluntary, I would still attend them

92. R.E. classesare poorly prepared and taught

93. R.E. teachers allow sufficient time for discussion

94. This school has a good R.E. programme for older students
95. R.E. is taught at a level comparable with that of other subjects
96. R.E. classes have helped me to understand the Gospels
97. R.E. classes have shown me the place of the Eucharist in Catholic life
98. R.E. classes have deepened my understanding of the Catholic tradition
99. Basic Catholic values and moral teachings are not taught in R.E. classes
100. Contemporary moral issues are given emphasis in R.E. classes
101. Christian marriage has been treated in sufficient depth in R.E. classes
102. R.E. classes help me to form my own conscience
103. Assessment through assignments or examinations shoudl form part of R.E.
104. R.E. classes have helped me to pray
105. I do not know my Catholic faith well enough
106. R.E. classes have helped me understand other religions and non-religious points of view
107. R.E. classes take up too much time which should be devoted to other subjects
108. R.E. classes help me to understand the meaning of life

SECTION 7 – Values, Beliefs and Faith

THIS SECTION REFERS TO CERTAIN ISSUES OR TO STATEMENTS WHICH PEOPLE MAKE.

Please consider each carefully and indicate the degree to which you agree, or disagree, with them:

| A. Certainly false |
| B. Probably false |
| C. Uncertain |
| D. Probably true |
| E. Certainly true |

109. It is all right to take a small item from a large department store if everyone else does it
110. The homeless and disadvantaged people in society don't concern me at all
111. I believe in God
112. Euthanasia, or the mercy killing of the sick or dying, is morally wrong
113. I try to be friendly and helpful to others who are rejected or lonely

114. It is all right for people who are not married to live together
115. People today should respect the environment
116. I would go to Mass on Sundays even if I were free to stay away
117. People should be respected whatever their race, nationality or religion
118. Abortion is a worse evil than the birth of an unwanted child
119. God is a loving Father
120. Trying out drugs is all right, as long as you don't go too far
121. I experience times of questioning when I am uncertain and confused about my faith
122. It is important for me to spend some time in prayer each day
123. I accept the church's teaching on birth control
124. The trust and love of my parents influences my approach to life
125. My faith helps me be a better person
126. The Gospel of Jesus influences the way I lead my life
127. I have rejected aspects of the teaching of the Church in which I once believed
128. Jesus Christ is truly God
129. I am disturbed at times by my lack of faith
130. I believe that God always forgives me
131. I try to follow the Catholic way of life without questioning it
132. Jesus Christ is truly present in the Eucharist
133. I have developed my own way of relating to God apart from the Church
134. The Church needs women priests
135. The Church is very important to me
136. Jesus does not mean anything to me
137. I think that Church services are boring
138. I know that Jesus is very close to me
139. I think that saying prayers does no good
140. I am coming to believe because of my own convictions rather than the beliefs of others

SECTION 8 – Influences on your Religious Development

THE FOLLOWING QUESTIONS REFER TO VARIOUS INFLUENCES ON YOUR RELIGIOUS DEVELOPMENT OVER THE YEARS.

How important have been the following influences:

A. No importance
B. Little importance
C. Some importance
D. Very important
E. Most important

141. The example and lives of your parents
142. The influece of your Parish
143. The influence of your friends and peers
144. The example and lives of your teachers
145. The Religious Education provided by your school
146. The effect of a school Retreat, Christian Living Camp, or similar
147. The influence of a youth group
148. The influence of your Catholic School
149. School liturgies (Masses, prayer sessions, etc.)

THE FOLLOWING QUESTIONS REFER TO RETREATS. (Omit if you have not made a retreat in this or the previous year. Go on to question 156.)

Please indicate the extent to which you agree, or disagree, with the following statements:

> A. Certainly false
> B. Probably false
> C. Uncertain
> D. Probably true
> E. Certainly true

150. The Retreat was uninspiring and boring
151. The Retreat has had a lasting influence on my life
152. During the Retreat I came to respect the views of others more
153. The Retreat helped to give me a sense of self-worth
154. The Retreat was the most important religious experience of my life
155. During the Retreat I experienced times when I felt close to God.

SECTION 9 – Practices

THE FOLLOWING ITEMS REFER TO VARIOUS PRACTICES.

Please choose the appropriate answer.

156. I usually attend Mass (excluding School Masses)
    A. Each Sunday at least
    B. On a few Sundays a month
    C. Once a month
    D. A few times a year
    E. Rarely or never
157. I normally receive the Sacrament of Reconciliation (Confession)
    A. More than once a month
    B. About once a month

C. About once in three months

D. A few times a year

E. Rarely or never

158. I normally spend some time in personal prayer to God

A. Each day

B. Regularly, several times a week

C. Sometimes, a few times a month

D. A few times a year

E. Rarely or never

159. I normally read some part of the Scriptures (Bible)

A. Each day

B. Regularly, several times a week

C. Sometimes, a few times a month

D. A few times a year

E. Rarely or never

SECTION 10 – Knowledge of Catholic Teachings and Terms

EACH QUESTION IN THIS SECTION IS FOLLOWED BY FOUR ALTERNATIVE ANSWERS.

In each case mark the answer which you think correctly represents the Catholic position.

160. The gift by which God shares his life with us is called:

A. Grace   B. Merit   C. Indulgence   D. Sacramental

161. God reveals himself most to people through

A. The Person of Jesus   B. Men and Women   C. Nature

D. Wonder of life

162. God's telling us about himself through the life of Jesus is called:

A. Faith   B. Belief   C. Revelation   D. Infallibility

163. The movement to restore unity among Christian churches is called:

A. Missionary work   B. Prophecy   C. Ecumenism   D. Evangelism

164. The freeing of people from sin and its effects through Jesus is called:

A. Salvation   B. Revelation   C. Inspiration   D. Incarnation

165. The Sacrament that helps us be witnesses and followers of Jesus in our lives is:

A. Penance   B. Holy Orders   C. Marriage   D. Confirmation

166. Our free response to God revealing himself to us is called:

A. Insight   B. Revelation   C. Justice   D. Faith

167. The Church honours Mary, the Mother of Jesus, primarily because of her:

A. Immaculate Conception   B. Virginity   C. Motherhood of God

D. Assumption

168. The Bible is best described as:

A. History book which describes important religious events

B. Collection of many books written at different times under God's inspiration

    C. Book written by the early Church about God's plan
        for all peoples

    D. Collection of books about the life of Jesus and his Apostles

169. Several Gospels were written instead of only one:
    A. Gospel writers were not able to agree on details
    B. Writers worked without knowlegde of other Gospel account
    C. Different Gospels were written for different Chistian
        communities
    D. Several Gospels were needed to ensure accuacy of detail

170. A proper Catholic attitude towards the world is:
    A. The world is an evil place which we avoid as much as possible
    B. The world our proper environment capable of meeting all our
        needs
    C. The world is our present home, made good by God and to be
        improved by the lives of good people
    D. The world is not important as men and women were made for hap-
        piness in heaven

171. Christian marriage exists principally for husbands and wives to:
    A. Enjoy sexual pleasure in a sinless manner
    B. Offer support and love to each other
    C. Preserve family values and traditions
    D. Share love and create families

172. Conscience is best described as:
    A. A feeling of guilt after a person has done something wrong
    B. A personal judgement that something is right or wrong
    C. The law of God which is contained in the Ten Commandments
    D. All the laws of God and the Church

173. What is the most important implication of the Biblical story of
    creation?
    A. The world was created in a brief period of time
    B. Good and evil were created by God
    C. Adam and Eve were the first human beings
    D. Everything depends on God for its existence

SECTION 11 – Personal Goals for the Future

HOW IMPORTANT ARE THE FOLLOWING GOALS FOR YOUR FUTURE
LIFE:

A. No importance
B. Little importance
C. Some importance
D. Very important
E. Most important

174. To make a lot of money
175. To find personal happiness and satisfaction in life
176. To serve other people
177. To be honest in my dealings with others
178. To be happily married and have a happy family life
179. To accept myself as the person I am
180. To be important and successful in life
181. To find God in my life and grow in faith in Him
182. To live up to the example and teachings of Christ

(i) What have you come to APPRECIATE and VALUE about the CATHOLIC SCHOOL YOU ATTEND?

_____

_____

_____

_____

_____

(ii) Are there any CHANGES which you would make at your school?

_____

_____

_____

_____

_____

(iii) How would you describe the UNIQUE SPIRIT which exists in your school?

_____

_____

_____

THANK YOU FOR YOUR CARE IN ANSWERING THIS QUESTIONNAIRE

Bibliography

Adams, R. and Haaken, J. (1987) 'Anti-cultural culture: lifesprings ideology and its roots in humanistic psychology', *Journal of Humanistic Psychology*, 27, 4, Autumn

Alexander, H. (2000) 'In Search of a vision of the good: values education and the postmodern condition', in R. Gardner, J. Cairns and D. Lawton (eds), *Education for Values: Morals, Ethics and Citizenship in Contemporary Teaching.* London: Kogan Page

Allen, R. and West, A. (2007) 'Religious schools in London: school admissions, religious composition and selectivity?' British Educational Research Association

Annette, J. (2005) 'Faith schools and communities' in J. Cairns, R. Gardner and D. Lawton (eds), *Faith Schools: Consensus or Conflict?* London: Taylor and Francis

Archbishop of Canterbury (1988), 'The importance of Church Schools' in *The National Society, A Christian Voice in Education: Distinctiveness in Church Schools.* London: The National Society

Archbishop of Canterbury, Dr Rowan Williams (2003) *The Times*, 12 September

Archbishop of Canterbury, Dr Rowan Williams (2004a) *The Times*, 1 May

Archbishop of Canterbury, Dr Rowan Williams (2004b) *The Sunday Times*, 21 November

Aristotle (350 BCE) *Nicomachean Ethics* 1106 b 36–1107 a 3. Quotations from Aristotle are from Barnes, J. (ed.) (1984) *The Complete Works of Aristotle: The Revised Oxford Translation*, vols 1 and 2, Princeton: Princeton University Press

Armstrong, K. (1993) *A History of God From Abraham to the Present: the 4000-Year Quest for God.* London: Heinemann

Arnove, R.F., Altbach, P.G. and Kelly, G.P. (eds) (1992) *Emergent Issues in Education: Comparative Perspectives.* Buffalo: State University of New York Press

Arrupe, Rev. P. (1994) 'Men for others', in Melrose, C. (ed.) *Foundations.* Washington, DC: The Jesuit Secondary Education Association

Arthur, J. (1995) *The Ebbing Tide: Policy and Principles of Catholic Education*, Leominster: Gracewing

Arthur, J. with Bailey, R. (2000) *Schools and Community: The Communitarian Agenda in Education.* London: Falmer Press

Arthur, J. (2005) 'Measuring Catholic school performance: an international perspective', in R. Gardner, J. Cairns, D. Lawton (eds), *Faith Schools: Consensus or Conflict?* London: Routledge

Assessment of Performance Unit (1982) *Personal and Social Development: A Map of the Territory* (discussion paper). London: Department of Education and Science

Ayer, A.J. (1946) *Language, Truth and Logic.* London: Gollancz

Balls, E. The Times 4 July 2008

Bartelt, D. (1995) 'The macroecology of educational outcomes', in L. Rigsby, M. Reynolds and M. Wang (eds), *School-Community Connections: Exploring Issues for Research and Practice.* San Francisco: Jossey-Bass

Barth, F. (1994) *Ethnic Groups and Boundaries: The Social Organization of Cultural Differences.* Long Grove, Ill: Waveland Press

Bassey, M. (1999) *Case Study Research in Educational Settings.* Buckingham: Open University Press

Bates, R. (1986) *The Management of a Culture and Knowledge.* Melbourne: Deakin University Press

Baudrillard, J. (1993) *The Transparency of Evil.* London: Verso

Baumann, G. (1999) *The Multicultural Riddle: Re-thinking National, Ethnic and Religious Identities.* London: Routledge

Beck, C. (1991) *Better Schools.* London: Falmer

Beem, C. (1999) *The Necessity of Politics.* Chicago: The University of Chicago Press

Bell, D. (1996) *The Cultural Contradictions of Capitalism.* New York: Basic Books

Bellah, R., Madsen, R., Sullivan, W., Swidler, A. and Tipton S. (1996), *Habits of the Heart*, 2nd edition. Berkeley: University of California Press

Bellah, R. (1992) *The Broken Covenant: American Civil Religion in Time of Trial*, 2nd edition. Chicago: University of Chicago Press

Belsen, W. (1986) *Validity in Social Research.* Aldershot: Gower

Berger, P. and R.J. Neuhaus (1996) *To Empower People: From State to Civil Society*, 2nd edition. Washington DC: American Enterprise Institute Press

Berry, P. (1992) 'Introduction', in P. Berry and A. Wernick (eds), *Shadow of Spirit: Postmodernism and Religion.* London: Routledge

Biesta, G. (2003) 'How general can Bildung be? Reflections on the future of a modern educational ideal', in L. Lovlie, K.P. Mortensen and S.E. Nordenbo (eds), *Educating Humanity: Bildung in Postmodernity.* Oxford: Blackwell

Bocock, B. and Thompson, K. (1985) *Religion and Modernity.* Manchester: Manchester University Press

Bourne, J., Bridges, L. and Searle, C. (1994) *Outcast England: How Schools Exclude Black Pupils.* London: Institute of Race Relations

Bousted, M. (2007) BBC News, 10 September. London: BBC

Bruner, J. (1996) *The Culture of Education.* Cambridge, MA: Harvard University Press

Bryk, A. (1996) 'Lessons from Catholic high schools on renewing our educational institutions', in T. McLaughlin, J. O'Keefe and B. O'Keeffe (eds), *The Contemporary Catholic School: Context, Identity and Diversity.* London: Falmer

Bryk, A.S. and Lee, V.E. (1989) 'A multilevel model of the social distribution of high school achievement', *Sociology of Education*, 62, 3: 172–92

Bryk, A.S., Lee, V.E. and Holland, P.B. (1993) *Catholic Schools and the Common Good.* Cambridge, MA: Harvard University Press

Busher, H. (2001) 'The micro-politics of change, improvement and effectiveness in schools', in A. Harris and N. Bennett (eds) *School Effectiveness and School Improvement: Alternative Perspectives.* London: Continuum

Cairns, J. (2000) 'Schools, community and the developing values of young adults: towards an ecology of education in values' in J. Cairns, R. Gardner and D. Lawton (eds), *Values and the Curriculum.* London: Woburn Press

Cairns, J., Gardner, R. and Lawton, D. (eds) (2005) *Faith Schools: Consensus or Conflict?* London: Taylor and Francis

Callan, E. (1998) 'The politics of difference', in D. Carr (ed.), *Education, Knowledge and Truth: Beyond the Postmodern Impasse.* London: Routledge

Campbell, A.C. (1978) 'A brief history of School A's local area', School A's magazine, pp. 14–17

Cantle, T. (2001) *Community Cohesion: a report of the independent review team*, London: Home Office

Carey, G. (2000) 'Moral values: the challenge and opportunity', in J. Cairns, R. Gardner and D. Lawton (eds), *Values and the Curriculum*. London: Woburn Press

Carr, D. (ed.) (1998) *Education, Knowledge and Truth: Beyond the Postmodern Impasse*. London: Routledge

Carr, D. (2003) 'Three conceptions of spirituality for spiritual education', in D. Carr and J. Haldane (eds), *Spirituality, Philosophy and Education*. London: Routledge Falmer

Carr, D. (2004) 'Problems of values education', in J. Haldane (ed.), *Values Education and the Human World*. Exeter: Imprint Academic

Carr, D. and Haldane, J. (eds) (2003) *Spirituality, Philosophy and Education*. London: Routledge Falmer

Carr, D. and Steutel, J. (1999) 'Pointers, problems and prospects', in D. Carr and J. Steutel (eds), *Virtue, Ethics and Moral Education*. London: Routledge

Carr, D. and Steutel, J. (1999) *Virtue Ethics and Moral Education*. London: Routledge

Carter, S. (1993) *The Culture of Disbelief*. New York: Basic Books

Chodorkoff, D. (1990) 'Social ecology and community development', in J. Clark (ed.), *Reviewing the Earth: the promise of social ecology*. London: Greenprint

Christie, P. and Potterton, M. (1997) *School Development in South Africa: A Research Project to Investigate Strategic Interventions for Quality Improvement in South African Schools*. Johannesberg: University of the Witwatersand

Church of England (2001) Board of Education *Response to White Paper Schools Achieving Success*. London: Church House Press Office, 5 September 2001

Church Schools Review Group (2001) *The Way Ahead: Church of England Schools in the New Millennium*. London: Church House Publishing

Cohen, A. (1985) *The Symbolic Construction of Community*. Manchester: Manchester University Press

Cohen, L. and Manion, L. (1994) *Research Methods in Education*, 4th edition. London: Routledge

Coleman, J. (1981) 'Public schools, private schools, and the public interest', *The Public Interest*, 64, Summer

Coleman, J., Hoffer, T. and Kilgore, S. (1982) *High School Achievement: Public, Catholic and Private Schools Compared*. New York: Basic Books

Coleman, J. and Hoffer, T. (1987) *Public, Catholic and Private Schools: The Importance of Community*. New York: Basic Books

Coleman, J. (2001) 'Social capital in the creation of human capital', in A.H. Halsey, H. Lauder, P. Brown and A.S. Wells, *Education: Culture, Economy, Society*. Oxford: OUP

Comer, J.P. (1987) 'New Haven's school-community connections', *Educational Leadership*, 44, 6: 13–16

Commission for Social Justice (1994) *Social Justice: Strategy for National Renewal*. Vintage: IPPR

Cornick, D. (2003) *Inside Out: Journal of the Council for World Mission*, August

Country X 'National Development Plan 8, 1997/8–2002/3' Gox

Country Z (2003) 'Education Act', Goz

Cowen, R. (2000) 'The market-framed university', in J. Cairns, R. Gardner and D. Lawton (eds), *Values and the Curriculum*. London: Woburn Press

Cox, E. (1983) *Problems and Possibilities for Religious Education*. London: Hodder and Stoughton

Cox, E. (1986) 'The belief system', in D. Lawton (ed.), *School Curriculum Planning*. London: Hodder and Stoughton

Crossley, M. and Watson, K. (2003) *Comparative and International Research in Education: Globalisation, Context and Difference*. London: Routledge

Dante, A. *Divina Comedia* 'Paradiso' XIII.115–123

Darmody, J. (1990) *Some Perceptions and Expectations of Young Catholics*, Melbourne: Centre for Family Studies, Christ Campus, Institute of Catholic Education

Dawson, C. (1967) *The Crisis of Western Education*. London: Sheed and Ward

Department for Children, Schools and Families (DCSF) (2007) *Faith in the system*. Online: www.dcsf.gov.uk

Department for Education and Skills (1998) *Teachers: Meeting the Challenge for Change*. London: HMSO

Department for Education and Skills (2001) *Schools Achieving Success*, Cm 5230, London: Stationery Office

Dewey, J. (1957) *Reconstruction in Philosophy*, enlarged edition. Boston: Beacon

Dorling, D. and Thomas, B. (2007) 'Cities in Transition'. *Britain's Increasing Plurality*. London: Burrow Cadbury Trust

Dowden, R. (2002) *The Times*, 26 June

Durkheim, E. (1986) *Moral Education: A Study in the Theory and Application of the Sociology of Education*. New York: Free Press

Eisner, E. (1993) 'Forms of understanding and the future of educational research', *Educational Researcher*, 22, 7 (October): 5–11

Eisner, E. (1979) *The Educational Imagination: On the Design and Evaluation of School Programs*. New York: Macmillan

Elshtain, J. (1995), *Democracy on Trial*. New York: Basic Books

Erricker, C. and Erricker, J. (2000) *Reconstructing Religious, Spiritual and Moral Education*. London: Routledge Falmer

Erricker, J. (2000) 'Moral education as relationship in community', in C. Erricker and J. Erricker (eds), *Reconstructing Religious, Spiritual and Moral Education*. London: Routledge Falmer

European Values Study, *EUROPEAN VALUES STUDY*, 1999/2000 (Computer file) 2003/ Release 1, The Netherlands, Germany: Tilburg University

Evans, M. (2008) 'Britain is world's 7th most stable nation', *The Times*, 25 March

Finch, J. (1986) *Research and Policy: The Uses of Qualitative Methods in Social and Educational Research*. Lewes: Falmer Press

Fine, G.A. and Sandstrom, K.L. (1988) *Knowing Children: Participant Observation with Minors*. Newbury Park, CA: Sage

Finegold, D., McFarland, L. and Richardson, W. (eds) (1992), 'Something borrowed, something blue? A study of the Thatcher government's appropriation of American education and policy' (part 1), *Oxford Studies in Comparative Education*, 2, 2

Finegold, D., McFarland, L. and Richardson, W. (eds) (1993) 'Something borrowed, something blue? A study of the Thatcher government's appropriation of American education and training policy (part 2), *Oxford Studies in Comparative Education*, 3, 1

Flanagan, K. (1999) 'Introduction' in K. Flanagan and P.C. Jupp (eds), *Postmodernity, Sociology and Religion,* 2nd edition. Basingstoke: MacMillan

Flynn, M. (1985) *The Effectiveness of Catholic Schools*. Homebush: St Paul Publications

Flynn, M. (1993) *The Culture of Catholic Schools*. New South Wales: St Pauls Publications

Flynn, M. and Mok, M. (1999) 'Catholic Schools 2000 Research', unpublished report presented to a meeting of the School of Religious Education. Sydney: Australian Catholic University, December

Flynn, M. and Mok, M. (2002) *Catholic Schools 2000*. New South Wales: Catholic Education Commission

Foddy, W. (1993) *Constructing Questions for Interviews and Questionnaires – Theory and Practice in Social Research*. Cambridge: Cambridge University Press

Forrest, R. and Kearns, A. (2000) 'Social cohesion and multilevel urban governance', *Urban Studies*, 37, 5–6 (1 May): 995–1017

Francis, L. (2001) *The Values Debate: A Voice from the Pupils*. London: Woburn Press

Francis, L.J. and Robbins, M. (2005) *Urban Hope and Spiritual Health: The Adolescent Voice*. Werrington: Epworth

Freire, P. (1972) *Pedagogy of the Oppressed*. Harmondsworth: Penguin

Freire, P. (1985) 'The process of political literacy', in P. Freire (ed.), *The Politics of Education: Culture, Power and Liberation*. Translated by D. Macedo. Massachusetts: Bergin and Garvey Publishers Inc.

Freire, P. (1994) *Pedagogy of Hope*. New York: Continuum

Freire, P. (1998) *Pedagogy of Freedom: Ethics, Democracy and Civic Courage*. Lanham, MD: Rowan and Littlefield

Freire, P. and Shor, I. (1987) *A Pedagogy for Liberation*. London: Macmillan

Furnivall, J.S. (1956) *Colonial Policy and Practice*. New York: New York University Press

Gadamer, H.G. (1989) *Truth and Method*, 2nd edition. London: Sheed and Ward

Gallagher, D. and Gallagher, I. (eds) (1976) *The Education of Man: The Educational Philosophy of Jacques Maritain*. Connecticut: Greenwood Press

Gallagher, T. (2005) 'Faith schools and Northern Ireland: a review of research', in J. Cairns, D. Lawton and R. Gardner (eds), *Faith Schools: Consensus or Conflict?* London: Taylor and Francis

Gamarnikow, E. and Green, A. (2000) 'Citizenship, education and social capital', in D. Lawton, J. Cairns and R. Gardner (eds), *Education for Citizenship*. London: Continuum

Garfunkel, H. (1967) *Studies in Ethnomethodology*. Eaglewood Cliffs, NJ: Prentice Hall

Geertz, C. (1975) *The Interpretation of Culture*. New York: Basic Books

Geertz, C. (1985) 'Ideology as cultural system', in B. Boocock and K. Thompson (eds), *Religion and Modernity*. Manchester: Manchester University Press

Gellner, E. (1992) *Postmodernism, Reason and Religion*. London: Routledge

Giddens, A. (1998) *The Third Way: The Renewal of Social Democracy*. Cambridge: Polity

Gilbert, A.D. (1980) *The Making of Post-Christian Britain*. London: Longman

Gill, A. (2005) 'Religious membership', in W. Schweiker (ed.), *The Blackwell Companion to Religious Ethics*. Oxford: Blackwell Publishing

Gilligan, C. (1982) *In Another Voice*. Cambridge, MA: Harvard University Press

Goffman, E. (1955) 'On face work', *Psychiatry*, 18: 213–31

Goffman, E. (1983) 'The interaction order', *American Sociological Review*, 48: 1–17

Gordon, P. and Lawton, D. (2003) *Dictionary of Education*. London: Woburn Press

Government of Country X (1994) *The Revised National Policy on Education: As approved by the National Assembly on 7 March*. Paper no 2

Government of Country X (GoX) (1997) *National Development Plan 8: 1997/8–2002/3*

Government of Country X Presidential Task Group (GoXPTG) (1997) *Long Term Vision for Country X: Towards Prosperity For All*.

Government of Country Y (1999) *Strategic Plan for Educational Enhancement and Development*

Government of Country Y (2000) *Code of Ethics for Members of the Teaching Service*, 4th draft copy

Government of Country Z (1996) *Ethical Code for Teachers*

Government of Country Z (2003) *Education Act*

Grace, G. (1996) 'Leadership in Catholic Schools', in T.H. McLaughlin et al. (eds), *The Contemporary Catholic School: Context, Identity and Diversity*. London: Falmer Press

Grace, G. (1998) 'The future of the Catholic school: an English perspective', in J.M. Feheney (ed.), *From Ideal to Action*. Dublin: Veritas

Grace, G. (2000) *Catholic Schools and the Common Good*. London: Institute of Education

Grace, G. (2002) *Catholic Schools: Mission, Markets and Morality*. London: Routledge

Grace, G. (2003a) *The Guardian*, 8 November

Grace, G. (2003b) Paper presented to the conference, *Faith Schools: Consensus or Conflict?* held at the Institute of Education, University of London

Grace, G. and O'Keefe, J. (2007) *International Handbook of Catholic Education*. Dordrecht: Springer

Graham, D. (2003) *Secular or Religious? The Outlook of London's Jews: Planning for Jewish Communities 3*. London: IJPR

Great Britain (1998) *Teachers Meeting the Challenge of Change*. London: DfES

Greeley, A.M. and Rossi, P.H. (1996) *The Education of Catholic Americans*. Chicago: Aldine.

Gutmann, A. (1993) 'Democracy and democratic education', *Studies in Philosophy and Education*, 12, 1 (March): 1–9

Gutmann, A. (1987) *Democratic Education*. Princeton: Princeton University Press

Haldane, J. (1993) 'A prologomenon to an unwritten philosophy of education: Catholic social teaching and the common good', paper presented to the conference, *The Contemporary Catholic School and the Common Good*, St Edmund's College, Cambridge, July

Halsey, A.H., Lauder, H., Brown, P. and Wells, A.S. (2001) *Education: Culture, Economy, Society*. Oxford: OUP

Halstead, J.M. (1996) 'Liberal values and liberal education', in J.M. Halstead and M.J. Taylor (eds), *Values in Education and Education in Values*. London: Falmer Press

Hammond, J., Hay, D., Moxon, J., Netto, B., Raban, K., Straugheir, G. and Williams, C. (eds) (1990) *New Methods in RE Teaching – an experiential approach*. Harlow: Oliver and Boyd

Hardy, A. (1975) *The Biology of God*. London: Jonathan Cape

Hare, R.M. (1955) 'Theology and falsification', in A. Flew and A. MacIntyre (eds), *New Essays in Philosophical Theology*. London: S.C.M. Press

Hare, R.M. (1992) *Essays on Religion and Education*. Oxford: Clarendon Press

Hargreaves, A. (1994) *Changing Teachers, Changing Times*. London: Cassell

Harris, A. and Bennett, N. (eds) (2001) *School Effectiveness and School Improvement: Alternative Perspectives*. London: Continuum

Hay, D. and Nye, R. (1998) *The Spirit of the Child*. London: Harper Collins

Haynes, J. (1998) *Religion in Global Politics*. London: Longman

Heelas, P. (1998) 'Introduction: on differentiation and de-differentiation', in P. Heelas (ed.), *Religion, Modernity and Postmodernity*. Oxford: Blackwell

Heelas, P. (1999) 'De-traditionalisation of religion and self: the new age and postmodernity', in K. Flanagan and P.C. Jupp (eds), *Postmodernity, Sociology and Religion*, 2nd edition. Basingstoke: Macmillan

Heritage, J. (1997) 'Conversation analysis and institutional talk: analysing data' in D. Silverman (ed.), *Qualitative Research: Theory, Method and Practice*. London: Sage

Heubner, D. (1985) 'Religious metaphor in the language of education', *Religious Education*, 80, 3 (Summer)

Hefner, R. (1998) 'Secularization and citizenship', in P. Heelas (ed.), *Religion, Modernity and Postmodernity*. Oxford: Blackwell Publishers

Hirst, P. and Peters, R. (1970) *The Logic of Education*. London: Routledge and Kegan Paul

Hirst, P.H. (1974) *Moral Education in a Secular Society*. London: Hodder and Stoughton

Hobsbawm, E. (1994) 'Age of extremes: the short twentieth century', in E. Baglin-Jones and N. Jones (eds), *Education for Citizenship*. London: Kogan Page

Hobson, P.R. and Edwards, J.S. (1999) *Religious Education in a Pluralist Society*. London: Woburn Press

Hollenbach, D. (1996) 'The common good, pluralism and Catholic education', in T. McLaughlin, J. O' Keefe, and B. O' Keeffe (eds), *The Contemporary Catholic School: Context, Identity and Diversity*. London: Falmer Press

Holmes, B. (ed.) (1967) *Educational Policy and the Mission Schools*. London: Routledge and Kegan Paul

Holstein, J.A. and Gubrium, J.F. (1997) 'Active interviewing', in D. Silverman (ed.), *Qualitative Research: Theory, Method and Practice*. London: Sage

Hull, J. (1999), 'The preface', in P.R. Hobson and J.S. Edwards, *Religious Education in a Pluralist Society*. London: Woburn Press

Hulmes, E. (1979) *Commitment and Neutrality in Religious Education*. London: Geoffrey Chapman

Hulmes, E. (1994) 'Society in conflict: the value of education', *Aspects of Education*, 51

Hume, B. (1986) *With You in Spirit*. London: Westminster Archdiocese

Ingraffia, B.D. (1995) *Postmodern Theory and Biblical Theology: Vanquishing God's Shadow*. Cambridge: Cambridge University Press

Jackson, R. (1997) *Religious Education: An Interpretive Approach*. London: Hodder and Stoughton

Jackson R. (2004) *Rethinking Religious Education and Plurality: Issues in Diversity and Pedagogy*. London: Routledge Falmer

Jenkins, P. (2002) *The Next Christendom: The Coming of Global Christianity*. Oxford: OUP

John Paul II (1995) Address to the United Nations General Assembly, 5 October

Judge, H. (2002) *Faith-based Schools and the State: Catholics in America, France and England*. Wallingford: Symposium Books

Kant, I. (1992) 'An answer to the question, What is Enlightenment?', in P. Waugh (ed.), *Postmodernism: A Reader*. London: Edward Arnold

Kearney, R. and Sanders, A. (1988) *The Wake of Imagination*. London: Routledge

Kelly, A.V. (1999) *The Curriculum: Theory and Practice*, 4th edition. London: Paul Chapman Publishing

Kerr, F. (1998) 'Truth in religion', in D. Carr (ed.), *Education, Knowledge and Truth*. London: Routledge

Khama, D. (2001) 'Church and state partnership in education: perceptions of education administrators and community members in secondary schools in Lesotho', unpublished PhD dissertation, University of Reading

King, E.J. (1979) *Other Schools and Ours*, 5th edition. London: Holt, Rinehart and Winston

King, U. (2002) 'Spirituality and Postmodernism', *Farmington Papers, Philosophy of Religion 11*. Oxford: Farmington Institute for Christian Studies

Kolakowski, L. (1982) *Religion: If there is no God . . . On God, the Devil, Sin and Other Worries of the So-called Philosophy of Religion*. London: Fontana

Kung, H. (1980) *Does God Exist? An Answer for Today*. London: SCM

Lacey, C. (1996) 'Renewing teaching', in T. McLaughlin, J. O' Keefe and B. O' Keeffe (eds), *The Contemporary Catholic School: Context, Identity and Diversity*. London: Falmer Press

Lankshear, C. (1997) *Changing Literacies*. Buckingham: Open University Press

Lauwerys, J.A. (1967) 'Preface', in B. Holmes (ed.), *Educational Policy and the Mission Schools*. London: Routledge and Kegan Paul

Lawton, D. (1996) *Beyond the National Curriculum: Teacher Professionalism and Empowerment*. London: Hodder and Stoughton

Lawton, D. and Cowen, R. (2001) 'Values, culture and education: an overview', in J. Cairns, D. Lawton and R. Gardner (eds), *Values, Culture and Education World Yearbook of Education 2001*. London: Kogan Page

Leach, F.E. and Little, A.W. (eds) (1999) *Education, Cultures and Economics*. London: Falmer Press

Leicester, M. and Taylor, M. (1992) *Ethics, Ethnicity and Education*. London: Kogan Page

LeVine, R. and White, M. (1986) *Human Conditions: The Cultural Bases of Educational Development*. London: Routledge and Kegan Paul

Lewis, H.R. (2006) *Excellence Without A Soul: How a Great University Forgot Education*. United States: Public Affairs

Longley, C. (1995) 'Introduction', in J. Sacks, *Faith in the Future*. London: Darton, Longman and Todd

Lovlie, L. and Standish, P. (2003) 'Bildung and the idea of a liberal education', in L. Lovlie, K.P. Mortensen and S.E. Nordenbo (eds), *Educating Humanity: Bildung in Postmodernity*. Oxford: Blackwell

Lyotard, J.F. (1984) *The Postmodern Condition: A Report on Knowledge*. Manchester: Manchester University Press

MacBeath, J. (1999) *Schools Must Speak for Themselves: The Case for School Self-Evaluation*. London: Routledge

MacGilcrhrist, B., Myers, K. and Reed, J. (2004) *The Intelligent School*, 2nd edition. London: Sage

MacIntyre, A. (1984) *After Virtue: A Study in Moral Theory*, 2nd edition. London: Duckworth

MacIntyre, A. (1990) *Three Rival Versions of Moral Enquiry: Encyclopaedia, Genealogy and Tradition*. London: Duckworth

Macquarrie, J. (1972) *Paths in Spirituality*. London: Harper and Row

Mallinson, V. (1975) *An Introduction to the Study of Comparative Education*, 4th edition. London: Heinemann

Manning, H.E. Cardinal (1888) 'The Catholic Church and modern society' in The North American Review, reprinted in *Miscellanies, III*. London, pp. 309–22

Maritain, J. (1951) *Man and the State*. Chicago: University of Chicago Press

Maritain, J. Gallagher, D. and Gallagher, I. (eds) (1976) *The Education of Man: The Educational Philosophy of Jacques Maritain/edited, with an introduction by Donald and Idella Gallagher*. Notre Dame, IN: University of Notre Dame Press

McClelland, V.A. (1988) ' "Sensus Fidelium": the developing concept of Roman Catholic voluntary effort in education in England and Wales', in W. Tulasiewicz and C. Brock (eds), *Christianity and Educational Provision in International Perspective*. London: Routledge

Mc Clelland, V.A. (ed.) (1992) *The Catholic School and the European Context*. Hull: University of Hull

McClelland, V.A. (1996) 'Wholeness, faith, and the distinctiveness of the Catholic school', in T. McLaughlin, J. O' Keefe and B. O' Keeffe (eds), *The Contemporary Catholic School: Context, Identity and Diversity*. London: Falmer Press

McCutcheon, R.T. (1997) *Manufacturing Religion: The Discourse on Sui Generis Religion and the Politics of Nostalgia*. Oxford: Oxford University Press

McGrew, A. (1992) 'A global society', in S. Hall, D. Held and A. McGrew (eds), *Modernity and its Future*. Cambridge: Polity Press

McKenzie, L. (1982) *The Religious Education of Adults*. Birmingham, Alabama: Religious Education Press

McKenzie, L. (1991) *Adult Education and Worldview Construction*. Malabar: Krieger

McLaughlin, T.H. (1994) 'Values, coherence and the school', *Cambridge Journal of Education*, 24, 3: 253–70

McLaughlin, T. (2003) 'Education, spirituality and the common school', in D. Carr and J. Haldane (eds), *Spirituality, Philosophy and Education*. London: Routledge Falmer

McLaughlin, T., O' Keefe, J. and O' Keeffe, B. (1996) *The Contemporary Catholic School: Context, Identity and Diversity*. London: Falmer Press

McLean, M. (1983) 'Educational dependency: a critique', *Compare*, 13, 1: 25–41

Meijer, W.A.J. (1995) 'The plural self: a hermeneutical view on identity and plurality', *British Journal of Religious Education*, 17, 2: 92–9

Meissner, W.W. (1970) 'Notes toward a theory of values: the place of values', *Journal of Religion and Health*, 9, 2 (April): 120–9

Miller, G. (1997) 'Building bridges: the possibility of analytic dialogue between ethnography, conversation analysis and Foucault', in D. Silverman (ed.), *Qualitative Research: Theory, Method and Practice*. London: Sage

Miller, J. and Glassner, B. (1997) 'The "inside" and the "outside": finding realities in interviews', in D. Silverman (ed.), *Qualitative Research: Theory, Method and Practice*. London: Sage

Miller, W.L. (1986) *The First Liberty: Religion and the American Republic*. New York: Knopf

Misztal, B. (1996) *Trust in Modern Societies*. Oxford: Polity

Mmolai, S.K. (1999) 'Religion and ethics in modern secondary education', unpublished PhD thesis. Lancaster: University of Lancaster

Modood, T. (1997) 'Difference, cultural racism and antiracism', in P. Werbner and T. Modood (eds), *Debating Cultural Hybridity*. London: Zed Books

Morley, L. and Rassool, N. (1999) *School Effectiveness: Fracturing the Discourse*. London: Routledge

Morrison, K. (2002) *School Leadership and Complexity Theory*. London: Routledge Falmer

Mortimore, P., Sammons, P. and Hillman, D. (1995) *Key Characteristics of Effective Schools: A Review of School Effectiveness Research*. London: Ofsted

Mott-Thornton, K. (2003) 'Spirituality, pluralism and the limits of common schooling', in D. Carr and J. Haldane (eds), *Spirituality, Philosophy and Education*. London: Routledge Falmer

Mtumbuka, M.A. (2003) 'An empirical study of Catholic secondary schools in Malawi: strengths, weaknesses and challenges', unpublished PhD thesis, University of London. London: Institute of Education

National Curriculum Council (1993) *Spiritual and Moral Development*. York: National Curriculum Council

Neal, D. (1997a) 'The effects of Catholic secondary schooling on educational attainment', *Journal of Labour Economics*, 15, 1: 98–123

Neal, D. (1997b) 'Measuring Catholic school performance', *Public Interest*, 127 (Spring): 81–7

Neave, G. (1988) 'Education and social policy: demise of an ethic or change of values?', *Oxford Review of Education*, 14, 3: 273–83

Nelson, C.E. (1967) *Where Faith Begins*. Atlanta: John Knox Press

Newman, J.H. (1852) 'The idea of a university', in M.H. Abrams (1986) (ed.), *The Norton Anthology of English Literature*, vol. 2. London: Norton

Newmark, J. (2004) 'Keeping the faiths', *Jewish Chronicle*, 9 April

Niblett, W.R. (2001) *Life, Education, Discovery*. Bristol: Pomegranate Books

Nietzsche, F. (1969) *Thus Spoke Zarathustra: A Book for Everyone and No one*. Harmondsworth: Penguin

Norman, E.R. (1984) *The English Catholic Church in the Nineteenth Century*. Oxford: OUP

Nozick, R. (1981) *Philosophical Explanations*. Oxford: Clarendon Press

Office for Standards in Education (1994) *Handbook for the Inspection of Schools*, Consolidated edition. London: Ofsted

O'Keeffe, B. (1992) 'Catholic schools in an open society: the English challenge', in V.A. McClelland (ed.), *The Catholic School and the European Context*. Hull: University of Hull

O' Keefe, J. (1996) 'No margin, no mission', in T. McLaughlin, J. O'Keefe and B. O'Keeffe (eds), *The Contemporary Catholic School*. London:, Falmer Press

Osler, A. (2007) *Interim report on Faith Schools and Community Cohesion*. London: Runnymede Trust

Parekh, B. (1989) *Gandhi's Political Philosophy; A Critical Examination*. London: Macmillan

Parker-Jenkins, M., Hartas, D. and Irving, B. (2005) *In Good Faith: Schools, Religion and Public Funding*. Aldershot: Ashgate

Pendelbury, S. (1998) 'Feminism, epistemology and education', in Carr, D. (ed.), *Education, Knowledge and Truth: Beyond the Postmodern Impasse*. London: Routledge

Peters, R.S. (1966) *Ethics and Education*. London: George Allen and Unwin

Pettifer, J. and Bradley, R. (1992) *The Missionaries*. London: BBC Publications

Pine, R. (1990) *Brian Friel and Ireland's Drama*. London: Routledge

Preston, R. (1997) 'Prisms, kaleidoscopes and realities: resolving dilemmas in educational research', in K. Watson, C. Modgil and S. Modgil (eds), *Educational Dilemmas: Debate and Diversity: Volume 4 Quality in Education*. London: Cassell

Price, M. (1997) 'Religious education: an engagement in and expression of imagination', a paper presented to the Farmington Institute. Oxford: Harris Manchester College

Priestley, J. (1996) 'Spirituality in the curriculum', *Hockerill Lecture 1996*. Frinton-on Sea: Hockerill Educational Foundation

Priestley, J. (1997) 'Spirituality, curriculum and education', *International Journal of Children's Spirituality*, 2, 1

Priestley, J. (2000) 'The foreword', in C. Erricker and J. Erricker, *Reconstructing Religious, Spiritual and Moral Education*. London: Routledge Falmer

Priestley, J. (2002) Discussion on 'the spiritual in education' at University of Warwick Seminar on the Spiritual in Religious Education

Priestley, J. (2005) 'The spiritual dimension of the curriculum: what are school inspectors looking for and how can we help them find it?', in C. Ota and C. Erricker (eds), *Spiritual Education: Literary, Empirical and Pedagogical Approaches*. Sussex: Academic Press

Pring, R. (1984) *Personal and Social Education in the Curriculum*. London: Hodder and Stoughton

Pring, R. (1996) 'Markets, education and Catholic schools', in T.H. McLaughlin et al. (eds), *The Contemporary Catholic School*. London: Falmer

Pring, R. (2000a) *Philosophy of Educational Research*. London: Continuum

Pring, R. (2000b) 'Institutional values and personal development', in J. Cairns, R. Gardner and D. Lawton (eds), *Values and the Curriculum*. London: Woburn Press

Pring, R. (2005) 'Faith schools: can they be justified?', in R. Gardner, D. Lawton and J. Cairns (eds), *Faith Schools: Consensus or Conflict?* London: Routledge Falmer

Quality Assurance Agency for Higher Education (2000) *Benchmark Statement for Theology and Religious Studies*. Gloucester: QAAHE

Ranson, S. (1994) *Towards the Learning Society*. London: Cassell

Rawls, J. (1987) 'The idea of an overlapping consensus', *Oxford Journal of Legal Studies*, 7 February: 1–25

Rawls, J. (1993) *Political Liberalism*. New York: Columbia University Press

Raz, J. (1986) *The Morality of Freedom*. Oxford: OUP

Reich, R. (1992) *The Work of Nations: Preparing Ourselves for Twenty-first Century Capitalism*. New York: Random House

Reissman, C.K. (1993) *Narrative Analysis*. Newbury Park, CA: Sage

Roberts, P. (2000) *Education, Literacy and Humanization: Explaining the Works of Paolo Freire*. Westport, CT: Greenwood Publishing

Rodger, A. (1982) *Education and Faith in an Open Society*. Edinburgh: The Handsel Press

Rutter, M., Maughham, B., Mortimer, P. and Ouston, J. (1979) *Fifteen Thousand Hours: Secondary Schools and their Effects on Children*. London: Open Books

Sacks, J. (ed.) (1991) 'Introduction', in *Orthodoxy Confronts Modernity*. Hoboken, NJ, in association with Jews' College London, England: Ktav Publishing House

Sacks, J., the Chief Rabbi (1995) *Faith in the Future*. London: Darton, Longman and Todd

Sacks, J. (2000) *The Politics of Hope*. London: Vintage

Sacks, J. (2002) *The Dignity of Difference*. London: Continuum

Sacks, J. and Sutherland, S. (1996) *Education, Values and Religion*, Victor Cook Memorial Lectures. St Andrews: St Andrews University

Sandel, M.J. (1982) *Liberalism and the Limits of Justice*. Cambridge: Cambridge University Press

Sandel, M.J. (1994) 'Review of political liberalism of John Rawls', *Harvard Law Review*, 107, 7: 1765–94

Schagen, I. and Schagen, S. (2005) 'The impact of faith schools on pupil perform-ance' in R. Gardner, J. Cairns and D. Lawton (eds), *Faith Schools: Consensus or Conflict?* London: Routledge Falmer

Schmack, B. (2006) 'Supporting the professional development of primary school teachers in spiritual education', unpublished PhD thesis. Liverpool: Liverpool Hope University

Schneiders, S.M. (2000) 'Religion and spirituality: strangers, rivals or partners?', *Santa Clara Lectures*, 6, 2: 13

Scholefield, L. (1999) 'A tale of two cultures: a dialogical study of the cultures of a Jewish and a Catholic secondary school', unpublished PhD dissertation. Institute of Education: University of London

School A (1949) *Chronicles*: School A

School A (1978) *School Magazine*: School A

School B (n.d.) *Prospectus: School B*

School C (2000) *Guidelines for Teachers*: School C

School D (1996) *Handbook* (in translation): School D

Sennett, R. (2003) *Respect for the Formation of Character in an Age of Inequality*. London: Allen Lane, The Penguin Press

Sherman, N. (1997) *Making a Necessity of Virtue: Aristotle and Kant on Virtue*. Cambridge: Cambridge University Press

Sherman, N. (1999) 'Character development', in D. Carr and J. Steutel (eds), *Virtue Ethics and Moral Education*. London: Routledge

Simons, H. (1996) 'The paradox of case study', *Cambridge Journal of Education*, 26, 2: 225–40

Skeie, G. (1995) 'Plurality and pluralism: a challenge for religious education', *British Journal of Religious Education*, 25, 1: 47–59

Slee, R. and Weiner, G. (eds) (1998) *School Effectiveness for Whom? Challenges to the School Effectiveness and School Improvement Movements*. London: Falmer

Stenhouse, L. (1988) 'Case study methods', in J.P. Keeves (ed.), *Educational Research, Methodology and Measurement: An International Handbook*. Oxford: Pergamon

Stiltner, B. (1999) *Religion and the Common Good*. Oxford: Rowman and Littlefield

Stoll, L. and Fink, D. (1996) *Changing our Schools: Linking School Effectiveness with School Improvement*. Buckingham: Open University

Sudman, S. and Bradburn, N.M. (1982) *Asking Questions: A Practical Guide to Questionnaire Design*. San Francisco: Jossey-Bass

Sutherland, S. (1985) 'Concluding remarks', in M.C. Felderhof (ed.), *Religious Education in a Pluralistic Society*. London: Hodder and Stoughton

Sutherland, S. (1996) 'Education, values and religion', in J. Sacks and S. Sutherland (eds), *Victor Cook Memorial Lecture*. Centre of Philosophy: University of St Andrews

Sutherland, S. (2004) 'Education, values and religion: prognosis? cure?', in J. Haldane (ed.), *Values, Education and the Human World: Essays in Education, Culture, Politics, Religion and Science*. St Andrews Studies in Philosophy and Public Affairs. Exeter: Imprint Academic

Swann, M. (1985) *Education for All: The report of the Committee of Inquiry into the Education of Children from Ethnic Minority Groups*. London: HMSO

Tacey, D. (2005) 'Encountering tradition in a postmodern context', in C. Ota and C. Erricker (eds), *Spiritual Education*. Sussex: Academic Press

Taylor, C. (1989) *Sources of the Self: The Making of Modern identity.* Cambridge: Cambridge University Press

Taylor, M. (1996) 'Values and values education in schools', in J. Halstead and M. Taylor (eds), *Values in Education and Education in Values.* London: Falmer Press

Taylor, W. (2001) 'Introduction', in W.R. Niblett, *Life, Education, Discovery.* Bristol: Pomegranate Books

Taylor Fitz-Gibbon, C. (1997) 'Monitoring with feedback: the democratization of data: a response to Lindsay Paterson', in K. Watson, C. Modgil and S. Modgil (eds), *Educational Dilemmas: Debate and Diversity: Vol four Quality in Education.* London: Cassell

Thiessen, E.J. (1993) *Teaching for Commitment.* Leominster: Gracewing

Thomas, R.M. (1994) 'Religious education', in T. Husen and T.M. Postlethwaite (eds), *The International Encyclopedia of Education*, 2nd edition. Oxford: Pergamon Press, pp. 4995–5008

Thomas, R.M. (1998) *Conducting Educational Research: A Comparative View.* London: Bergin and Garvey

Tilburg University (2003) *Third Wave of the European Values Study*

Timms, S. (2002) *Times Educational Supplement*, 25 June

Tsayang, G. (1992) 'Comparative studies: an overview', in *Proceedings of the Comparative Education Awareness Seminar.* South Africa

Trainor, D. (1995) 'The Inspection of SMSCD', *Governors Action*, April: 8–9

Tulasiewicz, W. and Brock, C. (1988) *Christianity and Educational Provision in International Perspective.* London: Routledge

Ungoed-Thomas, J. (1997) *Vision of a School: The Good School in the Good Society.* London: Cassell

United Nations Development Programme (2003) *Forging a Global South – 25 Years after the Buenos Aires Conference on Technical Co-operation among Developing Countries.* New York: United Nations

Walsh, P. (1993) *Education and Meaning.* London: Cassell

Warnock, M. (1976) *Imagination.* London: Faber and Faber

Waters, M. (1995) *Globalization: Key Ideas.* London: Routledge

Watson, K. (1982) *Education in the Third World.* London: Croom Helm

Watson, K. (2003) 'Comparative and international studies in education', in W. Kay, L.J. Francis and K. Watson (eds), *Religion in Education.* Leominster: Gracewing

White, L.A. (1949) *The Science of Culture: A Study of Man and Civilization.* New York: Grove Press

Williams, P.N. (1990) 'A more perfect union: the silence of the Church', *America*, 162, 12: 315–18

Wilson, J. (1990) *A New Introduction to Moral Education.* London: Cassell

Wintersgill, B. (2000) 'The contribution of schools to pupils' spiritual, moral, social and cultural development', in J. Cairns, R. Gardner and D. Lawton (eds), *Values and the Curriculum.* London: Woburn Press

Wittgenstein, L. (1921) *Tractatus Logico-Philosophicus.* Extracts edited by D. Cole (1999)

Wittgenstein, L. (1953) *Philosophical Investigations.* Trans. G. Anscombe. Oxford: Blackwell

Woodhead, L. and Heelas, P. (2000) *Religion in Modern Times: An Interpretive Anthology.* Oxford: Blackwell

Wright. A. (1999) *Discerning the Spirit: Teaching Spirituality in the Religious Education Classroom.* Abingdon: Culham College Institute

Wright, A. (2004) *Religion, Education and Post-modernity.* London: Routledge Falmer

Wrigley, T. (2003) *Schools of Hope.* Stoke on Trent: Trentham Books

Yin, R.K. (1994) *Case Study Research: Design and Methods,* 2nd edition. London: Sage

Young, I.M. (1990) *Janus and the Politics of Difference.* Princeton, NJ: Princeton University Press

Index

Lightning Source UK Ltd.
Milton Keynes UK
11 February 2010

149919UK00001B/40/P